Moody Minds Distempered

Moody Minds Distempered

Essays on Melancholy and Depression

JENNIFER RADDEN

OXFORD

UNIVERSITY PRESS

2009

OXFORD
UNIVERSITY PRESS

Oxford University Press, Inc., publishes works that further
Oxford University's objective of excellence
in research, scholarship, and education.

Oxford   New York
Auckland   Cape Town   Dar es Salaam   Hong Kong   Karachi
Kuala Lumpur   Madrid   Melbourne   Mexico City   Nairobi
New Delhi   Shanghai   Taipei   Toronto

With offices in
Argentina   Austria   Brazil   Chile   Czech Republic   France   Greece
Guatemala   Hungary   Italy   Japan   Poland   Portugal   Singapore
South Korea   Switzerland   Thailand   Turkey   Ukraine   Vietnam

Copyright © 2009 by Oxford University Press, Inc.

Published by Oxford University Press, Inc.
198 Madison Avenue, New York, New York 10016

www.oup.com

Library of Congress Cataloging-in-Publication Data
Radden, Jennifer.
Moody minds distempered : essays on melancholy and depression / Jennifer Radden.
p. cm.
Includes bibliographical references.
ISBN 978-0-19-533828-7
1. Melancholy.   2. Depression, Mental.   I. Title.
[DNLM: 1. Depression—Collected Works.   2. Depressive Disorder—
Collected Works.   3. Affect—Collected Works.   4. Depression—history—
Collected Works.   5. Depressive Disorder—history—Collected Works.
6. Philosophy, Medical—Collected Works. WM 171 R125m 2009]
BF575.M44R33   2009
128'.37—dc22   2008014454

9 8 7 6 5 4 3 2 1

Printed in the United States of America
on acid-free paper

Dedicated to the memory of my father

William Whayman Leavett Radden

1900–1970

ACKNOWLEDGMENTS

Almost an adult lifetime of work is represented in these pages: there is no way I can do justice to the assistance I have received—from my own teachers, from professional colleagues and friends in the United States, Europe, and Australia, and from my valued students at the University of Massachusetts. I am grateful to every one of them, aware that without their knowledge, insights, ideas, encouragement and support, this book would not have been possible.

More specifically and more recently, I thank Peter Ohlin at Oxford University Press for his astuteness over, and enthusiasm for, this project. And incisive assistance from my friends in PHAEDRA also needs to be acknowledged: Jane Roland Martin, Janet Farrell Smith, Ann Diller, Beatrice Kipp Nelson, Susan Douglas Fransoza and Barbara Houston. In addition, Joan Fordyce, Gerrit Glas, James Phillips, Alec Bodkin, Jeff Poland, Suzanne Phillips, John Sadler, Amélie Rorty, David Brendel, Rachel Cooper, Chris Megone, Stephen Wilkinson, Marlies ter Borg, Louis Charland, Peter Kramer and David Healy have all helped me better understand melancholy, depression and the category of disorder; and the ideas on emotional pain were clarified by Murat Aydede and Larry Kaye.

My debt to libraries and librarians is also great: in particular, I want to thank librarians at the Healey Library in Boston, the Bodleian at Oxford, and Wellcome Institute in London. The Boston Athenaeum has provided an unmatched setting for thinking and writing.

The idea for this volume came while I was on sabbatical leave in 2006, and I thank the University of Massachusetts Boston for releasing me, and Oxford's University College, Corpus Christi College and Merton College for receiving me - on the H.L.A. Hart Fellowship that allowed me to bring my plan into manageable shape. To the Warden of Merton College, Dame Jessica Rawson, and the Merton College

Fellows, I am especially grateful. Untold comforts and luxuries—intellectual, creature, and social—were afforded me during that Michaelmas term as a Visiting Research Fellow at Merton.

My final and special acknowledgment goes to my husband Frank Keefe, who has seen me through, unwavering, during the year and a half the book has taken to ready for press.

CONTENTS

Moody Minds Distempered

...But I forget me, I,
I am seducèd with this poesy,
And, madder than bedlam, spend sweet time
In bitter numbers, in this idle rhyme.
Out on this humour! From a sickly bed,
And from a moody mind distemperèd,
I vomit forth my love, now turn'd to hate,
Scorning the honour of a poet's state.
Nor shall the kennel rout of muddy brains
Ravish my muse's heir, or hear my strains,
Once more. No nitty pedant shall correct
Enigmas to his shallow intellect.
Enchantment, Ned, have ravishèd my sense
In a poetic vain circumference.
Yet thus I hope (God shield I now should lie),
Many more fools, and most more wise than I.

—John Marston,
The Scourge of Villainy,
Satire X, 1598

Introduction

The essays and discussions in this volume comprise a selection of my writing about melancholy and depression. Some of this work is historically oriented. I have attempted to place states of melancholy and depression within Western medical and cultural traditions that began with Hippocrates and Aristotle, and to uncover the theoretical implications of equating states of melancholy as we learn of them in these earlier, classical accounts with states of depression as they are characterized in our own time. Depictions of melancholic and depressive conditions in the classification and theories underpinning psychoanalysis, contemporary psychology, and psychiatry are also explored. Other writing analyzes concepts such as disease, disorder, and illness as they cast light on what we understand of melancholy and depression, and examines the phenomenology of the suffering so prominent in these conditions.

This writing forms part of a broader body of my work inquiring into the concepts and categories associated with mental disorder. Consciousness and mental processes, the self, agency, the emotions, and rationality are central themes for every philosopher interested in the field of the mental and psychological. Unlike many researchers within that field, however, I regard mental illness and psychopathology as natural, obvious, and even indispensable extensions and examples for such inquiries. (Any account of consciousness and self-identity must explain dissociated states, for example, and, in my opinion, theories of responsibility and agency need to accommodate disorders of impulse control.)

My particular interest in disordered affect traces to two research projects undertaken during my graduate training in the philosophy of mind. One concerned emotions. The intricate norms governing appropriate and warranted response as captured in "intentional" definitions of particular emotions (such as those in Descartes's *Passions of the Soul* and Spinoza's *Ethics*) directed my attention to the aberrant and incomplete responses found, for example, in the disordered affect of depression. In addition, thinking about feelings this way made me aware of what might distinguish affective from other psychopathology, a difference lost from sight when attention is

3

on the broader category of mental disorder that encompasses cognitive and behavioral, as much as affective, aberration.

My second project explored conceptions of rationality in Freud's 1911–1917 ("metapsychological") papers. Of these papers, "Mourning and Melancholia" (1917) prompted an interest in the ideas about self, love, and loss that are there shown to underlie melancholic and depressive suffering. It also alerted me to the intersection of gender and depression, along with the complex cluster of meanings that link depressive states with women and the feminine—this last, an interest nourished by the exciting feminist theorizing of the 1980s and 1990s in works such as Julia Kristeva's *Black Sun*. The force and ambiguity of the historical record had been brought home to us all by reading Michel Foucault's *Madness and Civilization* (1965), and for me, this yielded what has proven a long-lived fascination with early modern writing on melancholy and depression—the Elizabethans, for instance, and Robert Burton. Stanley Jackson's wonderful *Melancholia and Depression* (1986) became an indispensable guide when, with his encouragement and blessing, I set about compiling excerpts from historical sources on melancholy and depression for my 2000 collection, *The Nature of Melancholy*. Many of the essays that follow grew out of my research for that volume.

Late-nineteenth-century writing, especially, was influential. The ideas in the classical canon of writing about melancholy culminate, toward the end of the nineteenth century, with works that are the recognizable antecedents of today's psychiatry. Prominent here is Emil Kraepelin's *Textbook*, where we find prefigured twentieth- and twenty-first-century psychiatric classification, thinking, and lore. As a source and harbinger of things to come, late-nineteenth-century writing has directed my thinking about melancholy and depression, and it continues to be of enduring interest.

The subject of melancholy in Western traditions is one whose appeal reaches well beyond any particular disciplinary division, and, indeed, the study of melancholy long antecedes the advent of such disciplinary boundaries. For the historian of science, ideas, and medicine; for scholars of language and literature; for the art historian, and those engaged in gender studies, the psychologist and social scientist—for all these, treasures lie in the canon of medical and philosophical writing on melancholy that was inaugurated with Hippocratic humoral lore. For the philosopher, too, such writing yields a range of absorbing inquiries: epistemological, methodological and ontological, aesthetic, moral and cultural. The essays collected here stray into other disciplinary areas and in several cases lie somewhere between philosophy and intellectual history, but they were selected to illustrate some of the diverse philosophical concerns raised by writing about melancholy. As such, they engage with preliminary, though fundamental, issues: what melancholy is, the status of our knowledge of melancholy and claims made about it, how it is to be defined, its relation to modern-day depression, and the implications and cultural meaning, or meanings, of its distinctive subjectivity—the "moody distemper" of my title.

As its interdisciplinary interest suggests, the subject of melancholy may be approached in many different ways with notably differing methodologies. Reflecting my own training in analytic philosophy, the immediate stimulus for most of the essays gathered here was concern over problematic concepts and issues of method and epistemology.

Sketching the Conceptual Landscape

To appreciate the work of later times requires that we recognize its genealogy in earlier thinking. The early modern and modern era saw the emergence of science and medicine as we know them today. The sixteenth, seventeenth, eighteenth, and nineteenth centuries thus provide the immediate historical backdrop for many of my discussions. Because of the vitality and authority of classical and early medieval writing about melancholy, however, we must start further back. Our cultural understanding of melancholy was laid down in the humoral theories of the Greeks, the demonology of medieval Christianity, and the astrology and lore of renaissance humanism. This older background, then, calls for some introduction.

Past Themes from Classical and Early Medieval Times

Found in the Hippocratic corpus, and acknowledged by Aristotelian writing, Greek humoral lore was maintained and developed by Galen, court physician to the emperor Marcus Aurelius during the second century CE. Among the several diseases of the black bile was identified the eponymous disorder of melancholy itself, a condition whose symptoms included unwarrantedly dispirited and apprehensive affective states.

The black bile was one of four bodily humors (black and yellow bile, phlegm, and blood), imbalances of which, it was thought, influenced health and also explained temperament. There were normal individual variations here, with one or another humor predominating in each person. But by becoming excessive, overly heated, or dangerously viscous, these humoral fluids brought about disorder and even madness. The humors were also aligned with particular qualities (of heat, cold, wetness, and dryness); with elements (the earthy, airy, fiery, and watery); as well as with the seasons (winter, spring, summer, autumn) and even life stages (youth and old age, for example). The mood states, temperament, and nature of the man of melancholy were linked to the natural world in these multiple ways through a form of "associationism" that found commonality between, for instance, the coldness, dryness, and darkness of the humor and all else possessing those same qualities.

Moods of fear and sadness "without cause" became the hallmarks of melancholy subjectivity. From their first statement in Hippocratic writing—endorsed then by Galen and reaffirmed until well into the modern period—these feelings were invoked to characterize what we would today call the *psychological* symptoms of the disorder. In his great *Anatomy of Melancholy* (1621), Burton speaks of fear and sorrow as almost definitive of melancholy subjectivity—they are its "most assured signes, inseparable companions, and characters."

Another association, deriving from influential writing on melancholy and perhaps itself tracing to Platonic ideas about the inspired nature of madness, attributed these states to men of brilliance, greatness, and creativity. This, too, was a trope that clung to melancholy into the modern period and beyond.

Medical and philosophical learning were centered in the Middle East after the classical era, and there Galenic lore was faithfully preserved by such guardians as Ishaq ibn Imran, Haly Abbas, and Ibn Sina (Avicenna). When, later, their work was translated into medieval Latin, the humoral assumptions, symptom descriptions, and associations remained. In Western Europe, meanwhile, an additional set of concerns around states of despondency and inertia had arisen. Rather than melancholy, *accidia* and *tristitia* were a reflection of moral failings, even sins. For the early Catholic Church fathers Evagrius and Cassian, listlessness and dejection were inimical to the joyful attitude befitting a Christian.[1] As preoccupations of the medieval Christian church misogyny, witchcraft and demonology also changed how melancholia came to be attributed and understood. Melancholy was a morally dangerous state, a "devil's bath" inviting demonic influence. And, in a theme emphasized throughout the infamous *Malleus Malificarum* (1485), women's moral and intellectual inadequacies left them especially vulnerable to such demonic possession.

With the advent of humanistic neo-Platonistism, fresh motifs acquired prominence, and melancholy regained the glamour of its classical depiction. Marsilio Ficino's disquisition on the melancholy of the learned man and the man of genius, *Three Books on Life* (1482), fused Christian with humanist doctrines. And here, too, as part of the revival of classical learning, themes from the Greek authors were recalled, including the Aristotlian notion that melancholy accompanies outstanding brilliance and talent. By this time, astrological, occult, and magical associations had been added. The new renaissance conception of creative genius is conjoined to that of the man of melancholy, the link forged through astrology. *Homo melancholicus*, the brooding man of genius, was born under Saturn and influenced by Mercury. Arabic writing from Asia Minor, the source for these astrological embellishments, also provided Hellenistic lore on magic: now, rather than inanimate, the universe was believed alive with spirits, occult influences, and sympathies, and melancholy states formed part of an organic unity of interrelated and magically connected elements.

These then, were the ideas about melancholy that prevailed and were conserved, often with remarkable fidelity, until the early modern period. With a reverence for authorities alien to modern medical or scholarly approaches, these earlier ideas and motifs—humoral theory; the emphasis on dejected, dispirited, and apprehensive feelings; the link with astrology, inspiration, and genius; and the acknowledgment of demonic and magical influence—were for centuries reproduced and reflected, often uncritically, in later accounts of melancholy.

Early Modern and Modern Ideas

Trends and themes dominating writing about melancholy (and later depression) between the seventeenth and nineteenth centuries are less easy to characterize: now, the orthodoxy of the past fractures and gives way to the new epistemologies of the early modern and modern eras. Unquestioning confidence in authoritative texts from the past had diminished, for one thing, so that more reliance was placed on the author's own individual observations and on the variety of newer, scientific hypotheses that framed, and sought to explain, those observations. Although "black bile" lingered as a common metaphor for more than a century after Burton's time, it can be seen to function as little more than a metaphor in some passages of the *Anatomy*. And, while he continued to place faith in astrology, Burton was like other enlightened thinkers of the sixteenth and seventeenth centuries in eschewing explanations that smacked of magic and demonology. To the extent that the link with intellectual pursuits and brilliance remained, confidence in the idea that the exalted qualities accompanying it adequately compensated for melancholy suffering waned. Moreover, less glamorous, competing, causal hypotheses had come to acquire prominence. Modern ideas on effort and labor brought emphasis on the part played by a failure to participate in the work world. (There is no greater cause of melancholy than idleness, Burton assures us, "no better cure than business.") And new focus came to be placed on the melancholiac's unsociability, his love of solitude, and the discomforting self-consciousness that was acknowledged as both cause and symptom of his condition.

One facet of the earlier notions that remained undiminished was the framing of melancholy as a condition characterized by a subjective distress depicted, in particular, as mood states of apprehension and sadness.

Extensive transformations occurred between the end of the eighteenth and the last decades of the nineteenth century when, in the series of editions of his influential *Textbook*, Kraepelin created the disease category of "manic-depressive insanity," and early psychiatry took hold. Previous notions of melancholy were narrowed and adjusted to fit the expectations and demands of modern-day, scientific psychology and psychiatry. A sharper separation between observable behavior and subjective report came to be required, for example. The earlier association between feelings of sadness and despondency, on the one hand, and those of fear, anxiety, and apprehension, on the other, weakened in the face of new, anxiety-focused, "nervous" disorders such as neurasthenia (and later anxiety neuroses). The legacy of eighteenth-century faculty psychology fostered a division between those disorders affecting cognitive capabilities and those affecting the feelings and passions. And, as melancholia came to be seen as a disorder of affection and thus the fate of women, with their perceived emotionality, affective variability, and vulnerability, it became increasingly "gendered."

Melancholy and Depression as Medical, Psychological, and Moral Concepts

When melancholy is regarded as a condition attributed to particular individuals, one group of questions that arises relates to what might be termed its ontological status. Is it some kind of naturally occurring state—a "natural kind"? Is melancholy a definable category? What is its relation to the twentieth-century condition known as depression? The status of melancholy and depression as medical complaints raises further questions. How are they understood in relation to other diseases and to the disorders of modern-day diagnostic psychiatry? Are they dimensional conditions, shading imperceptibly toward normal and normative forms of suffering, or must they be understood categorically? And how should they be placed in the separation sometimes drawn between diseases and illnesses?

Melancholy as a Kind of Kind

Speaking of the natural world, philosophers of science have long presupposed that there are naturally occurring "kinds"—categories of stuff and things so distinctive and discretely bounded, so invariant, and so universally occurring as to encourage us to suppose their existence entirely independent of human observation and interpretation. What kind of kind is melancholy? Once, it was regarded in something of the same way as philosophers understand natural kinds today, premodern accounts seem to indicate. The terms "melancholy" and "melancholia"[2] referred to naturally occurring bodily states, brought about by changes in the black bile and to the effects of those changes. When severe, they were diseases, and as such likely found in any population at any time.

An additional commonality was recognized to unite melancholy states, placing them in a "natural" arrangement. A curious metaphysics of associations or qualities linked the properties of the man of melancholy with the natural world, as we saw earlier. Rather than a causal result of the darkness of his bile, the melancholiac's perceived swarthiness and darkened skin color were emblematic of the commonality of all dark things. Through an association that linked overheating to smoke-like fumes, his delusions resulted from the obscuring effect on his brain of the smoky vapors from overheated ("adusted") black bile. And when melancholia was associated with Saturn and Mercury, it was as much due to the coldness and dryness believed common to the humor and those planets as to any alignment of the heavens determining the melancholiac's horoscope.

Such ideas eventually proved misguided and sterile, with the humoral lore and associationist metaphysics being unscientific and contrary to modern ways of understanding the world. Without the anchoring presence of the imbalanced humor to provide a unifying causal center, and without their affinity to other dark, cold, and dry kinds of things, we must wonder to what extent the signs and symptoms previously understood as the varying effects of one distinctive state might have been a more arbitrary collection of disparate states and traits, without any real commonality.

Melancholy states were also long regarded as the symptoms of disease and biological variation, it is true. These early humoral theorists were doctors, after all, whose general understanding of the relation between an underlying biological state and its observable signs and symptoms was not significantly different from that forming part of modern-day pathology. Yet viewed from this perspective, melancholy states were still acknowledged to differ from simpler kinds of kind. Not only could the same symptoms betoken a range of organic causes, but also the same underlying state could produce a Protean diversity of manifestations. Understood as an inner state of imbalance that gave rise to more observable signs and symptoms, melancholy was not discretely bounded. The symptoms of melancholy, it was frequently complained, were endlessly—and for those studying it, frustratingly—various. Moreover, they merged without any clear demarcation into the variations attributable to normal moods and "natural" temperamental difference. So even setting aside the misapprehensions of previous eras and emphasizing only the conception of melancholy understood as a disease, we must conclude that it was at best an anomalous natural medical kind, less readily absorbed into that category than some other medical conditions.

Comparative Methods

How then to proceed? The approach that makes use of historical and cross-cultural comparison (which I have employed in several of the essays in this volume) is one with some considerable methodological heft. Were we to observe similarities between the symptoms of one era, or one culture, and another, when the disorder those symptoms were taken to bespeak seemed unchanged, we might be entitled to conclude that the *same disorder* occurred in these different populations. Hippocratic and Gallenic medicine make reference to some complaints that might be regarded as such natural medical kinds (gout, for example, and gallstones). But the complexities that arise when we attempt such comparison with melancholy require us to go slowly. Before concluding that melancholy was a natural medical kind, for instance, we must first determine whether the melancholia of old was the same disorder as depression. And the approach proper to answering such a question needs investigation. Despite the apparent surface similarity between past melancholy and today's depression, underlying methodological issues prevent us from easily equating the two.

The philosophical distinction between illnesses and diseases would perhaps allow us to say that there were two illnesses here (melancholia and depression) but only one disease—a solution employed when it is asserted that different cultures sometimes produce a variety of symptom profiles. The concept of masked depression is invoked, for instance, to explain why men's depression symptoms include none of the felt sadness and dispiritedness of women's. (Depression in China, it has been argued, takes the culturally acceptable form of somatized symptoms—headache, back pain, dizziness, and such—while Western men's acting out and excessive drinking are the depressive idiom permitted by their gender roles.) But the effectiveness of this solution depends on whether a descriptive or causal ontology is presupposed. Only by positing that underlying disease processes, as yet undetected, cause these divergent symptoms, do we seem able to easily think of each of these separate, local "illnesses" (of Western women's dejection, men's acting out, Chinese women's backache) as forms of depressive disease.[3] And in the same way, ontological presuppositions will affect attempts to determine the relation between past melancholy and today's depression.

Biological states may one day be discovered to confirm the ancient Greek doctors' confidence that hidden, organic states explained, united, and bound all forms of melancholy. Guided by the new brain science, in combination with responses to treatment, today's researchers continue to seek potential markers for affective disorder and its apparent subtypes, including one known as melancholia.[4] (As a subtype of depression, melancholia is defined in terms of its severity and its characteristic ahedonic subjective states—loss of pleasure in normally pleasurable experiences—as well as bodily signs such as sleep disturbance.)[5] Recent acknowledgment of the interaction between environment and the body have yielded stress and impaired resilience (often called diathesis-stress) models. Underlying states of biological fragility explained by genetics, damage, or deficit are understood as risk factors here, and depression results when some environmental trigger (a loss, a defeat, a trauma) occurs.[6] The applicability of this model to depressive states may be questioned, however. And some studies suggest that depression, like adjustment and posttraumatic stress disorders, is better accommodated by stress-based than by diathesis-stress models. Stressful conditions alone may cause pathologically depressive states.[7]

Even if some underlying risk factors were unfailingly present, their role in our understanding of the suffering associated with melancholy and depression would need to be more fully ascertained. Within the biological psychiatry that posits the presence of organic risk factors, conceptual uncertainties continue to divide nosologists; they also dog researchers. Controversy and disagreement surround the question of whether depression is a single condition rather than several different ones—whether severe and milder forms of the disorder rest on a continuum, for example. Diseases may be either categorical or dimensional. Depression is thought by some to be a unitary, dimensional disorder, akin to high blood pressure.[8] On this dimensional model, presupposed in much recent research, even mild depression is disease.[9] However, depression is a condition that is often self-limiting at its less-severe extreme; it is also one, placebo studies strongly indicate, whose course will be affected by suggestion.[10]

Research seeking to identify underlying organic states through responses to particular treatments—a common approach—will have to deal with the confounding effect of these factors that, at the milder end of the depression spectrum, are undeniable. A categorical model, or one that allowed for several distinct forms of depressive illness, could avoid these complexities and guide nosological decisions: if severe depression is unresponsive to placebo, that may indicate it is a distinct condition. Such a categorical model was presupposed in the once-orthodox separation between endogenous and exogenous depression. But that separation is now generally regarded as unsustainable, and despite considerable efforts to establish them, no alternative rubrics have received equivalent support. Whether depression includes one or several disorders, and if the latter, the nature of the proper, separate, characterization of each one, are questions that remain, thus far, without definitive answers.[11] And these fundamental conceptual uncertainties represent a serious deficit at the base of contemporary understanding and research.

Boundary Riding

An important philosophical task arises, I believe, when we consider the boundaries of concepts such as melancholy and depression. The suffering from which, as Burton says, "no man living is free" is different from melancholy understood as an entrenched disorder; moreover, normal melancholy or dour temperaments are different from disorders of temperament. States of melancholy and depression must be placed in relation to each of these more ordinary conditions. Understood in general terms, states of suffering and distress include both those that are an inescapable part of the human condition and those brought about by seemingly more preventable misfortune. In addition, trait-based conditions involving disordered temperament such as the chronic tendency toward unhappiness known as "dysthymia," differ from what appear to be two distinct kinds of more permanent personality style: those that occur naturally as individual temperament and those attributable to permanently souring or embittering life experiences.

Again, this is not a claim about differences that are, or may ever be, immediately observable. The penumbra around depressive illnesses makes for grey areas and a seemingly imperceptible shading from the frankly pathological to the normal (what we might expect) and normative (what is not only predictable but appropriate and fitting). It is tempting, because of this, to adopt the position of much "antipsychiatry" rhetoric that treats such separations as unwarrantedly arbitrary and thereby egregiously alienating. To the extent that the separation is emphasized, it seems likely to alienate people with depressive illnesses, it is true. And these risks and costs must not be forgotten. Still, I believe it behooves us to establish definitions and insist on conceptual boundaries in this way.

As today's consumer movements and the new forms of identity politics have demonstrated, there are a number of ways to recognize and even celebrate difference and disability that bypass the stigma, self-stigma, and discrimination that first come to mind when we think of such alienation. Moreover, there are other risks and costs to be considered. The often severely depressed inhabitants of refugee camps, who are treated with antidepressants, prompt us to envision such real life costs, in both overtreatment and undertreatment, that might arise from forgetting distinctions among different forms of human suffering. If all suffering were to be medicalized without recognition that it may have sprung from preventable human actions, we would risk losing sight of the nonmedical measures that should be sought: in this case, preventing the states of affairs that create refugees rather than merely medicating their suffering. Should genuinely medical conditions come to be seen as indistinguishable from the suffering that results from some combination of human nature, indifference, and oppressive conditions, they might go untreated, their sufferers left as much the hapless victims of their disorder as those who—punished for delusions they were helpless to avoid or understand—were once judged to be demonically possessed.

Other theorists' attempts to define disease, disorder, or mental illness represent further instances of such conceptual boundary riding, and in recent years these have been the focus of considerable effort. Best known are two: Christopher Boorse's definition of disease as dysfunction relative to norms of functioning in some reference group, and Jerome Wakefield's of mental disorder as harmful dysfunction understood in terms of evolutionary faculty psychology.[12] Neither of these approaches has survived the damaging criticisms to which they have been subject by analytic philosophers. Critiques of Boorsian accounts of dysfunction relative to a reference group emphasize the difficulties of fixing on a *suitable* reference group; those of Wakefield's on its unsubstantiated, empirical, essentialist assumptions about the way natural selection underlies natural function.[13]

A second boundary deserving attention is the one between the pain and suffering accompanying severe depression and more ordinary sensations of pain resulting from real or perceived tissue damage. Undoubted similarities unite emotional pain, so familiar from depression, with sensation pain. Yet conceptual and phenomenological differences distinguish them. This complex relationship was confusingly depicted, and dealt with, in philosophical discussions about "mental" and "physical" pain during the 1970s. And it has been neglected and bypassed in much recent pain research, whose exclusive focus has been on painful sensations.

Even sensation pain is a psychic state and not merely the stimulation of nociceptive centers, today's pain researchers have emphasized. But if this is correct, then we need to understand what makes it so and recognize how it differs from, and corresponds with, other kinds of painful experience. And this is an inquiry with particular practical weight. Emotional pain and suffering are common diagnostic symptoms of some psychiatric disorders such as depression and defining features of others (Pain Disorder). They also form part of the definition of mental disorder employed by the American Psychiatric Association's current diagnostic and statistical manual, the *DSM-IV*.

Melancholy as Subjective, Painful, Sad, and Apprehensive Moods

Throughout its long history, as we saw, melancholy was viewed as a condition of subjective distress and its particular, distinctive, affective nature was recognized as feelings of apprehension and sadness. This characterization has implications for several further philosophical inquiries and conclusions. That its basis in psychological symptoms should be so prominent situates melancholy as a condition that seems to demand a phenomenological approach to understanding it, for example. In addition, affective states find a special place in Western cultural ideas and ideals, where they form the basis of important moral, aesthetic, and social norms. And finally, those feelings—of fear and sadness without cause—often seem to betoken moods rather than more cognitive affective states, and moods have their own particular epistemology and links to self-identity.

The emotional suffering so definitive of melancholy and depressive subjectivity, at least as we recognize it in the West, may be a medical symptom, but it is much else besides. Each of the implications just sketched, then, requires further attention. Since phenomenological evidence adheres to its own rules, the emphasis on the patient's personal account of the symptoms suffered calls for a distinctive methodology. First-person claims about our subjective states are not infallible. But the distinctive way we reach such claims (immediately) rather than as others must do to confirm them, by way of evidence, position us for a certain type of authority in relation to such first-person claims, I believe. (Characterizations of the differences between self-knowledge and our knowledge of others' mental lives remain contested and unresolved. Hastening to distance themselves from the grandiosity of Cartesian assertions on behalf of self-knowledge, contemporary philosophers have staked out a wide range of positions, including some that would deny even the latter fairly modest claim to special, proprietary access.)

First-person symptom descriptions have a place in all clinical medicine, of course, and, indeed, the distinction between symptoms and signs is precisely this one: the patient complains of symptoms, whereas doctors, or machines, may identify signs. But, in my view, the part played by feelings among the criteria for both the melancholy of old and today's depression combine with the want of agreed-on and diagnostically dispositive signs or other organic or behavioral indicators of depressive disorders, to render the symptom-based psychological evidence especially vital to an understanding of these disorders.

As feelings, in addition, the subjective states comprising melancholy and depression are associated with a metaphysics that locates such subjectivity at the heart of identity and value. Feelings are often normative. The sadness of mourning is a socially appropriate response, for example: there is something morally wanting in the person who remains indifferent in the face of a loved one's death. No aspect of our mental life is more important to the quality and meaning of our existence than emotions. They are what make life worth living, or sometimes even worth ending—to paraphrase Ronald de Sousa.[14]

To be human is to suffer, certainly; but to suffer in the right way, in response to one's life experience, it is widely believed, is to possess the preconditions for character and right action. (Although most obvious as an implication of virtue-based accounts of character, one way or another, this tenet informs most other moral psychological accounts of personhood as well.) The outward similarity between suffering that is deemed pathological and suffering that marks us as human and can be seen as a reasonable and appropriate response to our human condition has important philosophical implications. The task of separating what are judged normal and appropriate responses from aberrant and pathological suffering, then, seems to me one of considerable significance, and these links between feelings and the moral life require us to pay attention to the features dividing the frankly "abnormal" from the normal and normative.

The sad and apprehensive feelings of melancholy and depression are also linked to some of the deepest of our cultural ideas and ideals. Such states find special echoes in philosophical views about human existence, for example. In a range of philosophical (and, of course, theological) traditions, the ultimate meaninglessness of life has been construed as supporting *attitudes* regarded as appropriate (such as despair) and right and fitting *behavior* (suicide), as well as reasonable, or warranted, *belief*. And the bleak and uncompromising stance known as the tragic view of life has often been judged the appropriate one to adopt in the face of the human predicament. That certain facts about the universe warrant particular *moods*, in particular, is a recognition we associate with Søren Kierkegaard and his critique of modernity. It is also to be found in other thinkers. William James, for example, likens our awareness of our own mortality to a worm at the core of all our usual springs of delight—one that might, at any time, turn us into "melancholy metaphysicians." This is not merely a claim about human psychology, I think: there may be metaphysical warrant for such affections, James implies. And these will color our every response and perception (*all* our usual springs of delight, as he says), imposing a mood of dejection.

In addition, the feeling states making up melancholy and depression have aesthetic resonance where, at least within our culture, a bleak gravity marks the "tragic" style, and framing, of—as well as what are judged appropriate responses to—much great art.

Moods

Before the modern era, writing about melancholy contained repeated themes, as I have observed, including the emphasis on subjective states of dejection and apprehension. Yet the historical evidence about melancholy has been variously interpreted, with some scholars going as far as questioning whether the earlier category of melancholia bears *any* correspondence to present-day diagnostic categories. (Certainly, the former was more encompassing than any of today's diagnoses,[15] and some evidence suggests it marked conditions with fewer or less-disabling symptoms.[16] In a similar way, the relationship between the apparently unipolar melancholia and bipolar disorder remains unresolved, even today, as does the force of the now-outmoded category of partial insanity that acknowledged the extent to which melancholy moods can leave most cognitive functioning unimpaired.[17])

The ambiguity of extant historical sources and the incompleteness of the record with which we are left have encouraged me to seek alternative, less-historical approaches to questions about the relationship between melancholia and other disorders. One such exploration, which has motivated my focus on melancholy subjectivity and its traditional characterization in terms of "fear and sadness without cause," asks whether melancholy might be different from other disorders in some way evident from its distinctive subjectivity. I believe that it is, and that the implications of the distinctiveness of melancholy and depressive subjectivity hold lessons about these states understood as mental states, as aspects of identity, and even as aspects of moral psychology.

The expression "without cause" contains ambiguity. With some uses of "cause" in that phrase, the emphasis was clearly to be placed on affective states that were ungrounded or unwarranted by the facts of the matter, exaggerated or inappropriate reactions based on misunderstanding or delusion. (This is "without *just* cause," as Burton sometimes puts it [my emphasis].) If fear and sadness are without sufficient cause, they are directed toward some proposition that the sufferer understands to be so, or to exist. They are accompanied, that is, by what are known as "intentional" objects—those things or states of affairs that they can be said to be over or about. In this case (without sufficient cause), however, their objects do not appear to warrant the degree of feeling attributed to them. Excessive fear over a clearly minimal risk, or extreme distress over what appears to be a trifling setback, illustrate fear and sadness without cause, on this reading. These are judgments reflecting cultural evaluations of appropriateness that in turn rest on rationality and moral norms. (It has been argued that these norms allow us to distinguish pathological depression from the more ordinary sadness that is a natural human response to certain life stressors, a conclusion to which I return later in this discussion.)[18]

A second interpretation of "without cause" presses on the initial term. If there were no (known) object of these states of fear and sadness, then a depiction emerges of something vaguer: pervasive "objectless" feelings that frame and color subjective experience. The technical distinction sometimes drawn between moods and emotions allows us to name this difference. If melancholic fear and sadness are entirely without an identifiable cause,[19] they are not over or about anything in particular. Rather, they are ways of apprehending and experiencing the world in its entirety. In moods of elation, as it has been put, *everything* is perceived as attractive and attainable, whereas in moods of depression, everything appears gloomy or irritating.[20] Because they color and frame all experience, moods are a particular *way* of experiencing, rather than a particular experience, it might be said.

Translators have used both "mood" and "state of mind" for the German word *Stimmung*, which, Heidegger reminds us, derives from the tuning of a musical instrument. As *Stimmung*, people's "moods" evoke their "attunement," or "temper." Just as an instrument is always tuned *in some way*, whether well tempered or ill, so we are always in some mood or another, and our moods are an inescapable way of being. This gives moods an ontological primacy over more cognitive states, Heidegger insists, although without the precision provided by intentional objects, our moods are not as transparent to us as our more cognitive states. (Feelings of melancholy blur into dull despair, elegiac states, nostalgia, and ennui, for example.) Moods are important and ubiquitous, but they are also elusive and unbounded. Like the mood of anxiety, to use one of Heidegger's examples, they are already "there" — and so close, as he puts it, that it stifles ones' breath — yet, at the same time, they are "nowhere."[21]

In the case of emotions, assessments as to appropriateness are directed toward and expressed in terms of a relation, usually that between the feeling or attitude and its object and or occasion. (Only in one who has been unnecessarily and seriously harmed, for example, will a feeling of anger be a fitting and proper response; anger over a trifling annoyance is inappropriate.) Moods, since they are apparently objectless, are not as readily, or as specifically, appraised as are emotions for appropriateness to the circumstances. (Moods have sometimes been described as possessing objects, but objects so encompassing as to be "the whole world" or "all of experience."[22]) Nonetheless, moods, too, as we saw, are sometimes judged in terms of general appropriateness. During the early medieval era, when *accidia* and *tristitia* were regarded as faults, it was because a joyful disposition was deemed suitable to the Christian. Dour moods were improper in the face of the Christian message of redemption and promise of eternal life. Similarly, if the world *is* devoid of meaning and human life of any real purpose, a generalized bleakness of mood will be apt and fitting.

The implications of this interpretation of melancholy subjectivity as sometimes involving objectless, "moody" affection, and the significance of the more general category of affective states are several, moreover. The broad division between affective and schizophrenic disorders that traces to the Kraepelinian division between manic-depressive disease and dementia praecox, I believe it can be shown, was derived less from direct observation than from the seemingly misleading and arbitrary distinction between disorders affecting cognition and affection, respectively. They were heirs to an earlier faculty psychology tracing to eighteenth-century emphasis on the division between the cognitive functions making up Reason and the affections comprising the Passions. The reification of these psychological functions was often found in crudely physiological and anatomical focus of late-nineteenth-century psychiatry. (It also explains the mistakes and absurdities of phrenology.)

Rather than being warranted by the misleading contrast drawn between affective and cognitive states, the broad Kraepelinian distinction between manic-depressive disease and dementia praecox better corresponds to that between nonintentional mood states and other, intentional, states. If depressive and manic-depressive states are helpfully separated from other disorders at all (and much suggests that these categories are still confusingly arbitrary), it may be because of the prevalence of nonintentional states, or mood states, involved in their subjectivity. The diagnostic label "mood disorder" found in recent classifications, then, is considerably better fitted than the earlier "affective disorder" to describe conditions involving depression and manic-depression, in my judgment.

There are several additional implications of construing melancholy and depression as mood states. We refer to landscapes as sad, or melancholy. This custom is not, or not alone, because natural sights evoke affective states in us, however, but because they evoke for us the rich lode of culturally transmitted associations and ideas about states like melancholy. It is also because such states connote something closer to a mood than an emotion. Indeed, it is their status as nonintentional and objectless moods that permits us to assign "melancholy," "gloominess," "sadness," and similar moodlike attributes to nonhuman phenomena, I suggest. A landscape cannot be grateful or resentful, but it can be cheerful or sad.

The distinctively "moody" nature of melancholy and depressive states is also implicated in another aspect of melancholy and depressive subjectivity. The narratives of those recounting their own experiences of mental disorder reveal how the self or subject is represented in relation to its psychological symptoms. "Symptom-integrating" depictions of that relation portray symptoms in proprietary terms: my symptoms are "part of me" or "mine." Depression memoirs more often than others, it seems, reveal a symptom-integrating structure. And again, the explanation why this should be so seems likely to rest, at least in part, with the distinctive, nebulous, pervasiveness of mood states that renders them close to "inalienable," from the perspective of self-identity. Moods cannot be separated from the subject in the way more precise, intentional states such as delusional beliefs are able to be. After the fact, we may doubt that a mood was ours ("that mournful pessimist—no, not me at all!"). But at the time, we are our moods, and they are us. In being "nowhere" as Heidegger puts it, they are (sometimes even stiflingly) present.

Culture

Whatever biological attributes may be located within the melancholy sufferer's body, melancholy and depression must be understood as shaped by culture. Indeed, whatever other kind of kind it may be, melancholy appears to have been an instance of what Ian Hacking has called an interactive kind—affected by its sufferers' awareness of themselves as so identified (or diagnosed).[23] So an additional inquiry, which takes us inevitably to cross-cultural and cross-historical ideas, considers the cultural tropes and associations (some of them old, and some new or recently revived) that attach to ascriptions of melancholy and depression. These include its association with inspiration, glamour, brilliance, and gender—particularly, the ostensible contrast between heroic and glamorous masculine melancholy and the abject and "feminine" suffering of today's depression. They also include its link to loss and its expression in self-denigrating attitudes.

As a central category in our culture, embedded in all Western traditions, gender represents an inescapable element to be considered as we appraise the cultural associations attaching to melancholy and depression. Both in terms of diagnostic fact and cultural imagination, the second half of the nineteenth century saw an increasing association between women, the feminine, and disordered passions or affects. Later, the twentieth century brought theorizing from post-Lacanian feminism. Thinkers such as Luce Irigaray, Julia Kristeva, and Judith Butler elaborate on loss analyses, each in a separate way attempting to explain, and at the same time valorize, women's depressive or melancholic subjectivity.

Foucault's "archeological" explorations into sixteenth- and seventeenth-century conceptions of insanity provide a guide for cross-cultural and cross-historical comparison. By considering the female depression sufferer of today in light of the glamorous melancholy man from those earlier times, we are able to discern some of the effect of culture and the social and cultural structures which, whatever bio-logical commonalities may be shared across times and places, tie the melancho-liac or depressive to a particular, local, cultural "moment." Freud's "Mourning and Melancholia" particularly invites "deconstruction" into its cultural assumptions and associations along these lines. It contains elements from the earlier traditions and is embued with renaissance tropes about *Homos melancholicus*, the brilliant, sagacious, charmed man of melancholy. Yet beside and drawn along by Freud's bold new theo-ries of introjection and narcissism, innovations are introduced and highlighted. Now, melancholia is depicted as an experience and a result of *loss* and is characterized by feelings of self-loathing. The force and influence of Freud's essay have been so great, I contend, that only with difficulty can we recognize that two constituents of much twentieth-century thinking about depression, loss, and low self-esteem emerged this way as implications of his theorizing and are in large part attributable to Freud.

Loss, particularly, has become a mainstay of twentieth- and twenty-first-century descriptions of melancholy and depressive subjectivity. Different strains of thinking grew out of Freud's emphasis on loss in "Mourning and Melancholia," however. One of these, object relations theory, continues to use "loss" in the sense of loss of a personified other, once loved. In much other psychology and psychiatry, by contrast, "loss" has come to cover the greater range signified by the term "lack." We find ref-erence to depression as a loss of self-esteem, loss of self, loss of relationships, loss of agency, loss of opportunity, and even loss of hedonic mood states. Thus almost trivi-alized, loss will not bear the theoretical weight sometimes placed on it, I believe.

Most recently, evidence of this reliance on—and weakening of—the concept of loss is found in work by Horwitz and Wakefield. In otherwise admirable efforts to emphasize the conceptual difference between (pathologically) depressive suffering and more normal and normative responses to life's vicissitudes, these thinkers characterize "normal sadness" as an appropriate response to loss, that ceases, in time, upon the cessa-tion of that loss. Loss, they allow, is of several different forms: loss of attachments; losses related to power, status, resources, and respect; and loss of "ideals, goals, meanings."[24] This broad interpretation is innocuous when it characterizes normal sadness as distinct from pathological depression, for surely normal sadness does involve every type and degree of loss-like suffering. But many contemporary loss-based analyses of pathologi-cal depression leach "loss" of substantive meaning, not only reducing it to the vaguer "lack," but even rendering it synonymous with terms like "setback," "upset," or "discom-fort." And these, I believe, reflect a betrayal and degradation of Freud's bold insight.

In an especially telling way, the issue of gender intersects with the "heroic" view of melancholy as a mark of brilliance, intellectual power, and inspiration. The pop-ularity of the heroic view has waxed and waned through different eras, but at least two iterations of the set of ideas linking melancholy with such glamorous attributes can be identified: the one beginning with Ficino and continuing through Burton and the other attitudes adopted with European Romanticism at the end of the eigh-teenth and the beginning of the nineteenth century. Arguably, we are even seeing a modest return of those attitudes today. An echo of Romantic characterizations is discernable in Foucault's writing, as it is (abetted by psychopharmacological adver-tising that names the poets believed to have suffered the same disorder),[25] in the newly articulate voices of depression sufferers recounting their own experiences in illness memoirs—in William Styron's *Darkness Visible*, Redfield Jamison's *Unquiet Mind,* and Andrew Solomon's *Noonday Demon*, for example.

Quite as significant as these occasional irruptions, however, is another trend. Through the last part of the nineteenth century the new category of depression that came to replace melancholy lost its appealing and heroic associations. Though still remembered, the glamorous aspects of melancholy were muted and even eclipsed when—and arguably because—depression became increasingly "gendered," a women's condition in epidemiological terms and linked, in cultural ones, with disvalued and disparaged feminine traits. This contrast, and transformation, is nowhere more evident than in "Mourning and Melancholia," where glamorous male examples from the past such as Hamlet are presented alongside the nameless, carping, self-hating, and foolish woman melancholiacs who were Freud's patients.

The heroic view of melancholy, so long-lived and arguably resurgent today, has much appeal. Who among depression sufferers could resist cultural tropes that link their disorder to artistic and intellectual achievement, to creativity, and to a profounder understanding and wisdom than is vouchsafed to more sanguine folk? In turn, who among the well could not welcome a return to more positive characterizations of those who endure depressive suffering? Some counter to the negative stereotypes (with their sequelae in self-stigma and discrimination), and some compensation for that suffering, can surely only be applauded. As today's new consumer, survivor, and "mad pride" movements have played an important part in recasting or "valorizing" some other symptoms of psychiatric disorder. so, too, it may be argued, we should celebrate the alignment of the symptoms of depression with these more culturally honored and valued traits of brilliance, creativity and wisdom.

This proposal runs entirely contrary to modern-day biological psychiatry. There, depression is a disease like any other, better not confused with heroic postures or unnecessarily tangled with gender associations. It is merely a matter of ill health—and a massive public health problem—that modern science will conquer and, with time, expunge. No scientific studies confirm a link between depression and these valued traits, moreover.

The heroic view of melancholy actually embodies several separate arguments, only some of which involve causal claims, however, and whose causal claims also differ significantly. The heroic view thus contains approaches and variations against which particular critiques carry more and less weight. If brilliance and talent come with depression or manic-depression, it has been pointed out, it would seem most likely due to cultural expectations, to the "interactive kind," status of these conditions, and to other effects only contingently related to such traits. (Difference and otherness help in the creative process, Kramer notes, and depression is a form of difference; if self-consciousness is the subject of art, then depressives make ideal chroniclers; literary achievements might even arise by default, when the stamina for a regular job cannot be mustered.[26]

Other causal claims introduce outcomes more difficult to evaluate. "I hated being depressed, but it was also in depression that I learned my own acreage, the full extent of my soul," says Andrew Solomon.[27] Romantic hyperbole, perhaps. But by whom, and how, could the truth of that remark be determined?

Moreover, causal links to creativity or brilliance must be separated from those to sagacity. The provocative findings of the "sadder but wiser" studies perhaps even provide some sort of empirical support for a particular causal link with accurate judgment. The mildly depressed make more realistic assessments of themselves and the world around them, these studies indicate.[28] While no more creative or brilliant as the result of their depression, then, these sufferers may yet possess "a keener eye for the truth," as Freud grandly put it when he attributed superior self knowledge to the melancholiac.[29]

The most impregnable of what Peter Kramer entitles the "charm" arguments in support of the heroic view need not even be construed as causal claims. The philosophical stance known as the tragic attitude may find unique resonance in depressive subjectivity, as Kierkegaard believed, without arising from the depressed mind or giving rise to it. Not all the glamour and charm of melancholy depends on causal claims, and entirely undoing the enchantment of melancholy and depressive states may yet be a challenge that eludes modern science.

Essays

History: Intellectual and Medical History of Melancholy and Depression

Until the early modern period, we saw, the canon of writing on melancholy remained faithful to classical and medieval ideas. Barely changed through the centuries, these earlier themes—the emphasis on dejected, dispirited and fearful feelings; the humors; the tie with inspiration and genius; and the acknowledgement of astrological, demonic, and magical influence—were each preserved in later accounts of melancholy if only, eventually, in the form of metaphors. Against the persisting orthodoxy of these canonical works, Teresa of Avila's scattered observations on the melancholy she observed within the cloister provide a revealing contrast (see chapter 1, "Melancholia in the Writing of a Sixteenth-Century Spanish Nun"). Teresa lacked access to that canon, written in Latin and the property of scholars. Her astute and sensitive depictions of melancholy, we must suppose, reflect either direct observation or the common lore of her time. Focused on preventing melancholy within the closed community of the convent, Teresa recognized and understood the effects of suggestibility on the spread of these afflictions. She also distinguished milder from more severe conditions, an important moral distinction that for her grounds and justifies radical differences in treatment. The severely melancholy nun should receive the compassion due to one with illness, she insisted, while those only mildly afflicted must be punished.

Outlined in "Melancholy: History of a Concept" (chapter 2) are some of the transformations that occurred between the end of the eighteenth and the last decades of the nineteenth century. The loose, earlier category of melancholy was narrowed and tightened to fit Kraepelin's disease type of manic-depressive insanity, I show, and these changes emerge through the series of editions of Kraepelin's *Textbook of Psychiatry*. Melancholy became more conspicuously "gendered" during this era, for example, and associated with the feminine and women. Viewed, thus, as a women's disorder, melancholia has received considerable attention in the last part of the twentieth century from post-Lacanian feminists such as Irigaray, Kristeva, and Butler, whose theories, each elaborating on loss analyses, are introduced. Among theories or models of depression such as these, a taxonomy can now be identified, I show here: theories concerning loss contrast with biological and imbalance analyses; with cultural causation theories and multicausal, diathesis-stress models; and with the claims of the cultural constructionists.

By viewing the female depression sufferer of contemporary times alongside the Elizabethan man of melancholy (in "Melancholy and Melancholia," chapter 3) we are able to discern some of the effect of culture, time, and place on ascriptions of melancholia. In particular, this discussion shows how women's role, and gender associations, might explain how sadness and despair came to be regarded as unmitigated defects today in a way that they were not when they were the fashionable complaints of the Elizabethan rake or scholar.

Categories: Melancholy and Depression as Medical, Psychological, and Moral Concepts

The relationship between melancholia of old and present-day depression is a complex and confusing one, not admitting of any easy analysis. "Is This Dame Melancholy?: Equating Today's Depression and Past Melancholia" (chapter 4) explores the approach proper to determining that relationship. Ontological presuppositions are implicated here, I try to demonstrate. We must determine what sort of thing melancholy is before determining its relation to depressive states. And although it might be supposed useful, the philosophical distinction between illness and disease is itself dependent on these deeper foundations. Only by positing that underlying disease processes, as yet undetected, cause these divergent symptoms, do we seem able to easily think of each of these separate, local, "illnesses"—melancholia of old and today's depression—as forms of depressive disease. Melancholia from past times cannot be simply equated with today's depression.

Quite profound conceptual and political tensions arise out of the "cross-cultural psychiatry" of medical anthropologist Arthur Kleinman. In a brief follow-up to commentary on my discussion about equating depression and melancholia (chapter 5, "The Psychiatry of Cross-Cultural Suffering"), I raise some of these. We want to avoid cultural relativism so as to recognize and respond to universal suffering in the way it deserves. Yet we also want to avoid cultural imperialism. And this may not be so easy to achieve.

Two distinctions which, while they are not always stressed in early modern writing, can be maintained through appeal to humoral presuppositions are highlighted and defended in "Epidemic Depression and Burtonian Melancholy" (chapter 6). The universal suffering that seems to be part of our human lot—and entirely normal and normative—is different from melancholy understood as an entrenched disorder. And normal melancholy, sour, or dour temperaments also seem to be properly distinguished from disorders of temperament.

The normal effects of adverse life experiences, such as oppression or the death of loved ones, are often indistinguishable from the effects of depressive disorder. Yet these forms of suffering are marked by morally relevant differences: such conceptual boundaries must be affirmed and maintained.

In part because others have adequately shown the flaws of efforts at definition of disorder or disease associated with Boorse and Wakefield, I approach the question of how to circumscribe mental, or at least affective, disorder by focusing on Cooper's less-well-known effort employing everyday normative concepts. Suitably qualified, I show, a definition of disease or disorder can take us some way toward excluding normal and normative states and personality styles.

In "Emotional Pain and Psychiatry" (chapter 7), I consider the pain and suffering accompanying depression from another perspective—this time examining its similarities with ordinary sensation pain. Emotional pain and suffering enter into much psychiatric theorizing and lore, so clarifying conceptual and phenomenological differences between these two sorts of pain and suffering is a task with immediate urgency. Pain is not merely the stimulation of pain receptors or a localized episode of sensory experience, it is now widely acknowledged, and painful sensations may have psychogenic causes. That said, "emotional pain" (e-pain) is not a metaphor; although it is analogous, sensation pain (s-pain) differs from e-pain in a range of ways that, taken together, constitute a significant set of differences. Rather than encouraging us to speak of the term "pain" as having two senses, as some philosophers have wanted to do, I conclude that these differences, explained and enumerated here, likely reveal that "pain" is a looser type of category, of which s-pain and e-pain represent recognizable variants.

The sources of present-day psychiatric classification—in particular, the broad division between affective and schizophrenic disorders that traces to the Kraepelinian division between manic-depressive disease and dementia praecox—are the subject of chapter 8, "Lumps and Bumps: Kantian Faculty Psychology, Phrenology, and Twentieth-Century Psychiatric Classification." To a considerable extent, I argue, this influential division reflected cultural presuppositions and assumptions traceable to the previous century's contrast between Reason and Passion and to the influence of faculty psychology (also discernable, during the nineteenth century, in the spectacular rise and fall of phrenology). Rather than a natural or universal division, the separation between emotion and cognition looks to be a creation of European, seventeenth- and eighteenth-century thinking. Kraepelin believed himself to be the consummate empirical scientist. But the misleading and arbitrary distinction between disorders affecting cognition and affection, respectively, seems to partly explain what Kraepelin found and how he chose to classify it.

Freud and Kraepelin were contemporaries. And like Kraepelin's famous classification, Freud's work also invites "deconstruction" into its cultural assumptions and associations, as I illustrate in "Love and Loss in Freud's 'Mourning and Melancholia': a Rereading" (chapter 9). "Mourning and Melancholia" is a confusing and multifaceted work, at once filled with old ideas about *Homo melancholicus*, and the vehicle by which are introduced breathtakingly new ideas, including those about introjection and narcissism that form the theoretical underpinnings for subsequent object relations psychology. These theoretical advances, in turn, can be shown to explain two characterizations of melancholia so central to later understanding of depression: its depiction as a response to loss (albeit a reduced conception of loss closer to the notion of any lack, deficiency, or setback) and its expression in feelings of self-loathing and guilt. Although this debt is not widely recognized, I emphasize that these two central constituents of much twentieth-century thinking about depression, loss and low self-esteem, originate more as implications of Freud's theorizing than as clinical observations.

Subjectivity: Melancholy as Subjective, Sad, and Apprehensive Moods

First-person accounts of experiences of melancholy and depression date to medieval times. They provide valuable source material on the distinctive subjectivity of affective disorder. I have appealed to such narratives in an attempt to better understand melancholy and depressive self-identity in "My Symptoms, Myself: Reading Mental Illness Memoirs for Identity Assumptions" (chapter 10). The particular question here is how the self or subject is represented in relation to its psychological symptoms—the feelings, impulses, or beliefs considered aberrant or pathological. I explore the theory of self and the perceived analogies with bodily symptoms guiding how the self is seen in relation to its psychological symptoms in such memoirs, where symptoms are to varying degrees woven into self-identity. The distinctive nature and cultural place of mood states, I propose, seem to explain why memoirs of depression reveal a more proprietary attitude toward symptoms. As intentional states with sharper delineation, aberrant beliefs and, perhaps, desires can be more easily detached or alienated from the self. But, together with their inchoate and amorphous nature, the pervasiveness of mood states render them almost "inalienable."

Some additional implications of construing melancholy and depression as mood states enter into the discussions that follow. In chapter 11, "Melancholy, Mood, and Landscape," I attempt to explain why we refer to landscapes as sad or melancholy. This effect is not, or not alone, because natural sights evoke affective states in us. Melancholy landscapes may also affect us with such mood states in a more direct way, but I argue that, primarily, we attribute melancholy to landscape by some alchemy derived from the associative attachment between visual and affective aspects of our conception of melancholy. Aspects of the landscape make us *think* of, not (or not merely) feel, melancholy. And it is the nonintentional and objectless status of moods, in fact, that allows us to attribute "melancholy," "gloominess," "sadness," and similar moodlike attributes to natural phenomena.

In *Against Depression*, Kramer takes on the long-held cultural tropes linking melancholy and depressive states to glamorous attributes such as brilliance, creativity, and sagacity. He sketches a future time at which depression will be regarded as no more attractive, charming, or profound than are, today, tuberculosis or heart disease. And he hints at a utopian era when, due to genetics and perhaps even social engineering, depression has gone the way of the Black Death and leprosy. In reviewing Kramer's book (chapter 12: Review of *Against Depression*,) I explore and challenge this critique.

Kramer's objections have force: I, too, recognize the danger of an emerging neo-Romanticism that misrepresents the suffering and limitations that all too often accompany any severe mental disorder. Yet, the heroic view of melancholy contains approaches and variations on which these sorts of critique act more and less persuasively, I explain. And because of the cultural resonance of the heroic view, several of these "charm" arguments about melancholy seem likely to persist, surprisingly invulnerable to Kramer's attacks.

The essays that follow were written over a period of more than twenty years, during which my ideas (indeed, my approach and even style) have changed to a considerable degree. Some recasting and restatement of points and themes was thus unavoidable. To minimize repetition, I have removed or shortened sections and paragraphs I thought unnecessary. Nonetheless, a certain amount of restatement remains, and the reader is urged to proceed selectively. Any inconsistencies or major shifts in emphasis have been noted in the preceding essay.

Notes

1. Daly 2007.
2. These terms were used indifferently, at least through the early modern period, and will be so used in what follows. Toward the end of the nineteenth century, I have argued, we find some tendency to preserve "melancholia" for the disease state.
3. Following the lead of Arthur Kleinman, cross-cultural studies have been taken to suggest that depression in non-Western cultures is almost always "somatized"—that is, experienced in the form of bodily ills rather than the conscious states of emotional pain and distress that are its central characteristics in our culture (Kleinman 1988, Gaw 1993, Kirmayer and Young 1998, Moerman 2002). Instead of a marginal case, it is suggested, masked depression may be the paradigm—and misleadingly named. This approach embraces a causal ontology. But the findings on which Kleinman relies have also been subject to damning reexamination in more recent years. For example, Horwitz and Wakefield 2007:197–202.
4. Kessing 2007.
5. In their recent taxonomy of causal theories about mental disorder, Zachar and Kendler point out that this "temporizing causalism" is not shared by all (Zachar and Kendler 2007:557).
6. Kendler, Karkowski, and Prescott 1999; Kramer 2005.
7. Mirowsky and Ross 2003; Turner and Lloyd 1999.
8. Kendler and Gardner 1998.
9. Kramer 2005.
10. For example, Healy 1997, Moerman 2002, Kessing 2007.
11. Shorter 2007.
12. Boorse 1975, Wakefield 1992.
13. Cooper 2002, Lilienfeld and Marino 1995, Gert and Culver 2004, Murphy and Woolfolk 2000, Poland 2002.
14. De Sousa (2007) says: " No aspect of our mental life is more important to the quality and meaning of our existence than emotions. They are what make life worth living, or sometimes ending."
15. Most notably, perhaps, it encompassed today's anxiety disorders.
16. Berrios and Porter 1998.
17. Jackson 1983.
18. Horwitz and Wakefield 2007.

19. They have causes, presumably, although these may not be causes known to their subject; importantly, their "causes" are not part of what, subjectively, the mood is recognized as over or about.

20. Taylor 1996:165; my emphasis.

21. Heidegger 1962:12–13.

22. For example, Solomon 1984:306.

23. Hacking 1999.

24. Horwitz and Wakefield 2007:28.

25. Healy 2006.

26. Kramer 2005.

27. Solomon 2001:24.

28. Alloy and Abramson 1979; Vazquez 1987; Ruehlman, West, and Pasahow 1985. These findings have not gone unchallenged, it should be noted. See, for example, Dunning and Story 1991; Fu, Koutstaal, Fu, Poon, and Cleare 2005.

29. Freud 1957:156.

References

Alloy, L. B., and Abramson, L. Y. 1979. Judgement of Contingency in Depressed and Non-depressed Students: Sadder but Wiser? *Journal of Experimental Psychology and Genetics* 108(4):441–85.

Berrios, G., and Porter, R. 1998. *The History of Clinical Psychiatry: The Origin and History of Psychiatric Disorders*. New York: New York University Press.

Cooper, R. 2002. Disease. *Studies in the History and philosophy of Biological and Biomedical Sciences* 38: 263–82.

Daly, R. W. 2007. Before Depression: The Medieval Vice of Acedia. *Psychiatry* 70 (1):30–51.

de Sousa, Ronald. 2007. "Emotion." In *The Stanford Encyclopedia of Philosophy* (Summer 2007 edition), ed. Edward N. Zalta. At http://plato.stanford.edu/archives/sum2007/entries/emotion/.

Dunning, D., and Story, A. 1991. Depression, Realism and the Overconfidence Effect: Are the Sadder Wiser When Predicting Future Actions and Events? *Journal of Personal and Social Psychology* 61(4):521–32.

Freud, S. 1957 [1917]. "Mourning and Melancholia." In *Collected Papers*, 4 authorized translation under the supervision of Joan Rivière. London: Hogarth Press, 152–70.

Fu, T., Koutstaal, W., Fu, C., Poon, L., and Cleare, A.J. 2005. Depression, Confidence and Decision: Evidence against Depressive Realism. *Journal of Psychopathology and Behavioral Assessment* 27(4):243–52.

Gaw, A. 1993. *Culture, Ethnicity, and Mental Illness*. Washington, DC: American Psychiatric Press.

Gert, B. and Culver, C. 2004 Defining Mental Disorder. In *The Philosophy of Physhiatry: A Companion*, ed. Jennifer Radden. Oxford: Oxford University press, 415–25.

Hacking, I. 1999. *The Social Construction of What?* Cambridge: Harvard University Press.

Haslam, N. 2002. Practical, Functional, and Natural Kinds. *Philosophy, Psychiatry, and Psychology* 9(3): 237–41.

Healy, D. 1997. *The Anti-depressant Era*. Cambridge: Harvard University Press.

Healy, D. 2006. The Latest Mania: Selling Bipolar Disorder. *PLoS Medicine* 3(4):1–4.

Heidegger, M. 1962. *Being and Time*. Trans. by John Macquarrie and Edward Robinson. New York: Harper and Row.

Horwitz, A., and Wakefield, J. 2007. *The Loss of Sadness: How Psychiatry Transformed Normal Sorrow into Depressive Disorder*. New York: Oxford University Press.

Jackson, S. 1983. Melancholia and Partial Insanity. *Journal of the History of Behavioral Science* 19:173–84.

Jackson, S. 1986. *Melancholia and Depression*. New Haven: Yale University Press.

Kendler, K., and Gardner, C. 1998. Boundaries of Major Depression: An Evaluation of DSM-IV Criteria. *American Journal of Psychiatry* 155:172–77.

Kendler, K., Karkowski, L.M., and Prescott, C.A. 1999. Causal Relationship between Stressful Life Events and the Onset of Major Depression. *American Journal of Psychiatry* 156(6):837–41.

Kessing, L. V. 2007. Epidemiology of Subtypes of Depression. *Acta Psychiatrica Scandinavica* 115(Suppl.433):85–89.

Kirmayer, and, Young, 1998. Culture and Context in the Evolutionary Concept of Mental Disorder. *Journal of Abnormal Psychology* 108:446–52.

Kleinman, A. 1988. *Rethinking Psychiatry: From Cultural Category to Personal Experience*. New York: Free Press.

Kramer, P. 2005. *Against Depression*. New York: Viking.

Lepinies, W. 1992. *Melancholy and Society*. Trans. by Jeremy Gaines and Doris Jones. Cambridge: Harvard University Press.

Lilienfeld, S. and Marino, L. 1995. Mental Disorder as a Roschian Concept. *Journal of Abnormal Psychology* 104(33):411–20.

Mirowsky and Ross 2003.

Moerman, D. 2002. *Meaning, Medicine and the "Placebo Effect."* Cambridge: Cambridge University Press.

Murphy, D. and Woolfolk, R. L. 2000. The Harmful Dysfunction Analysis of Mental Disorder. *Philosophy, Psychiatry & Psychology* 7(4):241–52.

Poland, J. 2002. Whither Mental Disorder? Unpublished Manuscript.

Ruehlman, L. S., West, S. G., and Pasahow, R. J. 1985. Depression and Evaluative Schemata. *Journal of Personality*. 53(1):46–92.

Shorter, E. 2007. The Doctrine of the Two Depressions in Historical Perspective. *Acta Psychiatrica Scandinavica* 115(Suppl. 433):5–13.

Solomon, A. 2001. *The Noonday Demon: An Atlas of Depression*. New York: Scribner.

Solomon, R. 1984. Emotion and Choice. In *What Is an Emotion? Classic Readings in Philosophical Psychology*, ed. Cheshire Calhoun and Robert Solomon. New York: Oxford University Press. 305–26.

Taylor, G. 1996. Deadly Vices? In *How Should One Live? Essays on the Virtues*, ed. Roger Crisp. Oxford: Clarendon.

Turner, R. J., and Lloyd, D. A. 1999. The Stress Process and the Social Distribution of Depression. *Journal of Health Soc. Behav.* 40(4):374–404.

Vazquez, C. 1987. Judgement of Contingency: Cognitive Biases in Depressed and Non-depressed Subjects. *Journal of Personal and Social Psychology* 52(2):419–31.

Wakefield, J. 1992. Disorder as Harmful Dysfunction. *Psychological Review* 99(2):232–47.

Zachar, P. 2002. The Practical Kinds Model as a Pragmatist Theory of Classification? *Philosophy, Psychiatry, and Psychology* 9(3):219–27.

Zachar, P., and Kendler, K. 2007. Psychiatric Disorders: A Conceptual Taxonomy. *American Journal of Psychiatry* 164(4):557–65.

PART I

HISTORY

*Intellectual and Medical History
of Melancholy and Depression*

Melancholia in the Writing of a Sixteenth-Century Spanish Nun

Since the time of Hippocratic writers, melancholia has fascinated its observers. From Greek doctors and philosophers through to Robert Burton in the seventeenth century, there has been a remarkably consistent focus on the humoral imbalances thought to underlie these conditions and on the subjective moods of apprehension and generalized dejection, long characterized as "fear and sadness without cause," through which they are identified. This set of ideas—found in the writings of Galen, the Greco-Arabic doctors such as Avicenna and Rhazes, and Renaissance thinkers such as Ficino, followed by Weyer and Paracelsus in the early modern era—is well known. Less well known are the unsystematic discussions of melancholy and melancholia by the Spanish abbess Teresa de Alhumada (1515–82), later Saint Teresa of Avila, who noted the apparently widespread melancholia that she encountered in the cloistered world of the nunnery. (The terms "melancholy" and "melancholia" were used interchangeably during this era, and no consistent language distinguished states of disorder from normal temperamental variations. I employ "melancholia" here, although some translations of Teresa's writing employ "melancholy.")

A mystical writer, poet, and reformer of prodigious energies and effectiveness, Teresa of Avila helped forge the Roman Catholic Church's own internal reform (the Counter-Reformation) by founding the Discalced (barefoot) Carmelite order. At a time of religious and political turmoil in Spain, when her efforts placed her at risk from the Inquisition, Teresa strove for a return to a more ascetic monastic practice; she challenged church authorities on doctrine; and, through the force of her own adroitness, intellect, and charisma, she accumulated considerable power and authority during her lifetime.

Teresa's writing on melancholia holds much intrinsic interest, especially if we remember that during her time, "melancholia" denoted a range of symptoms far

First published in *Harvard Review of Psychiatry*, Volume 12, No.5 (September/October) 2004: 293-297. Reprinted with permission of the publisher, Taylor & Francis Ltd.

exceeding that of today's mood disorders. Moreover, in exploring the identification and treatment of this condition in small communities of nuns, Teresa developed framing assumptions that stand in contrast both to the medical thinking of her own time and to that of present-day psychiatry. A consideration and explanation of the astute observations, distinctive purposes, and practical recommendations of this brilliant woman will cast light on the medical assumptions of her era and perhaps, too, contribute to our current understanding of mental disorder.

In the early modern period of the sixteenth century, melancholia included belief states that we would today recognize as psychotic; manic states; all kinds of delusions; paralyses and other somatic symptoms; and dissociated states.[1] Despite resemblances between melancholia from that era and today's diagnostic categories of depression or bipolar disorder, melancholia was not only far broader but was marked by differences of framing and underlying assumptions even in the medical writing of the time (as exemplified in the Low Countries doctor Johann Weyer's famous book on witches, witchcraft, and medical symptoms, *De Praestigiis Daemonum*,[2] a work that reflected the influence of [early] modern scientific and empirical method). Moreover, these sixteenth-century conceptions of a disordered imagination cannot easily be understood in terms of any faculty-psychology division between feeling and thinking; such distinctions came to be emphasized only in the eighteenth and nineteenth centuries.

Most of Teresa's discussions of melancholia occur in *The Foundations* (1573–82), in which she described her reforms and offered advice for prioresses in charge of nunneries, and *The Interior Castle* (1577), in which she made observations and recommendations on prayer and the spiritual life.[3,4] Some differences in her ideas on melancholia can be discerned between these two discussions, but they do not affect the broad themes noted here. There are also scattered references to melancholia throughout her letters[5] (where she made evident that she supposed melancholia to afflict men as often as women).

Teresa subscribed to several of the ideas and assumptions on melancholia found in the better-known medical works of her time, including an emphasis on the humoral nature of the disorder. Also shared with the medical writing of her contemporaries was the belief that the devil plays a role in producing the melancholiac's want of reason,[6] though the sincerity and literalness of these claims about demonic influence have been questioned by recent historians.[7] The devil, Teresa observed in *The Foundations*, "takes melancholy as a means for trying to win over some persons." The humane and sympathetic attitude toward the sufferer of melancholia—an attitude associated with the humanistic values of the Reformation—is also evident in Teresa's writing (at least when that sufferer is severely afflicted). Her sophisticated acknowledgment of the power of suggestion is found in the medical writing of some of her contemporaries (notably, Weyer) as well, though Teresa adapted and employed it to different ends. Finally, although Teresa had a less negative attitude toward women than is found in medical writing at the time, she, too, seems to have accepted the standard lore that women's natural intellectual frailties made them more prone to demonic influence and to the disorders of the imagination associated with melancholia.

Aside from these common assumptions that Teresa apparently shared with her contemporaries, several points in her references to melancholia and her recommendations for its treatment deserve special attention. Of note is the extreme seriousness with which she took this condition and its potentially damaging effects in a closed, religious community. In Teresa's writing, melancholia was a growing menace—in part because it was seen as on the rise, and also because it represented a kind of socially imparted disorder, a contagion. Over and over Teresa emphasized that acknowledging melancholia in even one nun presented a danger to the rest of the community; for example, in *The Interior Castle* she commented that such an afflicted nun could lead everyone around her to think "that she herself is a melancholic and that thus others must bear with her." What concerned Teresa was not the burden that the ailing nun would impose on the rest of the community but the fear that through suggestion, others would believe themselves similarly afflicted. (Although Teresa did not expressly state that small groups of women living together in close quarters in an atmosphere of religious fervor and extremism might be especially prone to such a dynamic, her discussions have an urgency implying that she recognized it.) In this reasoning we see an apparently sophisticated acknowledgment of the power of suggestion and of how the manner in which this disorder is represented in a community may influence its spread.

Another emphasis in Teresa's discussions was the need to distinguish melancholia from other, superficially allied psychic afflictions of more immediately supernatural origin (for example, trials sent by God, as well as mischief from the devil), at least to the extent that each kind of condition required different handling. (This qualification was an important one, we shall see below.) Although Teresa distinguished between severe and mild cases of melancholia, she believed that the latter, if left untreated, could become so serious that the power of reason could be lost and reason itself would become, in her word, darkened. That said, the darkening of reason that occurred with severe cases seems to be of little intrinsic interest; it was not fully described and was introduced only to explain when a differential treatment was required.

Teresa's attitudes toward, and treatment of, the two categories were markedly and consistently different. Milder cases of the disorder were characterized by a dangerous willfulness or disobedience and needed to be treated with strict, unyielding discipline. More serious cases, in contrast, were to be treated with sympathy and understanding because the sufferer was no longer capable of obedience. She regarded severe cases as involving serious illness that required an appropriate response: the sufferers needed to be given medicine, kept in the infirmary, and excused from blame.

In severe melancholia there was a loss of self-control—which was the basis for Teresa's judgment of relative severity—whereas in milder melancholia some degree of self-control remained (rendering these cases the greater treatment challenge). Teresa emphasized the need to dominate the nun suffering from milder melancholia, which was associated with willfulness or disobedience. What interested these milder melancholic persons most, Teresa observed in *The Foundations*, was getting their own way; they say "everything that comes to their lips...finding rest in what gives them pleasure; in sum, they are like a person who cannot bear anyone who resists him." Faced with this willfulness, the prioress needed to make use of the order's penances and to "strive to bring these persons into submission...to make them understand they will obtain neither all nor part of what they want." There was no remedy other than "to make these persons submit in all the ways and means possible."

While harsh discipline was recommended to extinguish, or at least manage, the willfulness associated with milder cases of melancholia, it should be emphasized that the disobedience at issue here typically involved matters of religious excess (e.g., too frequent and too extreme self-mortification). And the punishments typically involved deprivations, penances such as extra prayers, and being isolated in one's cell.

As to positive prescriptions and preventive measures, Teresa recommended moderate regimes concerning diet, work, rest, and prayer and discouraged extreme behavior, such as excessive self-mortification or religious devotion. Teresa recognized that these remedies might fail. Sometimes, she remarked in *The Interior Castle*, "there is no remedy in this tempest," and those afflicted can only be encouraged to hope for mercy from God.

In writing on the sources and limits of the self-control required to comply with the discipline that she wished to impose in less-severe cases of melancholia, Teresa's observations were especially insightful and promise to throw real light on our own limited understanding of self-control today. Thus, in a passage from *The Foundations* about such cases, she remarked, "Although [they] are not rational, they have to be dealt with as if they were." She seems to imply that between full rationality (with its accompanying self-control) and complete nonrationality (with its lack of control) lie incompletely resolved states where suggestion might play a part. If the nun were persuaded that she had the requisite rational control, she could perhaps actually gain such control. (On an alternative, but compatible, interpretation, it may be said that the obedience demanded by Teresa would have imposed an external order that could restore order to disordered minds.)

Some explanation for Teresa's ideas on melancholia might first be sought in aspects of that remarkable woman's life.[8–12] One such aspect concerns what she did *not* know. As a woman, Teresa was forbidden to study the classical languages, with the consequence that she can have known none of the classical and medieval works on melancholia. She would have been unfamiliar with the Aristotelian and Renaissance views that identified melancholia as the afflication of creative geniuses, with the Renaissance link between melancholia and Saturn, and with the rich visual tradition and iconography around melancholia in the fine arts. Some contemporary texts devoted to melancholia, which emphasized the humoral origin of the disorder, were available in her native Castilian, so she may have known of these texts. Moreover, she may have had access to doctors in Avila (most likely, Jewish converts to Christianity, known as *conversos*), and also to the medical knowledge of the Jesuits.[10] But she seems to have mainly relied on what her religious convictions, coupled with her perceptive observations of other people, taught her.

Teresa also knew melancholia or closely allied states from personal experience, which perhaps provided an additional source for her descriptions. Not all of Teresa's own complaints were identified as illnesses in a secular, medical sense (although descriptions of spiritual and religious states were, during that era, often cast in metaphors of health, illness, and disease). Nonetheless, some of those complaints were so construed, and her own and others' accounts indicate that she was plagued most of her life by despondent moods, inertia, concentration problems, headaches, total and partial paralyses, and digestive irregularities and pain for which she found it necessary to induce daily vomiting.

Another source of Teresa's ideas and assumptions on melancholia and human psychology may have been her idiosyncratic personal history. In the Spain of the sixteenth century, peopled with New Christians (the *conversos*) as well as Old, great emphasis was placed on what was described as "purity of blood" (*limpieza de sangre*). The Inquisition concerned itself with heresy, deceit, and secret Jewish practices.[13] Teresa was from a *converso* family—Jews who had been forced to convert to Christianity in her grandfather's time—and within whose ranks were included several charged with apostasy and punished by the authorities during her childhood and youth for secretly engaging in Jewish practices and maintaining Jewish beliefs while paying public tribute to Christianity. This transgression, known as "Judaizing," was frequently subject to severe punishment in the Spain of Teresa's time.

Teresa's own degree of ambivalence about her Jewish background remains, and will probably always remain, uncertain.[7,8] Since the expulsion of Jews and Moors from Spain in 1492, the powerful and pervasive Inquisition subjected "New Christians" to intense scrutiny and punished them on the merest suspicion.[14] In this setting of danger and deceit, Teresa was surrounded by the fractured identities of those whose public acts of Christianity covered, or were suspected of covering, private Jewish practices or beliefs. One source for Teresa's conception of the self and of the world around her thus seems to be her knowledge of the complex cultural identity of the *converso*. She would have likely conceived of the self as complex and layered, open to suggestion, and not always firmly in—or out of—control. This is not to suggest that Teresa suffered a disorder of identity. Her remarkable effectiveness as a reformer and manager of communities of nuns belies that notion. It is rather that, based on what she experienced and observed around her, and as she approached the problem raised by melancholia in her communities of nuns, she would have adopted a conception of the self that was more layered than unified.

Unlike the inductive method associated with medical writing today, which draws broader conclusions from the carefully accumulated evidence of the illness of particular individuals, Teresa appears to have had little interest in her melancholic nuns as "cases." Indeed, she avoided the use of identifying descriptions altogether. References are to a generalized other: "the afflicted nun," "the poor little thing." Moreover, Teresa's writing only partially reflects the individualism stimulated by the new cultural and political structures of sixteenth-century Europe.[15-17] Her style is strikingly individual, in being personal, direct, and idiosyncratic. Her signature voice leaps from the page as we read. Rather than subscribing to the individualistic conception of the self as an autonomous agent independent of all contingencies, however, Teresa seems to have understood the self in terms of, and as constituted by, its relationships with others. Whatever we may make of Teresa's own personality, the self in Teresa's writing about melancholia was construed less as an individual and more as part of a larger social whole.

Teresa's relational conception of self obviously reflected, in part, the structure of the convent, in which each nun was one element of an interdependent community. The limited and limiting place of women in Spanish society at the time—when entering the cloister represented ordinary women's sole means of avoiding the submissive roles assigned to most women (such as domestic ones) and of acquiring some education—would likely also have perpetuated collectivist models of the self.

Teresa's unwavering attention to the needs and goods of the community would have arisen, too, from her particular occupational and historical challenge. She founded new institutions throughout Spain and trained abbesses to manage these new monastic foundations; her role was consistently managerial in what became a large corporate entity.

Prioritizing these communal goals may have allowed Teresa to advocate deception and to show what seems to have been, from today's perspective, a failure of respect for the individuals involved. Melancholia was a condition to be named and interpreted to its sufferer selectively, if at all. Teresa went as far as to advocate a ban on the use of the term "melancholia" in all religious houses because the afflicted nun, once labeled, would have greater difficulty overcoming her complaint, and other nuns—through the power of suggestion—would be drawn to believe themselves similarly afflicted.

Teresa's practical, pragmatic approach is a second, notable feature of her references to melancholia. Rather than mapping and describing an independent reality as medical writing has traditionally aimed to do, Teresa was attempting to solve a practical, communal problem when she wrote about melancholia. Her writing was unsystematic; her discussions placed no importance on particular cases and individuating symptoms; and the causes of melancholia (black bile, the devil, and self-mortifications, such as fasting, that weakened the body) were isolated only vaguely and emphasized rarely. Rather like medical empiricists—who have appeared intermittently from Hippocratic times until the present, and who focus not on causes but on treatment results—Teresa was indifferent to causes and focused only on practicalities: What works?

Thus, melancholia was nowhere represented as a distinct phenomenon separable from the treatment context. And Teresa's interest in it was limited to two practical concerns: distinguishing it from the states of distress sent by God or the devil, which required alternative spiritual ministrations, and preventing its damaging effects on the whole community. In medical writing on melancholia from Hippocrates and Galen onward, divisions and subdivisions have typically been elaborate and, also, usually causally based. Teresa employed one division—severe versus mild—and that exclusively for the purpose of offering differential treatments.

Emblematic of her practical approach is the way that Teresa dealt with any questions about the reality of melancholia. Those who were severely afflicted should be treated *as if* they were sick—not, notice, because they actually were so. Similarly, at least in her work on prayer—*The Interior Castle*, written later than the passages on melancholia in *The Foundations*—Teresa insisted that, regardless of their source, locutions (private voices) needed to be ignored and treated as if they were temptations in matters of faith. That way, Teresa believed, they would go away and not influence their sufferers; if the melancholic nun was encouraged to treat her locutions as temptations from the devil, she would best be able to ignore and thus overcome them. Even if locutions came not from the devil but from the weak imagination (of melancholia), Teresa remarked in *The Interior Castle* that "it's necessary to treat them *as if* they were temptations in matters of faith, and thus resist them always. They will go away because they will have little effect on you" (emphasis added). Teresa proposed adopting a spiritual rather than a medical frame of reference, it seems, not because of any particular belief about the origins of the disorder but out of a conviction that a spiritual approach would be more effective in eliminating the problem, specifically by granting greater self-control to, and reducing distress in, the sufferer.

Recent scholarship has emphasized Teresa's vulnerability as an outspoken critic of the established religious and political order. It has been suggested that her writing and ideas must be read as carefully selected, defensive creations that were designed to protect herself and her communities of nuns from very real dangers.[7] This conception requires us to adopt some degree of skepticism as we interpret Teresa's remarks about melancholia, perhaps especially the harsh tone that she adopted when she wrote of enforcing submission and obedience in the willful, mildly melancholic nun. The strict obedience that Teresa demanded would have been the safest response to the threat imposed by the Inquisition, which played an increasingly menacing and invasive part in policing aberrant behavior by women outside, and within, the cloister.

Teresa of Avila's personal background and particular times likely shaped the attitudes and assumptions about the self and the world that distinguished her thinking about melancholia. These attitudes and assumptions may have contributed, in turn, to her distinctive insights into melancholia in the cloister. Such insights include the factor of self-control in its identification and treatment (as severe versus mild) and the element of suggestibility in its prevention. The issue of self-control needed to be at the center of treatment decisions, she insisted, yet self-control was not, she recognized, an all-or-nothing state. Rather, it could be fostered and strengthened through the right kinds of interventions by others. Precisely because the influence of others was so powerful, however, it could also weaken self-control and spread melancholia—and not just reduce it. Hence the importance of what was communicated—and how. Despite her emphasis on the power of communication, Teresa acknowledged that bodily weakness brought on by fasting, self-mortification, and religious excesses would likely have enhanced the effects of suggestion and influence. Although her broader causal analysis included supernatural elements, we can set those aside and admire her understanding of this range of the natural causes of melancholia.

References

1. Jackson S. *Melancholia and depression.* New Haven, CT: Yale University Press, 1986.
2. Weyer J, Mora G, ed., Shea J, trans. *Witches, devils, and doctors in the Renaissance: Johann Weyer: De Praestigiis Daemonum.* Binghamton, NY: Medieval and Renaissance Texts and Studies, 1991.
3. Saint Teresa of Avila; Kavanaugh K, Rodriguez O, trans. *The collected works of St. Teresa of Avila.* Washington, DC: Institute of Carmelite Studies, 1976–85.
4. Radden J, ed. *The nature of melancholy.* Oxford, New York: Oxford University Press, 2000.
5. Saint Teresa of Avila; Kavanaugh K, trans. *The collected letters of St. Teresa of Avila.* Vol. 1. Washington, DC: Institute of Carmelite Studies, 2001.
6. Weber A. Saint Teresa, demonologist. In: Cruz A, Perry ME, eds., *Culture and control in Counter-Reformation Spain.* Minneapolis: University of Minnesota Press, 1992.

7. Lindberg C, ed. *The Reformation theologians: an introduction to theology in the early modern period*. Oxford: Blackwell, 2002.
8. Ahlgren GTW. *Teresa of Avila and the politics of sanctity*. Ithaca, NY: Cornell University Press, 1996.
9. Medwick C. *Teresa of Avila: the progress of a soul*. New York: Knopf, 1999.
10. Perry E. *Gender and disorder in modern Seville*. Princeton, NJ: Princeton University Press, 1990.
11. Cruz A, Perry M, eds. *Culture and control in Counter-Reformation Spain*. Minneapolis: University of Minnesota Press, 1992.
12. Howells E. *John of the Cross and Teresa of Avila: mystical knowing and selfhood*. New York: Crossroad, 2002.
13. Gitlitz DM. *Secrecy and deceit: the religion of the crypto-Jews*. Philadelphia, Jerusalem: Jewish Publication Society, 1996.
14. Giles M, ed. *Women in the Inquisition*. Baltimore: Johns Hopkins University Press, 1999.
15. Burckhurdt J; Middlemore SGC, trans. *The civilization of the Renaissance in Italy*. Oxford: Oxford University Press, 1945.
16. Davis NZ. Boundaries and the sense of self in sixteenth-century France. In: Heller T, Wellbery D, eds. *Reconstructing individualism: autonomy, individuality, and the self in Western thought*. Stanford, CA: Stanford University Press, 1986.
17. Greenblatt S. *Renaissance self-fashioning: from More to Shakespeare*. Chicago: University of Chicago Press, 1980.

2

Melancholy: History of a Concept

Melancholy, Melancholia, and Depression as Affective States and Kraepelinian Diseases

Whatever their other association, melancholy and depression are today viewed as states suffered, not sought—conditions beyond voluntary control. The contrast between active and passive states, however, reflects a relatively recent emphasis.

Our mental categories are the product of faculty psychology. (In faculty psychology separable mental functions such as thinking, imagining, feeling, and willing were thought to be usefully conceptualized, if not explained, by positing mental faculties corresponding to each.) These faculty psychological divisions only solidified in psychology and philosophy since the seventeenth and eighteenth centuries. Other cultures and traditions and our own culture at earlier times can be shown to have employed different ways of dividing the person. It thus behooves us to examine premodern writing about melancholy attentive to the "modernist" framing by which depression is today a mood or feeling and beyond the power of the will. By comparing earlier with later writing we may identify the influence of these ways of constructing and dividing mental states and abilities.

The monastic failing of despondency and inertia known as "acedia," or *accidia*, and the related failing of the dejection, sadness, or sorrow known as *tristitia*, will serve to illustrate. Scholars debate the exact relation between these failings and melancholy, but their closeness cannot be denied. Later, acedia was also allied with or identified with the sin of sloth, or *desidia*. Acedia was a fate to be struggled against. The true Christian athlete, writes John Cassian, in the fifth century, "should hasten to expel this disease...and should strive against this most evil spirit" (Cassian 1995).

This chapter consists of selections from the introduction to *The Nature of Melancholy: Readings on Melancholy, Melancholia and Depression from Aristotle to Kristeva*. New York: Oxford University Press, 2000. Reprinted with permission from Oxford University Press, Inc.

If acedia is regarded as a temptation and later a sin, then one might suppose it to be a state which is within our power to prevent. And if acedia were akin to melancholy, perhaps melancholy once eluded the category of a state suffered passively, also.

May we conclude acedia was a state over which its sufferer exercised control? Not quite, apparently. Its later designation as a cardinal sin meant that there were moral injunctions against acedia, undoubtedly. One source, here, are the handbooks of penance ("penitentials") which became popular in the thirteenth century. Such handbooks frequently implied that confession was a form of healing and the sins of the penitent were afflictions for which, not literally, but employing a medical metaphor, the sufferer was to be "treated" and "cured" rather than chastised. This suggests that acedia is a condition falling midway between a disease to which its victims haplessly succumbed and a bad habit. In this respect, acedia might be said to resist the modernist categories to which we are inclined to subject it.

Alternative faculty psychological divisions, such as that between thought and imagination, can sometimes be identified in works of classification from the eighteenth century. But by the classifications of the following century, the grid imposed by the cognitive and affective faculties is widely and consistently evident and acquires greater prominence. For example, it is found in aspects of the construction of melancholia or depression as a clinical disorder that came with the emergence of clinical psychiatry at the end of the nineteenth century. Thus, the category of affective faculties appears to have influenced a fundamental psychiatric division—still found in the American Psychiatric Association's *Diagnostic and Statistical Manuals* and in the World Health Organization's *International Classification of Diseases* of the twentieth century: that between disorders of mood or affect, of which depression is one, and other disorders.

The late nineteenth century saw the emergence of psychiatry as a distinct medical specialization and with it a number of more or less authoritative psychiatric diagnostic classifications. Of these classificatory schemes, Kraepelin's system, as it is developed through the series of editions of his famous *Textbook of Psychiatry*, stands out as the most systematic and exhaustive, as the most influential in its time, and as the most clinically based. (As the director of an asylum, Kraepelin had for his empirical "database" the resources and meticulous records of a large, long-term, inpatient population.) It was due to these (among other) factors that Kraepelin's scheme became the most obvious source for subsequent twentieth-century classifications.

Kraepelin's ascendancy came at the end of a century of great change in thinking about every aspect of mental disorder. The growing medicalization of madness, the shift, documented by Foucault, from a conception of mental disorder as "unreason" to one in which it is a tamed, muted medical condition, has been widely portrayed (Foucault 1965, Scull 1979). During the first half of the nineteenth century, the "birth of the asylum" (Foucault) on the continent of Europe, and various English Acts of Parliament such as the Lunatics Act of 1845, reflected the "medical monopoly" (Scull) on madness. This gathering monopoly was not based on the success of medical treatments as much as on the emerging power of institutionalized medicine, historians have shown, together with an increasingly confident materialism and physiological psychology that posited exact parallels between mental and physical disorders. Localized lesions of the brain, it had come to be held, must be the source of mental disorder—although employing a notion of lesion more elastic and accommodating than our present one (Gosling 1987). While purely psychological "moral treatment" was not yet dismissed as worthless in curing the insane, only medical doctors understood the brain; doctors, then, became the rightful purveyors of care to the mentally afflicted.

As psychiatry became a distinct subdiscipline of clinical medicine, with its own practices and subject matter, writing about mental disorder becomes more precise. The distinction between melancholy moods, states, and dispositions attributable to most people and melancholia as mental disorder received increasing emphasis and served to delineate the subject matter of such texts. At the time of these broader changes, the relation between melancholia and depression also apparently underwent significant change. Hitherto, "melancholia" indicated a range of different conditions, some closer to today's delusional disorders, others to what we would distinguish as an affective or mood disorder. (One earlier usage, for example, in line with the eighteenth-century tendency to classify all mental disturbance as forms of cognitive disorder, depicted melancholia as a type of delusional thinking about some limited subject matter, a partial insanity [Jackson 1983].)

The narrower and more recent term "depression" originally referred only to a quality or symptom of melancholia. Samuel Johnson and others had spoken of a "depression" of spirits, but "depression" did not occur as a noun until toward the end of the nineteenth century and began to eclipse "melancholia," in referring to a disorder category, only by the twentieth century. Thus, writing of simple melancholia in Tuke's influential *Dictionary of Psychological Medicine*, the English doctor Charles Mercier merely spoke of a condition in which "the depression of feeling is unattended by delusion" (Mercier 1892:789)

By the time the term "depression" entered Kraepelin's writing, in contrast, it came to be used for a syndrome or symptom cluster rather than being merely one symptom of the broader category of melancholia. When in 1886 Kraepelin revised his nosological scheme in line with the separation between more- and less-optimistic prognoses, he used the term "periodic psychoses" for the collection of affective conditions that included mania, melancholia, and circular insanity. A year later, in the sixth edition of the *Textbook*, these became the "manic-depressive psychoses" that included "depressed states." By the eighth edition, published between 1909 and 1913, the depressive forms include five kinds of melancholia, divided primarily in terms of severity. "Depression" had taken its place as the name of a kind of symptom cluster.

Kraepelin's era also saw increased confidence in the "somatist" belief that mental disorder was a form of brain disease and that specific, localized lesions in the brain would eventually be identified with psychiatric symptom clusters. The discovery of the relation between syphilis and the dementing symptoms that were its sequelae (known as general paresis of the insane) provided the model. It fostered the assumption that, like physical diseases, mental diseases were a class of natural kinds: discrete and uniform symptom clusters that afforded ready and reliable identification. The analysis of diseases as syndromal entities and natural kinds was not of nineteenth-century origin. It is evident, for example, as early as the writing of Thomas Sydenham in England during the seventeenth century, who analogized diseases with the "determinate kinds" of botany. Nonetheless, it reached its high point two centuries later, during the historical era when psychiatric classification came of age.

The influence of Wilhelm Griesinger, and that of another important figure in the history of medicine, Rudolph Virchow, are reflected in these ideas. Griesinger had in 1845 published his somatist treatise arguing, against the "moralism" of the time, that psychological diseases are brain diseases and that the pathological anatomy of the nervous system and brain would prove to be the source of all mental or psychical disorder. Virchow had established the principles of cellular pathology in 1858, insisting that all diseases are localized. This German somatism, while at first (and subsequently) controversial, made a deep and lasting impression in America at the end of the nineteenth century. As the Americanist Elizabeth Lunbeck remarks, "However elusive the paradigm of general paresis would prove, the medical model of disease it underwrote attained a hegemonic position within psychiatric thought...[allowing] practitioners to order their observations as if disease—with its attendant etiology, course, and outcome—underlay what they could see" (Lunbeck 1994:117).

Two legacies from earlier eras acquired new significance when wedded to the nascent science of psychiatry, and together they encouraged a division of the brain and mental functioning into broad categories, including those concerned with cognition and those with affection. One was the legacy from faculty psychology (and later phrenology), in which functional divisions had been reified and concretized. Affection, or the affective faculty, corresponded with a localized part of the brain. Damage to or disease of that part of the brain accounted for diseases of the affective faculty (or as they were sometimes called, diseases of the passions). A second but related legacy was a strong set of *associations* growing out of the earlier, eighteenth-century distinction between Reason and Passion. These associations served to further polarize the mental functions of thinking or cognition, on the one hand, and feeling or affection, on the other.

The first of these legacies is well conveyed in the division of mental diseases enunciated by an American clinician of the first half of the nineteenth century, Rufus Wyman. Wyman was the physician superintendent of McLean Asylum, at Charlestown, a branch of the Massachusetts General Hospital, between 1818 and 1835. Writers on mental philosophy, Wyman remarks, "arrange the mental operations or states under two heads, one of which regards our knowledge, the other our feelings. The former includes the functions of the intellect....The latter includes the affections, emotions or passions, or the pathetical powers or states....This division of the mental states or functions has suggested a corresponding division of mental diseases of the intellect and diseases of the passions" (Wyman 1830/1970:810). Writing more than thirty years later in Germany, Griesinger speaks in almost the same terms: "From our observations," he remarks, "there are two groups of insanities: firstly, the affective ones, secondly the primary disturbances of perception and will, arising not from a problem of mood but from false thinking and will" (Griesinger 1867/1965:207). This passage is particularly important because of its influence on the Kraepelinian classification to follow. In his belief that mood disorder was an entity per se, it has been asserted, Griesinger prepared the ground for the Kraepelinean view (Berrios and Beer 1994:25).

Faculty psychology reflected functional divisions, as these passages from Wyman and Griesinger make clear. In addition, faculty psychology invited a "reification" of the functional units–entitled faculties, suggesting that the intellect and the passions corresponded with parts of the brain, each separately subject to disease. The flourishing "science" of phrenology, which localized all functions and traits, was an emblem of, and probably encouraged, this tendency to suppose real parts of the brain corresponded with each functional category. Nonetheless, not all who made use of faculty psychology to draw functional categories took the further, reifying step. For instance, the influential English psychiatrist of this period, Henry Maudsley, succeeded in avoiding it, warning that "the different forms of insanity are *not actual pathological entities*" (Maudsley 1867:323; my emphasis). This was because for Maudsley *all* insanity was inaugurated by a disturbance of the affective life.

The final division between disorders of affect (Kraepelin's manic-depressive diseases, which included melancholia), and disorders of the cognitive faculties (Kraepelin's dementia praecox), required a narrowing of the hitherto broader melancholia. Earlier than the nineteenth century, as we have seen, melancholia was often associated with fixed, false beliefs, or delusions—that is, with defects of reasoning and cognition. But now the delusional features of disorder were increasingly distinguished from the affective ones. Both a growing emphasis on the affective symptoms of melancholia and a corresponding neglect of its more cognitive delusional features occurred during the first half of the nineteenth century (Jackson 1986).

Kraepelin attempted to model psychiatry on the natural sciences: the task of psychiatric classification involved discovering and naming the naturally occurring kinds of mental disorder. He was famous for the care with which he established his generalizations on the basis of the long-term case studies he accumulated. Yet intent on a process of what he took to be discovering natural kinds, convinced that the disease entities of psychiatry would present symptom clusters in the same way as organic diseases, uncritical in his embrace of the division between cognition and affection, Kraepelin failed to recognize the possibility that the broad categories of affection and cognition were being imposed upon, rather than discovered in, his observation of the symptom clusters with which his patients were afflicted.

Because of his conviction that the course of every form of insanity included disordered affectivity, Maudsley did not fall prey to Kraepelin's error. But more than that, he also seems to have anticipated that particular error, and he warns of it with spectacular clarity. There is in the human mind, he remarks, "a sufficiently strong propensity not only to make divisions in knowledge where there are none in nature, and then to impose the divisions upon nature, making the reality thus conformable to the idea, but to go further, and to convert the generalizations made from observation into positive entities, permitting for the future these artificial creations to tyrannize over the understanding" (Maudsley 1867:323–24).

The second legacy from earlier eras inviting a separation of disorders of affection was an entrenched set of *associations* clustering around cognition, reason, and thought, on the one side, and affection, passion, and feeling, on the other. With the appearance of the modern scientific method in the sixteenth and seventeenth centuries had come emphasis on the distinction between human subjectivity and value in contrast to the observable and measurable objects of scientific study (Lloyd 1984). Reason had come to be regarded as the sole means to discovering an objective and value-free reality. Feeling and passion, in contrast, were increasingly depicted as forces beyond their subject's control and eluding rational understanding. Later, additional associations gathered around each pole: reason represented maleness and the masculine; passion was identified with femaleness and the feminine. (In Hegel's writing in the nineteenth century, for instance, male and female roles were organized around this contrast. Reason was associated with the public realm; passion with the private and domestic.)

Anthropologist Catherine Lutz has enumerated the range of associations that came to attach to the notion of affective states in the European Enlightenment period. They include not only the feminine, the private, and the domestic but also estrangement, irrationality, unintended and uncontrolled action, danger and vulnerability, physicality, subjectivity, and value (Lutz 1986). Such associations are evident in medical writing from the late nineteenth century period we are interested in, moreover. By midcentury, Thomas Laycock was analogizing women to children in their "affectability" when he wrote his book on the nervous diseases of women (Laycock 1840:131). And Robert Carter spoke of a "natural conformation" that causes women to *feel*, under circumstances where men *think*, and he built on this allegedly natural division a proneness to hysteria in women and to hypochondria in men (Carter 1853:33).

Out of this combination of ideas and assumptions of the late nineteenth century came the classificatory schema, still one of the most basic divisions in Western psychiatric nosological maps today, which separates disorders (or as Kraepelin has it, "diseases") of affect from other conditions.

The ascendancy of the distinction between affective as against other disorders outlined here did not take place without a struggle. One alternative classificatory heuristic posited a single type of psychosis, inaugurated by a phase of melancholia. This unitary psychosis hypothesis had had its supporters even among eighteenth-century thinkers, though in a rather different guise, and was associated with several important figures in the nineteenth century, including the early Griesinger. In addition, though none achieved lasting influence, classifications employing alternative faculty psychology divisions were proposed during the nineteenth-century period, positing diseases of the memory, will, personality, imagination, and moral faculties (for example, Ribot 1881, 1983, 1885).

The influence of the mental faculties can also be found in early-twentieth-century psychological accounts of emotion, such as the James-Lange theory, with their attempts to equate emotions with involuntary, noncognitive states of feeling and sensation. This view has been challenged both by cognitivists like Aaron Beck and by "cognitivist" theories of emotion long maintained within philosophy, in which emotions comprise cognitive and affective elements (Beck 1978). Beck's analysis is causal. The mood states associated with depression are responses to distorted cognitive states. Therapy addresses and alters these cognitive distortions to alleviate despondent affective responses. In contrast, philosophical cognitivist theories of emotion elevate the cognitive states to the status not of causes but of "constituents," the essential features whose presence either solely or together with affective features serve to define the emotions in question. (Thus, for example, my response is identified as "regret" rather than "sadness" in part, or wholly, by the cognitive specification of its object as a past event or events for which I have some degree of responsibility.)

Psychoanalytic thinking always and conspicuously avoided these mental faculty divisions between the cognitive and the affective, however, as is apparent in Freud's elaborate account of the mind afflicted with melancholia. The new—or at least sharpened—association of depression with loss and self-loathing that emerges from "Mourning and Melancholia" introduces to the subjective states under discussion a more closely formulated belief element. Earlier accounts of a simple, almost mood-like subjectivity of nebulous fear and sorrow is at odds with the frame of mind of Freud's melancholiac. So Freud's innovative emphasis on the cognitive attitudes toward the self in melancholia introduces a further turn, new to any psychiatric thinking about melancholia and depression and not consonant with the noncognitivist emphasis of the two decades of nonpsychoanalytic psychiatric thinking about melancholic states that preceded the publication of "Mourning and Melancholia" in 1917.

Melancholy as an Essentially Subjective Condition

Several aspects of the subjectivity of melancholy and melancholia require attention. One concerns feelings of melancholy when these are construed as momentary, felt, affective *occurrences* in contrast to *more habitual states*. Burton hints at something of this distinction when he speaks of "that transitory melancholy which goes and comes upon every small occasion of sorrow, need, sickness, trouble, fear, grief, passion or perturbation of the mind" (Burton 1621/1989:000).

Burton's purpose here, however, is to separate what he regards as normal, every-day subjective and behavioral manifestations of melancholy from more entrenched, and more serious, conditions. Thus, melancholy is either "in disposition" or "in habit" for Burton. The universal disposition, from which no man living is free, is ascribed when a man is "dull, sad, sour, lumpish, ill-disposed, solitary, any way moved or displeased." In contrast, this other kind of melancholy "is a habit,...a chronic or continuate disease, a settled humour...not errant, but fixed." Burton's division emphasizes the frequency and persistence of the subjective mood of melancholy. It is perhaps confusing to us in using the term "disposition" for the state cast in contrast to the "habit" of melancholy which is a more enduring trait: nowadays the term "disposition" is allied with the habitual tendency. Moreover, the settled humor Burton describes as subject for treatment may merely manifest itself in more frequent occurrences of the "sad, sour, lumpish, solitary" feelings found, as he says, in all men.

Burton here reveals one distinction: that between transitory and more settled forms of melancholy. Another distinction, however, remains unemphasized. This is the division we would today mark between the subjective and behavioral. The subjective captures what is able to be introspected—that which we alone know directly about our own mental and psychological states. The behavioral is that which may be known from the detached perspective of third-person observation, even in the absense of the subject's cooperation or verbal report. Like the modernist division between reason and passion, the division between the subjective and the behavioral is a product of a particular era (in this case, the nineteenth century), and of a particular set of purposes and practices—those of psychology. (In some behaviorist traditions, verbal behavior was included as reliable evidence; in others, even it was excluded.) As psychology separated from philosophy to become a distinct and distinctly empirical discipline, the experimentalists and behaviorists did battle with the introspectionists. These same contrasting sets of method and assumption were to harden, during the twentieth century, into the division between experimental and phenomenological approaches. Burton captures some of the subjectivity of melancholy in the *Anatomy*, but his focus is not on this methodological distinction. To be sad at least, if not to be sour, is to experience an essentially subjective condition determined, finally, from one's own subjective standpoint. In contrast, lumpishness and solitary tendencies may be identified as well by others as by oneself: "lumpish" and "solitary" are more behavioral terms.

The notion of melancholy as a subjective mood associated with literary work captures both the sense of a transitory and passing state, and the sense of an essentially subjective state. This notion gave rise to adjectival uses of "melancholy" of the kind Samuel Johnson notes in his dictionary: "Melancholy" as "a gloomy, pensive, discontented temper" yields the adjective "melancholy" indicating "gloomy" or "dismal," which is applied not only to persons but to landscape and events.

Klibansky, Panofsky, and Saxl identify in lyric writing, narrative poetry, and prose romances of the postmedieval era a poetic sense of melancholy as a passing subjective mood state (Klibansky et al., 1964). This poetic melancholy contrasts to the notion of melancholy as both a disease and a temperament, and in literary contexts the poetic notion of melancholy as a temporary mood of sadness and distress came partially to eclipse these earlier meanings. In all modern European literature, these authors assert, the expression "melancholy" lost the meaning of a quality and acquired instead the meaning of a "mood" that could be transferred to inanimate objects. Now we find references not only to melancholy attitudes but also to melancholy scenes, miens, and states of affairs.

The importance of melancholy subjectivity seems to gather force with the notion of Romantic melancholy, which emerged at the end of the eighteenth century. The man of melancholy in Romantic writing was, like Goethe's suffering Werther, all feeling, all sensibility. At times exaggerated emphasis fell on feelings—feelings of solitude, darkness, grief, suffering, despair, longing, and elegiac sadness.

Of the way the early modern poetic melancholy was transformed into late-eighteenth-century Romantic sensibility, it has been observed that the pressure of the religious conflicts of the sixteenth century rendered melancholy "a merciless reality, before whom men trembled...and whom they tried in vain to banish by a thousand antidotes and consolatory treatises." Only later was it possible for the imagination to transfigure melancholy into "an ideal condition, inherently pleasurable, however painful—a condition which by the continually renewed tension between depression and exaltation, unhappiness and 'apartness,' horror of death and increased awareness of life, could impart a new vitality to drama, poetry and art" (Klibansky et al., 1964:233). And it was not until after the excesses of the Gothic Revival "Graveyard School" of poetry with its ruins, churchyards, cloisters, yews, and ghosts, and after writing about melancholy had become stale in the convention, that Romanticism's "intensely personal utterance of profound individual sorrow" was possible (Klibansky et al., 1964:238). Only with the acuteness and vitality of early-nineteenth-century work as Keats's poetry, these authors believe, do we find writing on melancholy to match the Elizabethan's.

Alongside this flowering of Romantic ideas of melancholy with their emphasis on subjectivity, modern psychiatry was born. But in modern psychiatry's final and most definitive nineteenth-century analysis, that of Kraepelin's system of classification, the importance of melancholic subjectivity is diminished and the behavioral and bodily are increasingly privileged over the subjective.

The distinction between subjective and behavioral is reflected in the contrast between a symptom-based and a sign-based diagnostic emphasis in clinical medicine. The "symptom" is a patient's complaint, a description of inner states; a "sign," in contrast, is an outwardly observable feature of behavior or bodily condition. (A pain is a symptom; a rash a sign.) Maudsley's 1867 analysis of melancholia is psychological and symptom-based. Sixteen years later, Kraepelin's characterization of depression can be seen to deemphasize the subjective in favor of the behavioral. (That said, in contrast to the sparse subjective descriptions provided in today's textbooks of psychiatry, Kraepelin's accounts of the patient's subjective experiences are detailed and thorough.)

The trend foreshadowed in this Kraepelinian emphasis on more behavioral aspects of clinical depression is understandable. Later psychiatric nosology had cause to diminish the importance of what is sometimes known as the mood factor in depression: against subjective symptoms like felt sadness, directly observable signs like sleeplessness and weight loss better fit prevailing conceptions of scientific rigor. By the third edition of the American Psychiatric Association's *Diagnostic and Statistical Manual*, in 1980, clinical depression was characterized as much or more by certain behavioral manifestations (or "vegetative signs") as by the moods and feelings it involved: by a slowing or agitation of movement, by fatigue, loss of appetite, and sleep disturbance. Moreover, with this emphasis on behavioral and directly observable signs came refinement on the notion of depression. Now "agitated depression," marked by restless overactivity, was distinguished from "retarded depression," where activity was slowed down or inhibited. The fourth edition of the diagnostic and statistical manual in 1994 has continued this behavioral emphasis, despite some resistance. And a more recent empirical study observes that psychomotor disturbance is "both the most consistently suggested and most discriminating feature, especially when measured as an observed sign," across *"all assessment approaches to melancholia"* (Parker and Hadzi-Pavlovic 1996:25; my emphasis).

A theme in contemporary feminist writing on melancholy and depression emphasizes the contrast between loquacious male melancholy and the mute suffering (or as Schiesari has it, the mourning) of women. An emphasis on women's loss of speech is found in the work of Julia Kristeva, Judith Butler, and Luce Irigaray, as well as in Lacanian ideas (Kristeva 1989; Butler 1990, 1993; Irigaray 1991). In turn, women's estrangement from language is explained by an estrangement from the self, associated with the inevitably masculine "author" of the "self-narrative." Without embarking here on an analysis of these complex ideas, I would note that a disorder increasingly understood in terms of its behavioral manifestations will also serve to "silence" its sufferers. As, and to the extent that, emphasis is placed on observable signs over subjective and voiced symptoms, so the silence of that mute suffering must be even more profound. Whether as its cause, or one of its effects, the trend toward a behavioral analysis of clinical depression would likely accompany the "silencing" of depression.

Melancholic States as Mood States

Renaissance and later writing about melancholia concerns as much nebulous, pervasive, and nonintentional *moods* of fear and sadness (no cause) as fear and sadness in excess of their occasions (without sufficient cause). If melancholic fear and sadness are entirely without an identifiable cause felt to be what the mood is about or over, and are rather over or about nothing in particular—or everything—then they are moods, on a standard philosophical distinction.

Medical accounts of the early modern period contain reference both to fears and sorrows "without cause" and "without apparent cause" (Jackson 1986). This is readily illustrated through the copious case-notebooks of Richard Napier (1559–1634), presented and analyzed in contemporary times by McDonald (McDonald 1981). Napier was a medical man and clergyman who saw many patients "troubled in mind" during the first thirty-five years of the seventeenth century. Napier's melancholic patients sometimes suffered what appear to have been delusions and hallucinations, although demonic possession may have complicated people's attitudes toward, and preparedness to acknowledge, these more severe symptoms. But the majority of Napier's patients complained of melancholy, mopishness (a kind of dullness and sour failure of interest commonly attributed during the seventeenth century), anxiety, fear, gloom, sadness, despair, heavy-heartedness, inertia, and disinterest. (One patient was "solitary...and will do nothing," in Napier's words.) Much here suggests moods (without cause) rather than more cognitive and belief-based states (without sufficient cause).

Although nebulous, moods of anxiety, fear, and apprehension form a cluster distinguishable from moods of despondency, despair, and sadness. And like earlier Greek and Renaissance symptom descriptions, early modern accounts such as Napier's give equal emphasis to the two kinds of feeling. With the more medical focus of the nineteenth century, however, descriptions of melancholia seem to place stronger emphasis on the latter feeling-cluster (despondency, despair, and sadness). The "depressed" mood of early psychiatry is more of groundless sadness and despondency than of groundless fear and anxiety. Arguably, this narrowing is invited by new diagnostic categories. Neurasthenia and hysteria, and later obsessional and anxiety disorders, are more closely associated with groundless and irrational fears.

Gender: Depressive Subjectivity as Feminine

Reinforcing the isolation of diseases of the passions from other disease categories was a set of associations, of which one association was with the female and the feminine.

This legacy directs us to the intriguing twentieth-century "gendering" of depression understood as a clinical and subclinical disorder.

Today's depression sufferer seems to be female. Not only is this gender link true as diagnostic, and likely as epidemiological, fact; it also seems to be entrenched as part of our cultural imagination. Yet in one identifiable pattern, beginning at least as early as medieval times and still evident in eighteenth-century writing, women were considered not more but less susceptible to melancholy than men. Galen's contemporary in second-century Rome, Areteus of Cappadocia, believed that men are the more frequent sufferers of melancholy, as did the Persian doctor Avicenna, and, writing in the sixteenth century, Johann Weyer (although by using women for case illustration more frequently than he does men, Weyer seems to belie his own generalization). Benjamin Rush noted that partial insanity or "tristimania" (his term for melancholia) affects men more than women (Rush 1812). Sometimes added is a qualification: because of their nature, women are more severely affected when they experience melancholia.

This alignment between men and melancholic states is also found in eighteenth-century nonmedical writing, although it was not always accepted without question. First, in a poem titled "On a Certain Lady at Court" (1735), Alexander Pope identified "the thing that's most uncommon," a reasonable woman. Such an unusual woman, he remarks, would be:

> Not warped by passion, awed by rumour,
> Not grave through pride, or gay through folly,
> An equal mixture of good humour,
> And sensible soft melancholy.

Sensible, soft melancholy, we may infer, is more common in men. Writing sixty years later than Pope's poem, that astute observer of cultural roles Mary Wollstonecraft identified the same alignment between maleness and melancholy. She, however, protested the suggestion, that she attributes to an (unnamed) contemporary author, that "durable," steady, and *valuable* passions, like melancholy, are masculine traits, while women are subject only to fickle, changeable, and valueless passions (Wollstonecraft 1792/1988).

In apparent contradiction to this gender pattern linking melancholy with the masculine, iconic conventions between the early modern and the eighteenth-century periods seem to favor the notion of "Dame Melancholy" and "Dame Tristesse" as a woman, Dürer's famous series on melancholia offering perhaps the best known, but by no means the only, example. However, experts on such images insist that these female figures and depictions of what came to be known as "Dame Melancholy" represented, at most, the "feminine" within man, and a metaphor of male sorrow (Klibansky et al. 1964:349–50; Schiesari 1992); or the *cause* and *source* of male melancholy (Benjamin 1977:151). Moreover, the link reconnecting melancholy with genius through the Italian humanist period inevitably represents melancholy in the *man* of genius and genius in the *man* of melancholy. The category of genius had no more place for women than had the category of melancholy.

Drawing from the writing and iconic representation of the pre-nineteenth-century period to determine actual prevalence rates of melancholia in women and men

must be speculative and imprecise. It does seem fairly widely accepted that somewhere late in the nineteenth century, along with the emergence of melancholia
as something close to today's depression, melancholic subjectivity became—or
became increasingly and identifiably—feminine. This link between women, the
feminine, and present-day depression has two aspects, distinguishable in principle
but entwined in practice: the first is associative; the second, however, is epidemiological, concerning the actual prevalence rates of disorder in women and men.

The affective life of emotions, moods, and feelings was deemed unruly, unreli-
able, capricious, and beyond voluntary control; it was irrational and disordered, it was
associated with the bodily, with subjectivity, and with the feminine. These associations,
as we have seen, had been accruing since the eighteenth century. (Generalizations
such as this oversimplify, of course. For example, eighteenth-century attitudes distinguished among the different passions, as we have seen. Nonetheless, the preceding generalization is not a distortion. The more steady and enduring passions, which
were admired, were those associated with the masculine.)

Undeniably, the overall effect of this set of dualities was to identify the feminine
and women with madness more generally. But some evidence, at least, encourages us to consider that melancholia and depression may have been gender linked.
Because of women's "constitutional gentleness and the mobility of their sensations
and desires," for example, Esquirol remarks, writing in 1845, as well as "by the little
application which they make with reference to any matter," women seem at first to
be less vulnerable to melancholy than men are. And yet, are not "the extreme sus-
ceptibility and sedentary life of our women," the predisposing causes of this malady,
he asks? "Are not women under the control of influences to which men are strang-
ers, such as menstruation, pregnancy, confinement?, and nursing?" The amorous
passions "so active in women," together with religion, "which is a veritable passion
with many [women]," render girls, widows, and menopausal women prone to erotic
and religious melancholy (Esquirol 1845:211). Esquirol's discussion of the prevalence
rates of women suffering melancholia, or what he termed lypemania, reveals a particularly explicit part of this evidence. Later in the century, however, customs of
diagnostic classification obscured such straightforward correlations.

Although he offers case studies of both sexes in his essay on mourning and
melancholia, Freud does not align melancholia in any clear way with the feminine. Indeed, a case can be made that his account of melancholic subjectivity was
associated with the masculine rather than the feminine, just as earlier Renaissance
traditions had been (Schiesari 1992). Freud's contemporary Kraepelin, in contrast,
while he aimed to be an empirical scientist through and through, reveals occasional
glimpses of gender links connecting the affective with the feminine in his volumi-
nous writing about manic-depression. Among ourselves, he remarks, referring to
the patient population at his institution "about 70% of the patients (suffering manic
depressive insanity) belong to the female sex *with its greater emotional excitability*"
(Kraepelin 1920:174; my emphasis).

Lunbeck's discussion of the case materials of the Boston Psychopathic Hospital
from this period illustrates the gender association a different way: she shows case
descriptions of manic-depression that note the unmanly and effeminate traits of
men who suffered this disorder (Lunbeck 1994:149–50). The cultural trope on which

such judgments rest was a pervasive one. We see it in revulsion over the degenerate, sickly, and *unmanly* excesses of feeling associated with "Wertherism" and "green sickness" during the same period. This reaction against Romantic notions allowed no place for manly men among the passive, helpless, unhappy subjects of melancholic disorders.

As early as Kraepelin's writing, the epidemiological identification between women and the affective disorder known as manic-depression had been established, as the above passage from Kraepelin illustrates. This is not to be confused, however, with the more general link between women and madness associated with the second half of the nineteenth century. Concerning that more general link, a review of historical records from Victorian England concludes that this era saw insanity's "feminization": "the mid-nineteenth century is the period when the predominance of women among the institutionalized insane first becomes a statistically verifiable phenomenon" (Showalter 1985:52). The accuracy of such assertions has recently been challenged (Scull 1998). But several factors seem to confirm a perceived, if not an actual, gender link during this period. The rising numbers of women believed diagnosed as suffering mental disorder were a source of concern on the part of reformers (Showalter 1985). More significantly, attributions of women's proneness to mental disorder to the phases of female reproductive biology—puberty, pregnancy, childbirth, menopause—were now receiving emphasis in medical texts. Vulnerability to mental disorder had come to be seen as women's biological destiny. This connection between the female reproductive system and the brain was believed to make women the victims of "periodicity." Thus, according to one medical authority of the time, women became insane during pregnancy, after parturition, during lactation, at the age when menses first appear, and at menopause: and "the sympathetic connection existing between the brain and the uterus is plainly seen by the most casual observer" (Blandford 1871:69).

Most familiar to us today from the several maladies to which women's bodies were believed to leave them prone was a range of symptoms occurring after confinement and known as "puerperal" (childbirth) insanity or fever, of which at least some involved mild and severe depression leading to suicide and even infanticide. In puerperal insanity can be traced the sources of today's postpartum depression. Other authorities, including Maudsley, drew direct connections between women's reproductive cycles and melancholia in particular.

Despite Esquirol's bold insistence that melancholia was a women's disorder, late-nineteenth-century historical data must be approached very cautiously. The more specific link between women and affective disorders such as melancholia or depression is not so easily discerned as the larger alignment between women and madness. The link between women and manic depressive illness is supported in historical records and affirmed by present-day historians of psychiatry. Lunbeck, for example, speaking at least of North America, concluded that "from the start, manic-depressive insanity was interpreted as a peculiarly female malady" (Lunbeck 1994:148). Hospital charts, she points out, show women diagnosed with manic-depressive insanity almost twice as often as men. But this Kraepelinian classification, which includes the categories of melancholia as one of several subdivisions of manic depressive illness, does not permit us to keep track of a gender link with melancholia alone, considered as a unipolar condition, for example. There is another difficulty, moreover. Women were identified with certain forms of madness, including hysteria and neurasthenia. But these appear to have been ill-defined and overlapping conditions, neither one clearly distinguished from melancholia (Gosling 1987). Thus diagnostic reliability seems doubtful, at best.

Later observers continued to affirm women's particular proneness to depression into the twentieth century (Chessler 1972; Howell and Bayes 1981; American Psychiatric Association 1980, 1994); some continue to explain manic-depressive disorder in terms of problems peculiar to female reproductive organs (Gibson 1916, Howell and Bayes 1981). These observations must be approached critically also. The extent of the sex link that makes women more likely sufferers of depression than men in today's culture has been challenged (Howell and Bayes 1981, Corob 1987, Hartung and Widiger 1998–99). So has the stability of the epidemiological profile. (Some studies suggest a shift, with fewer women relative to men suffering depression since the 1980s [Klerman and Weissman 1989, Paykel 1991]). And studies have pointed to obvious confounding factors, such as women's greater tendency to engage in help-seeking behavior, although research methods now employed are believed to control for the distortion these factors introduce. Such reservations notwithstanding, however, most epidemiological assessments today continue to assert that depression is strongly gender-linked, a women's disorder.

Narcissism, Self-loathing, and Loss

Freud portrays melancholia as a narcissistic disorder of loss intrinsically directed toward the self. In this respect he introduces a new kind of theory, not hitherto encountered in the range of imbalance theories of depression tracing from Greek humoral theories to the biochemical models of present-day medicine.

Contemporary theorists point to an emphasis on self-identity and on loss in the language of male melancholy from the early modern period predating Freud. As Enterline says of the early modern writing she examines, "'melancholia'...as a kind of grieving without end or sufficient cause, is a state that disrupts the *subject's identity* as a sexual and as a speaking being" (Enterline 1995:8; (my emphasis)). For Schiesari, also, the Renaissance *Homo melancholicus* represents the "ego's warring over the object of loss, such that the loss itself becomes the dominant feature and not the lost object" (Schiesari 1992:11). (For Schiesari, though, the loss entailed in melancholy is a privileged form of male expression from which mourning women are precluded.) And for Kristeva, depression is "the hidden face of Narcissus" so that "I discover the antecedents to my current breakdown in a loss, death, or grief over someone or something that I once loved." Again, Kristeva observes that we see "the shadow cast on the fragile self, hardly dissociated from the other, precisely by the loss of that essential other. The shadow of despair" (Kristeva 1989:5). Melancholy and melancholic states appear as disorders of self and self-identity and conditions of loss.

The emphasis on loss, on the one hand, and the link with the self, on the other, are separable. But in Freud's essay, these two are firmly conjoined, and the conjunction has affected both diagnostic symptom description and literary themes for melancholia and depression until our day.

It seems widely agreed that the Renaissance ushered in greater emphasis on the individual subject, or even that it saw the birth of the modern subject in the individualistic sense we understand today. Thus, the presence of narcissistic concerns in Renaissance literary writing on melancholy, which theorists like Schiesari and Enterline trace, is undoubtedly part of the tradition long before Freud. Also, the self is a theme given additional prominence during the Romantic movement. But accounts of melancholic states reveal a greater emphasis on narcissistic concerns, loss, and themes of self-loathing, *only after Freud's essay on mourning and melancholia*. Freud's writing on melancholia construes melancholy and melancholic states in significantly different terms. From a condition of imbalance and a mood of despondency, melancholia becomes a frame of mind more centrally characterized by two things: a lack or want of something, or rather *someone*—that is, a loss—and, also, self-critical attitudes.

Sources and authorities from Freud's own time indicate that, at least for the kinds of case Freud is concerned with, self-accusation was not then a widely acknowledged feature of melancholia. Despite their apparently "observational" status, Freud's remarks about his melancholiac's attitudes of self-loathing seem to have been invoked as much by his loss theory of melancholia as by his patients' complaints. Rather than clinical records, his cases seem to have served as convenient illustrations of conceptual and theoretical implications.

In more recent psychoanalytic writing, Julia Kristeva has developed and expanded Freud's analysis on the element of loss in melancholia. Kristeva inherits Freud's model of "mourning" for the maternal object, but her analysis moves further in its insertion of gender into this experience of loss. We are all alike, subject to the loss of the object, she suggests, and thus inclined, as Freud believed, to incorporate or "introject" the "other." But women's fate is different. As well as the introjection of the maternal body, the "spectacular identification" with the mother peculiar to the female infant is a source of women's particular proneness to depression. Here, then, is a theory that explains not only melancholic loss but also the particular affinity between melancholia and the feminine.

Discussions and theories that posit melancholia or depression as loss in writing since Freud's "Mourning and Melancholia" have come in two identifiable strains. One, associated first with object-relations thinkers like Klein, Fairbairn, and Winnicott and with the attachment theory of John Bowlby, and later with such thinkers as Kristeva, faithfully continues the ideas expressed by Freud in "Mourning and Melancholia," where "loss" is used in its more-specific sense of a loss of a personified other, once possessed. (I would insist that "loss" does connote the more-limited notion. We may lose persons and things once possessed; we may lack but not lose almost anything at all, including qualities and things never possessed, like courage and country houses.)

Another strain, associated less with the psychoanalytic traditions and more with mainstream psychology and psychiatry, including Martin Seligman and Aaron Beck, has seen a broadening and even a trivializing of the notion of melancholia or depression as loss. Here "loss," like "lack," refers to any want of something desired or desirable, not necessarily something once possessed and not necessarily a personified other. We find reference to depression as a loss of self-esteem, loss of self, loss of relationships, loss of agency, loss of opportunity, and even, rendering such accounts entirely tautologous, a loss of hedonic mood states! Noting this broad use of the concept of loss, Beck has drawn attention to its link with its slang cognate "loser." A loser is someone *lacking* in every way: lacking opportunity, success, relationships, or happiness, for example. While it pervades present-day writing about clinical depression, then, the legacy of Freud's loss theory often bears little resemblance to its source in "Mourning and Melancholia."

From Melancholy to Melancholia and Depression

It has been proposed that the era between the Renaissance and our own times represents the historical boundaries of a "great age of melancholia," a tradition "inaugurated by the Renaissance, refined by the Enlightenment, flaunted by Romanticism, fetishized by the Decedents and theorized by Freud" before its current resurgence with postmodern writing on melancholy (Schiesari 1992:3–4). This may be so. But another deep divide occurs at the end of the nineteenth century, as human, redeeming, ambiguous (and masculine) melancholy pulls apart from aberrant, barren, mute (and feminine) depression.

First, there is a slight shift in language, at least in English-language patterns: "melancholy" becomes more firmly related to the normal condition; "melancholia" to the abnormal. (In an exception to this trend, some feminist and literary writing during the 1990s, such as Judith Butler's, reblurs the distinction between normal and abnormal melancholic states and makes "melancholy" and "melancholia" again interchangeable [Butler 1990, 1993, 1997]). In due time, the term "depression," of more recent origin and conveying another set of graphic and shaping metaphors, largely replaces "melancholia." By the time we reach the end of the nineteenth century, melancholy's different meanings appear to produce a tension: the term "melancholy" cannot connote these distinct and disparate states and conditions.

The trend toward regarding melancholia as a disease brought reasons to diminish the importance of its intrinsically subjective symptoms in favor of a behavioral, sign-based analysis. Introspectionism was eclipsed by experimentalism and behaviorism in the emerging academic psychology of this era. In light of that, the defeat of more subjective symptom-based analyses of mental diseases in favor of more behavioral sign-based analyses was inevitable. Moreover, with the strong disease model that influenced Kraepelin, there was no more reason to emphasize the subjective distress and suffering which had for so long characterized melancholic states.

At this point, we witness the divergence between "melancholia" and "melancholy." Melancholia the disease comes increasingly to be regarded as behavior and bodily states. In contrast, while the subjective suffering associated with melancholy as a condition of poets, artists, and men, and as part of normal human experience, continues to be affirmed. Even to the extent that melancholy subjectivity is acknowledged, moreover, it is increasingly limited to the cluster of moods associated not with groundless fear and anxiety but with a sorrowful despondency and despair.

Freud's work on melancholia was at odds with the trends identified thus far. In "Mourning and Melancholia" a certain aspect of melancholic and depressive subjectivity, hitherto of little importance, was attenuated, elaborated, and changed. There is increased emphasis on melancholia (and later depression) as analogous to mourning in being subjective states of loss and in being a condition associated not only with mood states but also with attitudes of self-loathing.

At the same time as this series of changes, melancholia became associated with feminine gender. This derives in part from empirical observation—although today we want to question the science of such data collection—as well as from Freudian and more recent psychoanalytic theorizing. It may also come from deeper structures, as feminist theorists have suggested. Melancholy with its loquacious male subject leaves little room for the mute suffering of women. Women, instead, are victims of depression.

Since Freud: Clinical Depression

After Freud's 1917 essay, at least in the English-language diagnostic traditions, melancholia became an increasingly rare disorder category, little more than a footnote to nosological schemes, and, as the years went by, it was less and less frequently described in clinical case material. In its stead we find emphasis on the condition today known as clinical depression. Now cast as a major mental disorder or disease, depression has been the subject of unceasing research and theorizing in both medical and nonmedical fields of study since the first decades of the twentieth century.

The melancholic states of past eras bear no simple relation to today's clinical depression, as the preceding discussion has aimed to show. Even melancholic subjectivity, for so long "fear and sadness without cause," has become sadness without cause, loss, and self-loathing.

Nonetheless, earlier theories of melancholy and melancholia foreshadow, at least in broad form, most if not all twentieth-century analyses of the disorder known as clinical depression. Historically, it is possible to identify a few decisive trends. Within psychoanalysis, certain aspects of the theory inaugurated in Freud's essay were deepened and developed in the work of Melanie Klein. In turn, the Kleinian stress on early object relations gave its name to a vital and influential neo-Freudian school represented by thinkers like Fairbairn and Winnicott; it also spawned the "attachment" theory associated with Bowlby and others, which posits early severing of relational connection as the source of subsequent depression (and other disorders).

For several decades, medical theorizing came to be dominated by notions of what (if we allow the term "imbalance" the elasticity it enjoyed in humoral accounts) looks like biological imbalance. While no longer humoral, biomedical analyses depend on the presence of deficit, excess, or dysfunction in biological states to explain the presence and persistence of at least the more severe, intractable, "endogenous" depression without apparent psychological origins. Thus, depletion of biogenic amines, on one hypothesis, accounts for the symptoms of depression. As well as biological imbalance theories, accounts in recent years propose structural changes in the brain as the source of clinical depression: in these we can see the heirs to the "brain lesion" hypotheses of the late nineteenth century.

These more biologically oriented theories did not go unchallenged, even at the start, and within medical psychiatry. Due to the influence of thinkers like Karl Bonhoeffer in Europe and Adolf Meyer in America, some depression as a response to psychological trauma has been acknowledged. In the decades to follow, "reactive" or "exogenous" depression was often relegated to a lesser role. Severe, "endogenous" depression was widely maintained to be organically caused.

In contrast to this orthodoxy, not only "reactive" depression but also the presence of more severe "endogenous" depressive states were sometimes explained by social and psychological factors. One such challenge to biological theories proposed that depression was "learned helplessness" (Seligman 1975). On this account, the inertia characteristic of depression was a response to a sensed loss of efficacy: it was "giving up." Although it incorporates elements of loss theory as well, Seligman's hypothesis may be seen to illustrate a new kind for our taxonomy of theories, a cultural causation theory—as does the cognitivist theory of depression introduced by Beck in the 1960s. (Interestingly, Beck's theory also echoes earlier theorizing about melancholy. With its emphasis on distorted and disordered belief, it is reminiscent of eighteenth-century attempts to construe all mental disorder as forms of false belief, or delusion, such as Boerhaave's and Kant's.)

The explosion of feminist sensibility and scholarship in the late twentieth century was a remarkable catalyst for studies in melancholia and depression. It yielded new theories of depression. Within the psychoanalytic tradition, it instigated further elaboration of loss theories and even a revival of interest in melancholy in work such as that of Irigaray, Kristeva, and Butler. Outside psychoanalytic traditions, it led to expanded empirical and theoretical focus on cultural causation, and also it incorporated "loss" theory, more loosely understood, to develop explanations of depression acknowledging gender roles and women's socialization. (Jean Baker Miller's early and influential writing on women's psychology demonstrates this development.) It prompted research on the gender link between women and depression, research that today proceeds within each of the three kinds of theoretical model distinguished in this essay.

Our taxonomy of theories now contains several categories: imbalance and biological theories, loss theories, cultural causation theories and cognitivist ones. And today theorizing and empirical research emphasizing each theoretical model is burgeoning—separately and in combination.

Complex multicausal accounts of depression posit an interaction between socially wrought trauma and biological, and even genetic, predispositions of the brain (for example, Akiskal and McKinney 1973, Kandel 1998). Such trauma, moreover, is frequently construed as loss, using the broader, nonpsychoanalytic notion of loss that covers any lack. Sometimes regarded as permanent, the resultant biological changes, in turn, are believed to affect psychological states in a complex feedback system. (The sense of closure promoted by these multitheoretical studies is perhaps inflated. Even the fundamental distinction between organic correlates of subjective distress and organic etiology of such distress is ignored, or collapsed, in much theorizing.)

Attempts to evaluate different models and analyses of depression seem to lead us inevitably to a question for anthropology: Is depression a constant across cultures? If we only knew the answer to this question, it would seem, then we could adjudicate between the different etiological accounts and emphases in the range of different and potentially incompatible models jostling in the field of depression studies today. Far from offering a quick remedy to this confusion of models and theories, however, the work of cultural anthropologists interested in the concept of depression has served to highlight the oversimplification and sketchy science implicit in the question. To ask about a person's emotional functioning, whether in a remote culture or in our own, they have demonstrated, is to ask as many as six questions, not one (Shweder 1985): What types of feelings are these? Which kinds of situations elicit these feelings? What do the feelings signify for those experiencing them? How are the feelings expressed? What rules of appropriateness guide the expression or display of these feelings? When they are not expressed or displayed, how are these feelings handled? Emotions have meanings, it has been insisted. To understand a person's emotional life, it is necessary to engage in conceptual analysis. Moreover, causes and cures may be in some important ways secondary: "it is possible to understand what it implies to feel depressed without knowing what 'really' brought it on or how 'really' to get rid of it" (Shweder 1985:199).

The cultural constructionism whose possibility is raised by these anthropological studies is orthogonal to the types of theory of depression outlined thus far. On radical constructionism, meanings constitute reality, making reality "independent of biology" in the words of Arthur Kleinman (Kleinman and Good 1985:494). So to the more standard ontologies of the types of depression theory reviewed thus far, we must add another which privileges meanings above other entities.

Melancholic states always strained the lineaments in which medicine attempted to clothe and contain them, and melancholia and allied states have from earliest times been the subject of intense theorizing and dispute. After his lifetime pursuit of the nature of melancholy, Burton was left with an overabundance of theories, explanations, categories, and runaway observations. The unflagging activity and theoretical disarray marking depression studies since Freud leave us similarly placed. About clinical depression we have more questions than answers.

References

Akiskal, H. S. , and McKinney, W. I. 1973. Depressive Disorder: Toward a Unified Hypothesis. *Science* 5(October):20–29.

American Psychiatric Association. 1980. *Diagnostic and Statistical Manual of Mental Disorders*, 3rd ed. Washington, DC: American Psychiatric Press.

American Psychiatric Association. 1994. *Diagnostic and Statistical Manual of Mental Disorders*, 4th ed. Washington, DC: American Psychiatric Press.

Beck, A. 1978. *Cognitive Theories of Depression*. Philadelphia: University of Pennsylvania Press.

Benjamin, W. 1977. *The Origin of German Tragic Drama*. Trans. John Osborne. London: New Left Books.

Berrios, G. E., and Beer, G. 1994. The Notion of Unitary Psychosis: A Conceptual History. *History of Psychiatry* 5:13–36.

Blandford, G. F. 1871. *Insanity and Its Treatment*. Philadelphia: Henry C. Lea.

Bucknill, J., and Tuke, D. H. 1858. A *Manual of Psychological Medicine*. Philadelphia: Blanchard and Lea.

Burton, R. 1621/1989. *The Anatomy of Melancholy*. Ed. Thomas Faulkner, Nicolas Kiessling, and Rhonda Blair. Oxford: Clarendon.

Butler, Judith. 1990. *Gender Trouble*. New York: Routledge.

—— 1993. *Bodies That Matter*. New York: Routledge.

—— 1997. *The Psychic Life of Power: Theories in Subjection*. Stanford, CA: Stanford University Press.

Carter, Robert Brudenell. 1853. *On the Pathology and Treatment of Hysteria*. London, n.p.

Cassian, J. 1955, *The Foundations of the Cenobitic Life and the Eight Capital Sins*. Grand Rapids, MI: Eerdmans.

Chessler, P. 1972. *Women and Madness*. New York: Doubleday.

Corob, Alison. 1987. *Working with Depressed Women: A Feminist Approach*. Aldershot: Gower.

Enterline, L. 1995. *The Tears of Narcissus: Melancholia and Masculinity in Early Modern Writing*. Stanford, CA: Stanford University Press.

Esquirol, E. 1845. *Mental Maladies: A Treatise on Insanity*. Trans. E. K. Hunt. Philadelphia: Mathew Carey et al.

Foucault, Michel 1965. *Madness and Civilization: A History of Madness in the Age of Reason*. New York: Vintage.

Freud, S. 1917/1953. Mourning and Melancholia In *Collected Papers*, vol. 4. London: Hogarth Press.

Gibson, G. 1916. The Relationship between Pelvic Disease and Manic Depressive Insanity. *American Journal of Obstetrics and Diseases of Women and Children* 74:439–44.

Gosling, F. G. 1987. *Before Freud: Neurasthenia and the American Medical Community* 1870–1910. Urbana: University of Illinois Press.

Griesinger, W. 1867/1965. *Mental Pathology and Therapeutics*. A facsimile of the English edition of 1867. New York: Hafner.

Hartung, C., and Widiger, T. 1998–99. Gender Differences in the Diagnosis of Mental Disorders: Conclusions and Controversies of DSM-IV. *Psychological Bulletin* 123(3):250–78.

Howell, Elizabeth, and Bayes, Marjorie (eds.). 1981. *Women and Mental Health*. New York: Basic Books.

Irigaray, Luce. 1991. *The Irigaray Reader*. Ed. Margaret Whitford. Oxford: Blackwell.

Jackson, Stanley. 1983. Melancholia and Partial Insanity. *Journal of the History of Behavioral Science* 19:173–84.

—— 1986. *Melancholia and Depression*. New Haven: Yale University Press.

Johnson, Samuel. 1755/1805. *Dictionary of the English Language in Which the Words Are Deduced from Their Originals, and Illustrated in Their Different Significations by Examples from the Best Writers*. 4 vols. 9th ed. London: Longman, Hurst, Rees, and Orme.

Kandel, E. R. 1998. A New Intellectual Framework for Psychiatry. *American Journal of Psychiatry* 155(4):457–69.

Klein, Melanie. 1975. *Love, Guilt and Reparation and Other Works*. London: Hogarth.

Kleinman, Arthur, and Good, B. (eds.). 1985. *Culture and Depression: Studies in the Anthropology and Cross-Cultural Psychiatry of Affect and Disorder*. Berkeley: University of California Press.

Klerman, G., and Weissman, M. 1989. Increasing Rates of Depression. *Journal of the American Medical Association* 261(15): 2229–35.

Klibansky, Raymond, Panofsky, Erwin, and Saxl, Fritz. 1964. *Saturn and Melancholy: Studies in the History of Natural Philosophy, History and Art*. New York: Basic Books.

Kraepelin, E. 1883. *Compendium der Psychiatrie*. Leipzig: Abel. First edition of what later became *Lehrbuch der Psychiatrie*.

—— 1887. *Textbook of Psychiatry*. 6th ed. Leipzig:abel.

—— 1920. *Manic-Depressive Illness*. Trans. Mary Barclay. Ed. George Robinson. Edinburgh: E. & S. Livingstone.

Kristeva, Julia. 1989. *Black Sun: Depression and Melancholy*. Trans. Leon Roudiez. New York: Columbia University Press.

Laycock, Thomas. 1840. *A Treatise on Nervous Diseases of Women*. London: Longman, Orme, Brown, Green & Longmans.

Lloyd, G. 1984. *The Man of Reason: "Male" and "Female" in Western Philosophy*. Minneapolis: University of Minnesota Press.

Lunbeck, E. 1994. *The Psychiatric Persuasion: Knowledge, Gender, and Power in Modern America*. Princeton, NJ: Princeton University Press.

Lutz, C. 1986. Emotion, Thought, and Estrangement: Emotion as Cultural Category. *Cultural Anthropology* 1:287–309.

Maudsley, H. 1867. *The Physiology and Pathology of the Mind*. New York: Appleton.

McDonald, M. 1981. *Mystical Bedlam: Madness, Anxiety, and Healing in Seventeenth-Century England*. Cambridge: Cambridge University Press.

Mercier, C. 1892. *A Dictionary of Psychological Medicine in Two Volumes*. Ed. D. Hack Tuke. Philadelphia: P. Blackiston.

Parker, G., and Hadzi-Pavlovic, Dusan (eds.) 1996. *Melancholia: A Disorder of Movement and Mood*. Cambridge: Cambridge University Press.

Paykel, E. S. 1991. Depression in Women. *British Journal of Psychiatry* 1958:22–29.

Pope, Alexander. 1714/1963. "The Rape of the Lock." In *Pope*. New York: Dell.

Real, Terrence. 1997. *I Don't Want to Talk about It*. Cambridge: Harvard University Press.

Ribot, T. 1881. *Maladies de la Memoire*. Paris, n. p.

—— 1883. *Maladies de la Volonte*. Paris, n. p.

—— 1885. *Maladies de la Personnalite*. Paris, n. p.

Rush, Benjamin. 1812. *Medical Inquiries and Observations upon the Diseases of the Mind*. Philadelphia: Kimber and Richardson.

Schiesari, Juliana. 1992. *The Gendering of Melancholia: Feminism, Psychoanalysis, and the Symbolics of Loss in Renaissance Literature*. Ithaca, NY: Cornell University Press.

Scull, Andrew. 1979. *Museums of Madness: The Social Organization of Insanity in Nineteenth-Century England*. New York: St. Martins.

—— 1998. Interview by Emily Eakin for an article entitled "Who's Afraid of Elaine Showalter?: The MLA President Incites Mass Hysteria." *Lingua Franca* Sept:28–36.

Seligman, M. 1975. *Helplessness: On Depression, Development, and Death*. New York: W. H. Freeman.

Showalter, Elaine. 1985. *The Female Malady*. New York: Random House.

Shweder, Richard. 1985. Menstrual Pollution, Soul Loss, and the Comparative Study of Emotions. In *Culture and Depression: Studies in Anthropology and Cross-Cultural Psychiatry of Affect and Disorder*, ed. Arthur Kleinman and Byron Good. Berkeley: University of California Press. 182–215.

Virchow, Robert. 1858/1971. *Cellular Pathology as Based upon Physiological and Pathological Histology*. Trans. Frank Chance. New York: Dover.

Wollstonecraft, Mary. 1792/1988. *A Vindication of the Rights of Women*, 2nd ed. Ed. Carol Poston. New York: Norton.

World Health Organization. 1991. *International Classification of Diseases*. 10th ed. New York: World Health Organization.

Wyman, Rufus 1830/1970. A Discourse on Mental Philosophy as Connected with Mental Disease. Delivered before the Massachusetts Medical Society, Boston. Reprinted in R., Hunter and I., Macalpine (1970), *Three Hundred Years of Psychiatry 1535–1860*. London: Oxford University Press 810–11.

3

Melancholy and Melancholia

Foucault's dense and brilliant "archaeological" analyses of the structures of insanity[1] reveal suggestions of a sixteenth-and seventeenth-century understanding of that condition as "unreason" *(déraison)*. The notion of insanity as unreason invites some interesting comparisons with its later medical understanding, the ascendency of which Foucault so closely documented.

I shall draw these comparisons in relation to one particular kind of mental disturbance, excessive sadness or depression, looking at two categories of sufferer: the melancholy man of the sixteenth and seventeenth centuries and today's clinically depressed woman. By exploring Elizabethan melancholy and contemporary melancholia or depression, I shall assess some of Foucault's claims about the transformation by which, as he pictured it, unreason became mental illness.

Unreason

On a superficial analysis, the history of madness during the past 800 years breaks where the medieval religious understanding gave rise to the secular, medical one that prevails today. In the former, madness was evil, caused by demonic possession and cured by the ministration of religious authorities; in the latter, it came to be seen as akin to illness or disease—the unforseeable misfortune of a victim more pitiable than blameworthy.

But Foucault's analysis of the history of madness in the "Age of Reason" belies this superficial division, for it reveals ways of viewing madness that came between the end of the religious understanding of the medieval or "Gothic" period and the full flowering of the later medical one. The concept of "unreason" is introduced to describe one such conception: that which prevailed briefly in the sixteenth and

This chapter is from *Pathologies of the Modern Self: Post Modern Studies in Narcissism, Schizophrenia and Depression*, edited by David Levin. New York: New York University Press., 1987, pp. 231-250.Reprinted with permission from New York University Press.

seventeenth-century period described by Foucault as "pre-Classical," only to disappear with the "Classical" experience of madness in the eighteenth century.[2]

Foucault described the concept of unreason as emerging with the emphasis on human reason and its powers that followed the Renaissance. He described the madhouse, where each form of madness "finds its proper place": "all this work of disorder, in perfect order pronounces, each in his turn, the Praise of Reason."[3] A state of unreason was seen as somehow especially hospitable to the entertainment of illusions. The illusory, said Foucault, is itself "the dramatic meaning of madness,"[4] and in madness "equilibrium is established, but it masks that equilibrium beneath the cloud of illusion, beneath feigned disorder; the rigor of the architecture is concealed beneath the cunning arrangement of these disordered violences."[5] Yet in these very illusions of madness was thought to lie a truth more profound than that known to the sane. There was a secret delirium underlying the chaotic and manifest delirium of madness, a delirium that is "in a sense, pure reason, reason delivered of all the external tinsel of dementia."[6]

The ordinary, unfrightening, and human quality of madness was emphasized with a conception of the manifestations of madness as a failure of reason, since such failures were universally experienced. There came to be "no madman but that which is every man, since it is man who constitutes madness in the attachment he bears for himself and by the illusions he entertains."[7] The similarity between madness and other forms of "folly" was stressed, and with this stress came a concern with the manifestations of these failings that leaves out as insignificant the question of their moral status or causal explanation. The long series of follies, "stigmatizing vices and faults as in the past, no longer attribute them all to pride, to lack of charity, to neglect of Christian virtues,"[8] as they had done in the earlier period under the influence of a religious understanding of madness. Instead, they came to be attributed to "a sort of great unreason for which nothing, in fact, is exactly responsible, but which involves everyone in a kind of secret complicity."[9] This concern with the manifestations of madness gives its unreasonableness a place as the defining characteristic of madness and provides the category through which it must be viewed. Unreason had, as Foucault put it, a nominal value: it "defined the locus of madness's possibility." Only "in relation to unreason, and to it alone"[10] could madness be understood.

Many facets of the notion of madness as unreason can be derived from Foucault's references to the attitudes and ideas of the pre-Classical period, but I wish to concentrate on one suggestion: that madness and its sufferers were seen at that time as less divorced from everyday experience than they are today.

In general terms, one point made by Foucault seems undeniable. However it may have been regarded earlier, madness today is a remote and unfamiliar phenomenon that strikes fear, perplexity, suspicion, and unease in the sane. Madness today is alienating. Moreover, some of this alienation seems to be attributable to the medical point of view from which it is standardly understood. True, the adoption of that point of view is associated with serious efforts to understand madness, with attempts to alleviate suffering, and with the lifting of moral blame. But in other ways the medical analysis is guilty of ignoring and obscuring the sense of madness as a familiar and unpuzzling feature of ordinary human life. Identifying and controlling the "disease," for example, and so labeling and isolating its sufferer, introducing widespread institutionalized professionalism into the management of madness—these have increased our sense of the mad person as unlike ordinary sane people whose deviations—unreasonableness, strange ideas, and excesses of feeling—we think of as like enough to our own weaknesses to be dealt with as normal human conditions.

Thus Foucault rightly attributed to the medical understanding a certain rarifying of madness. With the emergence of the medical point of view something was lost. *Déraison* (unreason) was transformed to become what it is today: obscure, puzzling, and remote from everyday human experience.

We shall now explore more closely the mechanics of that loss in the case of one kind of mental disorder—excessive sadness or despair. To do this, I wish to look at melancholy as it was understood in England during the period Foucault described as pre-Classical—Elizabethan times. Though only part of the "pre-Classical" period Foucault singled out is, strictly, Elizabethan (1558–1603), the term "Elizabethan melancholy" has come to connote the condition that gained prominence under that sovereign—and its influence in fact continued well into the eighteenth century. Moreover, my emphasis on England may be warranted by melancholy's other title, "the English malady."

Elizabethan Melancholy

The last quarter of the sixteenth century saw what some scholars have judged an epidemic[11] of the condition known as melancholy, and it became the experience and concern of poets and scientists alike. Melancholy continued to be a concept and category of major significance, both in England and on the Continent until the mid-eighteenth century,[12] but I shall restrict my discussion to the post-Renaissance period between the end of the sixteenth century and the middle of the seventeenth in order to remain in conformity with the "pre-Classical" era to which Foucault's analysis applies.

Melancholy is described, though never completely defined, in Burton's famous *Anatomy* published in 1626: its main symptoms are listed as sadness and fear ("without a cause"), suspicion and jealousy, inconstancy, proneness to love, and humorousness.[13] Sorrow and fear, particularly, Burton designates as melancholy's "true characters and inseparable companions."[14] And from an earlier scientific account, Timothy Bright's *Treatise on Melancholy* (1586),[15] comes the same emphasis on unwarranted black and apprehensive moods: those affected by melancholy "are in heaviness, sit comfortless, fear, doubt, despair and lament, when no cause requireth it."[16]

Reference here to the uncaused nature of the moods of despondency and apprehension that Bright and Burton and other commentators single out as primary features of melancholy seems to imply two things. Moods of melancholy are so pervasive as to be directed at or felt over no one particular thing. They were without objects, in Hume's terminology[17]—although they clearly have causes of one kind, as the humoral and other explanations Burton offers attest. And, more generally, they are at least unwarranted or unjustified in the sense of being disproportionate or inappropriate to their occasion.

In the literary tradition, the same moods of melancholy reveal themselves in feelings of sadness and apprehension, distress, misery, and world weariness. "Come heavy sleep, the image of true death," the poet sings:

> And close up these my weary weeping eyes,
> Whose spring of tears doth stop my vital breath,
> And tears my hart with sorrows high swoln crys:

Come and possess my tired thoughts-worne soule,
That living dies, till thought on me be stoule.

Come shadow my end: and shape of rest,
Alied to death, child to this black fac't night,
Come thou and charme these rebels in my brest,
Whose waking fancies doth my mind affright.
O come sweet sleepe, come or I die for ever,
Come ere my last sleepe coms, or come never.[18]

The mood is dark:

In darkness let me dwell, the ground shall sorrow be,
The roofe Despaire to all cheerful light from me[19]

And suicide has charm:

My thoughts hold mortal strife;
I do detest my life,
And with lamenting cries,
Peace to my soul to bring,
Oft call that prince which here doth monarchise:
—But he, grim, grinning King,
Who caitiffs scorns, and dost the blest surprise,
Late having decked with beauty's rose his tomb,
Distains to crop a weed, and will not come.[20]

A serious impediment to understanding the notion of melancholy during this period rests in its breadth and scope. Speaking of the varied symptoms of melancholy, Burton remarked that "Proteus himself is not so diverse; you may well make the Moon a new coat, as a true character of a melancholy man; as soon find the notion of a bird in the air as the heart of a melancholy man."[21] Moreover, present-day commentaries[22] place emphasis on the varying meanings or interpretations intended by that commodious term. Not only does "melancholy" seem to have been extended to cover a broader spectrum of mental abnormalities than those that would today be classified as clinical depression. In addition, melancholy traits were represented as ranging from despair and the black moods described by the poets to wit, wisdom, and inspiration. And, finally, "melancholy" refers as much to a passing or long-term attribute of a normal person as to mental disturbance. To our contemporary minds, the concept of melancholy at that period is at first so broad as to be almost meaningless.

Let us look more closely at each of the areas of ambiguity introduced. First, melancholy seems sometimes to be used so broadly as to cover several different kinds of madness or derangement. One present-day historian has gone as far as to conclude that "'melancholy' was constantly used as a synonym for madness."[23] Burton, on the other hand, decried this equation with every form of madness, and "new and old writers who have spoken confusedly of [melancholy], confounding melancholy with madness...that will have madness no other than melancholy in extent, differing in degrees.[24] And despite the apparently disparate symptoms of melancholy cited even by Burton himself, there seem to run through these accounts two shared themes: blackness of mood and feeling, and a humoral explanation. We shall return to these unifying themes presently.

Second, the melancholy man was as likely a poet, rake, or scholar as a madman. Alongside the tragic melancholic like Hamlet, in dramatic imagery, it has been pointed out, there stood the "fashionable melancholic."[25] There was "scarcely a man of distinction who was not either genuinely melancholy or at least considered as such by himself and others."[26] The figure of the melancholy man was fashionable and common, seen both in life and art. Characteristic poses and motifs, like the drooping head in Dürer's *Melancholia*, were associated with the condition in the stock melancholy characters of the stage and in painting.

The fashion of melancholy suggests there were compensations to this condition, despite the subjective distress it brought. Melancholy was an object of interest and respect. The melancholic character, it has been said, "had something about it of sombre philosophical dignity, something of Byronic grandeur."[27] Moreover melancholy was associated with other esteemed traits. The melancholic man will suffer, for he is "morose, taciturn, waspish, misanthropic, solitary, fond of darkness...extremely wretched and [he] often longs for death."[28] But he is also, as Burton said, "of deep reach, excellent apprehension, judicious, wise and witty."[29] A person of melancholy mood or disposition was likely to be marked by his wit and wisdom—his wit and wisdom, indeed, may have occasioned his melancholy.[30]

Emphasis on the two sets of traits sketched here derives from one of two distinct traditions contributing to the Elizabethan notion of melancholy. Of these, the first, primarily medical in orientation and origin, was more concerned with melancholy as the sadness and despair of mental abnormality, while the second, which emphasized the link between sadness and wit and wisdom, was associated more with normal psychology, where intellectual pursuits were believed to increase a person's vulnerability to such despondency.

Stemming from Galen and Aristotle, respectively, each of these different emphases had been influential during the preceding Renaissance period. The early physician Galen described the effects of black bile as an unrelieved blackness of mood and demeanour. But to Aristotle, or more exactly to one of his disciples, is attributed the question, "Why is it that all those who become eminent in philosophy or politics or poetry or the arts are clearly of an atrabilious temperament and some of them to such an extent as to be affected by the diseases caused by black bile?"[31] Melancholy in the Aristotelian tradition is the world weariness of the sensitive and creative. In the words of one historian, "Renaissance physicians and psychologists, although they believed that melancholy is likely to produce blockish stupidity and absurd irrationality, do not question the Aristotelian dictum...in general they agree that there is a relationship between melancholy and mental capacity."[32] This same belief seems to have prevailed during the post-Renaissance period we are considering. Burton himself acknowledged it in suggesting that love of learning and overmuch study were causes of melancholy.

Finally, as the picture of the melancholy rake or scholar suggests, melancholy was attributed to ordinary people in the absence of any suggestion of mental disturbance. The term "melancholy" came to describe not merely a "melancholy habit" (Burton) in an otherwise sane person—a long-term character trait or disposition— but also what Burton described as a "transitory melancholy disposition." Momentary or short-lived moods of sadness, of the kind that must be seen as normal emotional responses, were also attributed to melancholy. Indeed, in everyday settings, according to one authority, there has occurred a shift in traditional usage. In the earlier Medieval period melancholy had referred solely to a long-term disposition, whether disturbed or normal. In the post-Medieval period at which we are looking, however, it tended more and more towards "the subjective and transitory meaning, until at length it was so overshadowed by the new 'poetic' conception that this last became the normal meaning in modern thought and speech."[33] Thus a man might be melancholy for a morning or a lifetime; moreover, his lifelong melancholy might reflect either a normal but splenetic character or a serious mental abnormality.

Whether the various emphases considered here reflect, as present-day authorities seem to suggest,[34] differing meanings or senses of the notion of melancholy, or whether, instead, we are dealing with a concept so loose as to have no present-day equivalent, I shall discuss later. Let us first note two features of Elizabethan melancholy that may be appealed to in explaining the breadth and looseness of the notion: the humoral explanation apparently holding together each of the varying understandings of the condition, and the *feelings* associated with melancholy.[35]

Shared by all the different notions of melancholy is the causal principle appealed to in explaining them: black bile, described as "a heavy, viscid humour, so thick and adhesive that physicians have great difficulty evacuating it."[36] Other factors were also appealed to in explaining melancholy—for example, divine and planetary intervention—but the humoral explanation seems to have been the most widely accepted. A balance of the four humors (bile, blood, choler, and phlegm) was thought to determine a person's temperament. This tradition, which had influenced the understanding of health and illness alike since pre-Socratic times, allowed that a melancholic person had excessive black bile from the spleen. Thus wrote one contemporary physician, "If the spleneticke excrement surcharge the bodie, not only being purged by the help of the spleen, then are these purturbations far more outrageous, and hard to be mitigated...by persuasion."[37] Black bile proved a versatile explanation since variations in its condition according to temperature and viscosity accounted for a wide variation of effects, including the daily fluctuations in mood as well as more long-term states and dispositions.

In the case of melancholy, however, the humors provided causal explanations in a curious sense, since no bile ever was or would be black. Black bile, several authors have argued, was a kind of metaphor for the dark mood of melancholy rather than a reference to any actual substance. It was explained that there are associations among the notions of anger, darkness, blackness surging up with anger, and blackness as poisonous (thus *cholos* [anger] and *cholē* [bile] often overlap in poetic and literary usage): and "the black bile theory seems to have developed when subjective experience led to a search for causal agents that had some sort of intrinsic connection with the quality of the experience. If there is a black mood, there must be a black substance."[38]

We might conclude today that black bile was closer to a description than an explanation of melancholy.

Foucault hinted at a similar point in his discussion of melancholy when he insisted that it was "the phenomenology of melancholic experience"[39] which gave the concept of melancholy its coherence:

> A symbolic unity formed by the languor of the fluids, by the darkening of the animal spirits and the shadowy twilight they spread over the images of things, by the viscosity of the blood that laboriously trickles through the vessels, by the thickening of vapors that have become blackish, deleterious and acrid, by visceral functions that have become slow and somehow slimy—this unity, more a product of sensibility than of thought or theory, gives melancholia its characteristic stamp.[40]

Thus the apparently unifying function of the humoral explanations, Foucault seemed to suggest, is illusory.

This notion leads us to the second feature of melancholy apparently sufficient to unite the disparate manifestations to which it referred: the feelings associated with it. The purely affective qualities of melancholy—its phenomenology, in Foucault's phrase—may be appealed to directly in linking the conditions of the melancholy madman, the rake (albeit his affectations were self-induced and perhaps more perceived than real), and the sufferer from an isolated mood of sadness. The concept of melancholy was closely wedded to what Burton called its true characters and inseparable companions: sadness and fear without a cause. This may seem obvious, especially since in present-day usage the faintly archaic "melancholy" means little beyond the subjective mood of sadness. But it is a point worth observing, nevertheless, as we shall see when we come to compare the Elizabethan notion with our contemporary concepts of clinical depression and melancholia.

Melancholy and Melancholia

Our contemporary notions offer some interesting comparisons with the earlier ideas of melancholy we have been considering. Most obvious is that where the all-encompassing "melancholy" spanned, several terms must now be distinguished. "Melancholy" remains, but now it seems to be restricted for the most part, to the sad or dejected frame of mind of a normal person: my melancholy may be dispositional or momentary, but it is always within the normal range of emotional responses. In contrast, there is the term "melancholia," now itself somewhat outmoded, as we shall see, to cover the pathological or clinical dimensions of the condition. Thus Freud, in his 1917 paper "Mourning and Melancholia," characterized the mental features of the "melancholiac," or sufferer from melancholia, as "profoundly painful dejection, abrogation of interest in the outside world, loss of the capacity to love, inhibition of all activity, and a lowering of the self regarding feelings to a degree that finds utterance in self reproaches and self-revilings, and culminates in a delusional expectation of punishment."[41] We recognize a parallel between the feelings described here and those experienced in the earlier melancholy—even though "melancholy," by Freud's time, was a term already restricted in the way described above. Anyone may be melancholy, but only the mentally disturbed are described as melancholiacs or as suffering melancholia.

For today, we also have the concept of depression, both to describe the disposition or passing mood of sadness and despair of a normal person and, with certain qualifications, to mark off clinical abnormality. Anyone may experience momentary depression. But the condition of depressive illness or depressive reaction affects those requiring treatment.

Thus today's term "melancholy" more closely corresponds to "depression," and "melancholia" to depressive illness: the cognates of each term have been introduced to mark the distinction between ordinary sadness on the one hand and pathological or clinical sadness on the other. These terminological distinctions, I shall argue, permit—and encourage—the class of those suffering melancholia or clinical depression to be set apart from the person who is merely depressed or melancholy. They seem to reflect—and abet—an attitudinal separation between these two groups that is not as consistently stressed in the earlier period we have been considering.

We are familiar with the conditions of sadness, despair, and dejection that affect ordinary people; they need no introduction. But contemporary clinical concepts of depression and melancholia require a closer examination. Let us consider the official nosology of the American Psychiatric Association (DSM III), revised in 1980, which employs the terminology of the *depressive episode* to classify this kind of "affective disorder."[42]

Psychological states, both affective (moods and feelings) and cognitive (beliefs), as well as behavioral symptoms are introduced here. Thus a major depressive episode is said to be marked by:

A. the psychological "dysphoric" mood, or loss of interest or pleasure in all or almost all normal activities or pastimes

and

B. some of the following behavioral symptoms: poor appetite, insomnia, psychomotor agitation or retardation, slowed thinking or indecisiveness, fatigue

or psychological states:

feelings of worthlessness or self-reproach or excessive guilt or wishes to be dead.

Confusingly, the notion of melancholia enters here as an adjunct to some but not all major depressive episodes of the kind just defined, but it is introduced as adding identical or closely similar symptoms:

loss of pleasure, mood worse in the morning, psychomotor retardation or agitation, weight loss or insomnia

Thus it is left unclear what real difference, if any, marks the major depressive episode when accompanied by melancholia[43] and the major depressive episode without it.[44] The distinction seems to hint at the notion—implied, for example, in the concept of "masked depression"—that there might be a depressive episode in the absence of any of the subjective feelings of sadness and dejection usually taken to be central to melancholia. But at least as it is formulated here, this extreme behaviorist interpretation cannot be adopted, since the subjective feelings described in item A are presented as necessary conditions for the diagnosis (of major depressive episode), as its broader status as an "affective disorder" would lead us to expect.

In a comparison of the melancholy of the earlier period with today's depressive conditions, one issue seems apparent. The same moods of sadness predominate subjectively: we seem to be dealing with the same kind of feelings. And this is true, also, of the contemporary category of normal depression. The sad feelings of the normal melancholy or depressed person parallel those of the sufferer from depressive reactions or illness. So it is by a matter of degree that the clinically depressed person not subject to grosser abnormalities of hallucination or delusion is distinguished, affectively, from the merely sad or disheartened or dejected one. The mood's relative persistence, pervasiveness, and intensity alone mark the "pathology" of the former from the normal states of the latter. However, the contemporary concept of depressive episode as put forward in DSM III does suggest a lessening of emphasis on the subjective and particularly the affective side of this condition—despite its treatment of the presence of the feeling of "dysphoric mood" as a necessary diagnostic criterion. For there is now a strong emphasis on the assorted behavioral symptoms by which a clinician might detect the condition. While the patient's avowal of his or her feelings is presented as an essential ingredient in that diagnosis, the overall picture is as much of a behavioral disturbance as one of mood or "affect."

Some explanation of this trend toward a behavioristic analysis of depression may be found in the very subjective similarity between normal sadness and clinical depression, noted earlier. Emphasis on various cognitive and particularly the behavioral symptoms apparently better permit a sharp distinction to be drawn between the two categories. In a study of the factors distinguishing normal from clinical depression, it has been concluded that "the factors in social behaviour profile...which most clearly distinguish the severely depressed patient from the depressed normal one are: the extent to which self accusatory feelings are present; the level of 'helplessness', e.g. inability to make decisions; and, finally, the pace and tempo of his behaviour, i.e. overly retarded or overly agitated." Thus, "It is primarily the behavior...that distinguishes the two groups [normal people who are very depressed and those subsequently diagnosed as clinically ill], *not the central mood factor*. They can, in other words be equally sad, lonely—equally depressed in mood"[45] (emphasis added). So in order better to isolate, and thus, to treat, those who are clinically depressed, it has become useful to clinicians to emphasize the nonaffective features of the condition.

The development of the notion of depression as a behavioral condition also goes some way to explain the widespread adoption of the term "depression" rather than "melancholia," which occurred during the twentieth century. With the shift of emphasis away from the purely psychological toward behavioral and directly observable symptoms, the notion of depression gained currency and refinement. Thus *agitated depression*, marked by restless overactivity, came to be distinguished from *retarded depression*, where activity is slowed down or inhibited.[46]

Inviting this emphasis on observable symptoms at the expense of affective states was Freudian depth psychology. With the widespread acceptance of a psychoanalytic version of the unconscious state and early origins of depression, it was possible to account convincingly for the link between disparate behavioral symptoms.

The new terminology not only corresponds to an increasingly behavioristic emphasis in symptomatology; in addition, with its etymological suggestion of pressure and heaviness, the term "depression" conveys a physical and behavioral metaphor. We saw that "melancholy" suggested darkness, a purely psychological apprehension. But the weight and pressure upon the afflicted person conveyed by the term "depression" (Latin *deprimere*—to press down) carries images of physical as much as psychological burden and oppression.

Clinical depression, then, unlike the earlier melancholy, is characterized as much or more by certain behavioral manifestations as by the moods and feelings it involves: by a slowing or agitation of movement and by fatigue, loss of appetite, and insomnia. And despite the etymology of "depression," remarked earlier, most of these manifestations do not have the symbolic power to reinforce and remind us of the mood underlying them. Loss of appetite, fatigue, insomnia, and agitated movement do not as naturally seem to suggest dejection to an untrained observer as do the formalized melancholy gestures and motifs of the literature and painting of the seventeenth century, such as the drooping head.

Another difference between the earlier melancholy and today's clinical depression is that the latter is a women's complaint. One analysis has proposed that twice as many women as men suffer from depression in middle- and upper-class America;[47] other authorities suggest higher figures.[48] Our current image of the depression sufferer is, or ought to be—assuming those who complain of depression suffer accordingly—a woman. But although no comparable figures are available for the earlier period, the reverse seems true of melancholy.[49] While Dürer's series depicts a woman, the rakes, poets, scholars, and artists who suffered melancholy were men; the stage *melancholique* was standardly a male figure.

Moreover, it is presumably not unconnected with this change in gender association that contemporary clinical depression has lost its link with what was characterized earlier as the Aristotelian tradition: the notion that the other side of this mood of sadness and despair was intellectual depth, wisdom, and learning, even genius. It is not today fashionable to affect the women's condition of depression, in the way that it was once to affect melancholy. Now depression is a scourge and an "illness"—something, in many circles, to be concealed and denied.

As the differences of terminology suggest, emphasis in the early twenty-first century is placed on the dissimilarities between normal states of sadness and melancholy and the clinical depression at the other end of the scale. The rationale for this has been introduced already and has some force. By being distinguished in this way, those who require treatment for their condition can more easily receive it. When little stress was accorded to the separation of the clinically melancholy from the everyday, nonclinical melancholy sufferer, we might suppose the neglect of the former group. But nevertheless, this stress on the differences between the sufferer from clinical depression and the normal sad person invites the kind of alienation of the former that Foucault suggested.

Finally, it seems necessary to insert a corrective to the contemporary discussions of the earlier concept, with their emphasis on the disparity of meanings and traditions found in the commodious concept of melancholy. We seem to be asked to read the different emphases in the use of "melancholy"—its reference to normal states and dispositions, as well as to the suffering of the mentally disturbed, and its Aristotelian and Galenic meanings, for example—as reflecting a term used ambiguously. But the sense of "melancholy" that prevailed during the sixteenth and seventeenth centuries may, and perhaps ought, to be understood as univocal, even though it covered and connected both the more severe conditions on the one hand and variations of normal, though splenetic, character and mood on the other.

The Alienated Depressive: A Feminist Analysis

The contrast between the melancholy of the earlier period and today's notions of clinical and normal depression seems to provide added support for Foucault's contention: much that was ordinary and familiar about madness was lost with the emergence of medical structures, With emphasis on the behavior rather than the affect of depression, expressed in the new terminology, the element of feeling that seems to have united the various strands of the Elizabethan concept has relinquished its central place. And rather than an ordinary, familiar, and everyday figure, the *depressive* of today is increasingly rendered remote and alien, her condition unrelated to ordinary experience.

Contemporary feminist analyses of female depression may be appealed to in part to explain two of the features of our present notion of clinical depression distinguished here: its apparent prevalence among female sufferers on the one hand and its alienation from more ordinary states of sadness and despair on the other.

Let us set aside the question of how these feelings should be described and look instead at the explanation of why women might be expected to experience reactions of sadness and despair more frequently than men do in this society.

Theories as to why women are depressed appeal, either directly or indirectly, to their oppression. Thus, according to one authority, women are depressed because of their deprivation: "[They] are in mourning—for what they never had."[50]

At the simplest level, this analysis attributes sadness as a reasonable response by women in patriarchal society to the lack of freedom, opportunity, self-expression, respect, and esteem.[51] A slightly more complex explanation attributes female sadness to male oppression by introducing the notion of internalized anger. The oppressed woman, according to this theory, is subject to feelings of anger and rage—both (a) those whose legitimate object should be her oppressors, and (b) those that are the internalized reflection of that hostility and contempt felt by her oppressor for her. In the face of this anger, her response is sorrow and self-loathing. Thus Greenspan appealed to each kind of anger. She spoke of the real cause of woman's depression as "an abiding, unconscious rage at our oppression which has found no legitimate outlet."[52] But she also introduces the notion of societal anger turned inward: "Internalization of oppression is the crux of women's depression and self-hate. It is as though every impulse of a depressed woman's consciousness is finely tuned to a view of herself that is in accord with that of the dominant culture's view of women as inferior."[53]

Here, then, is a theory sufficient to explain why, in today's society, more women than men might be prone to depression. But this is not adequate to account for all the differences between today's notion of depression and the earlier one we have been considering. As far as can be determined from the scant historical evidence, we saw that, in the Elizabethan period, melancholy was not distinguished as a woman's condition—rather, it was associated with men. Yet it must at least be questioned whether there was less oppression for women in that era. Why, then, might women be peculiarly susceptible to depression today?

Evidence from the history of medicine suggests that women have long been subject to ideologically colored diagnoses and forms of treatment, and these have apparently differed extensively from period to period. But one theme remains constant: medicine's prime contribution to sexist ideology, as Ehrenreich and English put it, has been "to describe women as sick, and as potentially sickening to men."[54] To regard women as sick and requiring treatment was to wield a form of social control: it reflects sexist oppression exerted through the male-dominated medical establishment.

Ehrenreich and English proposed the following historical analysis. Throughout early medicine, and well past the earlier Elizabethan period we have been considering, this emphasis on women as sick centered on women's bodily and, particularly, reproductive organs and functions. But nineteenth-century advances in physiology eventually precluded many of the obviously false theories supporting these accounts—for example, the wandering uterus theory, which had held sway since ancient times. And the social control that Ehrenreich and English described as the "medical management of women" took an altered form by the end of the nineteenth century. Women's illness came to be seen as a psychic rather than bodily nature. The tendency of doctors to diagnose women's complaints as psychosomatic, it is argued, shows "that the medical view of women has not really shifted from 'sick' to 'well'; it has shifted from 'physically sick' to 'mentally sick'."[55] Today, these writers conclude, it is psychiatry rather than gynecology that upholds "the sexist tenets of women's fundamental defectiveness."[56]

Thus we see an explanation for the separation noted between ordinary moods experienced by normal people in response to everyday situations, on the one hand, and the "pathological" condition of clinical depression, on the other. Women's moods of sadness and despair are now the focus of this form of social control; women's responses have become "medicalized."

Whether or why women feel more sad and despairing in contemporary times than earlier is not something about which we can have any certainty. But it is now clearer why contemporary sadness and despair might have come to be regarded as illnesses and defects today in a way that they were not when they were the fashionable complaints of the Elizabethan rake or scholar.

I have shown here that the contrast between the unreason of Elizabethan melancholy and today's notion of clinical depression confirms Foucault's claims. That contrast has also illuminated ways in which earlier notions have been transformed with twentieth-century psychiatric thinking—a transformation that may be partly explained by appeal to contemporary feminist accounts of clinical depression.[57]

Notes

1. Michel Foucault, *Madness and Civilization: A History of Insanity in the Age of Reason*, trans. Richard Howard (New York: Vintage, 1973). First published as *Histoire de*

la Folie (Paris: Libraire Plon, 1965). All page references are to the Howard translation and Vintage edition.

2. Before introducing Foucault's view, I need to give one disclaimer. Nowhere in his work did Foucault systematically develop the thesis I am going to attribute to him, and what follows is an interpretation only.

3. Foucault, 36.

4. Ibid., 34.

5. Ibid., 34.

6. Ibid., 97.

7. Ibid., 26.

8. Ibid., 13.

9. Ibid., 13.

10. Ibid., 83.

11. L. Babb, *Sanity in Bedlam: A Study of Robert Burton's Anatomy of Melancholy* (East Lansing: Michigan State University Press, 1959), 3.

12. See C. A., Moore, "The English Malady," in *Backgrounds of English Literature* 1700–60 (Minneapolis: University of Minnesota Press, 1953), 179: "No characteristic of English poetry in the mid-eighteenth century is more familiar...than the perpetual reference to melancholy. Statistically this deserves to be called the Age of Melancholy."

13. R., Burton, *The Anatomy of Melancholy* (London: J. E. Hodson, 1621; 11th ed., 1806), 330.

14. Ibid., 149.

15. T. Bright, *A Treatise of Melancholy* (London: Thomas Vautrolier, 1586).

16. Ibid., 100.

17. D. Hume, *A Treatise of Human Nature*, ed., Selby Bigge, (Oxford: Clarendon, 1958), book 2, section 3.

18. Anonymous, in N. Greenberg, ed., *An Anthology of Elizabethan Lute Songs, Madrigals and Rounds* (New York: Norton, 1955), 104.

19. Ibid., 121.

20. H. Gardner, ed., *The New Oxford Book of English Verse* (Oxford: Clarendon, William Drummond of Hawthornden, in 1972), 230.

21. Ibid., 469.

22. For example, V. Skultans, *English Madness: Ideas on Insanity* 1580–1890 (London: Routledge and Kegan Paul, 1979).

23. V. Klibansky, F. Saxl, and E. Panofsky, *Saturn and Melancholy* (Cambridge: Heffer & Sons, for Nelson, London, 1964), 218.

24. Ibid., 153.

25. Ibid., 232.

26. L. Babb, "Melancholy and the Elizabethan Man of Letters," *Huntington Library Quarterly* (1940–41) 4:261.

27. Babb, L. *Sanity in Bedlam*, 3.

28. Ibid.,

29. Ibid., 451.

30. For example, Robert Anton, *The Philosophers Satyrs* (London, 1616), 14 ("Want makes the worthy *Artist* dull and sad, And *rare deserts*, most melancholy mad.") and Babb, "Melancholy and the Elizabethan Man of Letters," 252 ("Melancholy is the scholar's occupational disease.").

31. Aristotle, *Problemata* xxxi, in W. D. Ross, ed., *Aristotle's Works* (Chicago: Encyclopedia Brittanica, 1955).

32. Babb, "Melancholy and the Elizabethan Man of Letters," 253.

33. Klibansky et al., 218.

34. For example, Skultans, 19.

35. I do not wish to suggest that an essentialist analysis would be required here, but merely that, contrary to the implications of several modern commentators, evidence indicates that in this case one was available.

36. L. Babb, *The Elizabethan Malady: A Study of Melancholia in English Literature from* 1580 *to* 1642 (East Lansing: Michigan State College Press, 1951), 54.

37. Bright, 109.

38. B. Simon, *Mind and Madness in Ancient Greece: The Classical Roots of Modern Psychiatry* (Ithaca: Cornell University Press, 1978), 236; also Kudlien, "Beginn des med-izinischen Denkens," 77–99, and "Schwartzliche Organe," cited in Simon.

39. Foucault, 122.

40. Ibid., 124.

41. Sigmund Freud, *Collected Papers* (London: Hogarth, 1957), 153.

42. Distinguished from the lesser dysthymic disorder or depression neurosls (300.40), only by severity or duration.

43. American Psychiatric Association, *Diagnostic and Statistical Manual of Mental Disorders*, 3rd ed. (Washington, D.C.: American Psychiatric Association, 1981), Axis 1, 296.23.

44. Ibid., Axis 2, 296.22.

45. M. M. Katz, ed., "The Classification of Depression," in M. Katz, ed., *Depression in the 1970s: Modern Theory and Research* (Amsterdam: Ronald R. Fieve, 1971), 6.

46. Other considerations also influenced the elimination of the term "melancholia." See E. Stainbrook, "A Cross Cultural Evaluation of Depressive Reaction," in P. Hoch and J. Zubin, eds., *Depression* (New York: Grune & Stratton, 1954).

47. H. Lehmann, "Epidemiology of Depressive Disorders," in M. Katz, ed., *Depression in the 1970s: Modern Theory and Research* (Amsterdam: Ronald R. Fieve, 1971).

48. For example, P. Chessler, *Women and Madness* (New York: Avon, 1972), See also the National Institute of Mental Health reference tables on Patients in Mental Health Facilities, reproduced by Chessler on pp. 42–43, where women diagnosed as psychotic depressive out-numbered men in general hospitals, 69 percent to 31 percent, respectively; in outpatient clin-ics, 73 percent to 27 percent, respectively; in private hospitals, 73 percent to 27 percent; and in state and county hospitals, 68 percent to 32 percent.

49. As has been noted (Skulkans, 81).

50. Chessler, 44.

51. See also J. B. Miller, *Toward a New Psychology of Women* (Boston: Beacon, 1976), 90–91.

52. M. Greenspan, *A New Approach to Women and Therapy* (New York: McGraw-Hill, 1983), 300.

53. Ibid., 303.

54. B. Ehrenreich and D. English, *Complaints and Disorders: The Sexual Politics of Sickness* (Old Westbury, NY: Feminist Press, 1973), 5.

55. Ibid., 79.

56. Ibid., 79.

57. For help in writing this essay, I am grateful to Margaret Rhodes, Frank T. Keefe, Jane Roland Martin, Meredith Michaels, and David M. Levin.

PART II

CATEGORIES

*Melancholy and Depression
as Medical, Psychological,
and Moral Concepts*

4

Is This Dame Melancholy?

*Equating Today's Depression
and Past Melancholia*

A SUPERFICIAL CONTINUITY LINKS today's *clinical depression* with *melancholy* and *melancholia* (the latter two terms were used interchangeably until the nineteenth century). Indeed, an equation between the two is often assumed. The relationship between today's depression and melancholic states of old is an ambiguous and problematic one, however. Twentieth-century descriptions of depression and pre-nineteenth-century accounts of melancholia show some surprising similarities, but they also differ tellingly. Moreover, whether we see them as the same condition under different guises—reflecting differing cultural idioms of distress, perhaps—is itself a complex methodological and even ontological question. It rests not only or perhaps not at all on how much descriptions of these two conditions resemble one another but on what kind of thing conditions like depression and melancholia are judged to be.[1]

This inquiry into the theoretical implications of equating or even comparing depression with melancholia exposes and spotlights the tenets of the descriptive psychiatry, so influential in twentieth-century psychiatric classification and theorizing, which attempts to classify and understand mental disorders without reference to underlying causes.

The following discussion provides an overdue analysis and evaluation of the methodological and ontological presuppositions underlying descriptive psychiatry. In the process, it throws light on two widespread trends in current psychiatric classification, neither of which has received the critical attention it demands. The first of these is the tendency to attribute various forms of underlying *masked depression* to those with a symptom picture contrary to the one portrayed in traditional (Western) classifications. Cross-cultural psychiatry has identified women in China who do not feel depressed but experience a cluster of somatic symptoms, for example, and

First published in *Philosophy, Psychiatry & Psychology.* Vol 10, No.1 (March 2003): 37-52. Reprinted with permission from Johns Hopkins University Press.

these are commonly judged indicative of an underlying depression, as are the acting out, substance abuse, and antisocial behavior, exhibited predominantly by men, in our own society. Developments in psychopharmacology since 1990 have spawned the second trend that I call *drug cartography*: a remapping of psychiatric categories based not on traditional symptom clusters but on psychopharmacological effects. Here, depression becomes any condition that antidepressants alleviate. Whether different forms of masked depression should be deemed depression is a methodological question complicated by some of the same epistemological and ontological implications as the question of whether melancholia is depression. Moreover, these aspects of the theoretical infrastructure of the category of depression also arise when we ask whether depression can be defined via drug cartography.

In exploring the cross-historical comparison between melancholia and depression, this discussion provides a much-needed analysis of the presuppositions and methodology of descriptive psychiatry and examines its application to cross-cultural psychiatry and drug cartography. Then, from an evaluation of the relative merits and demerits of a descriptivist ontology, it is concluded that, despite their similarities, melancholia and depression are not to be understood as one and the same.

Similarities Between Melancholia and Depression

The canonical writing on melancholia in the long tradition beginning with Hippocrates, Aristotle, and Galen comprises theorizing, usually about humoral states, and descriptions of signs and symptoms illustrated, in varying detail, by reference to cases (Berrios and Porter 1995; Hunter and MacAlpine 1982; Jackson 1986; Radden 2000a). Humoral medicine retains only faint historical interest today. The descriptions of signs and symptoms are likely of quite substantial importance, however; apart from their remarkable immediacy and vitality, these descriptions could illuminate several disputed issues in psychopathology and classification.

A comparison between today's depression and the melancholia portrayed in these descriptions of signs and symptoms yields at least four similarities. First, prominence is given to a clustering of sadness, dejection, and despondency symptoms with fear, anxiety, and apprehension symptoms. These two kinds of feelings are portrayed as unfailingly present in melancholia in the following passage from Timothie Bright (1550–1615), writing in England in the sixteenth century, for example, "the perturbations of melancholie are for the most parte, sadde and fearfull, and such as rise of them: as distrust, doubt, diffidence, or despair" (Bright [1569] 2000:122). Noted as early as the Greek philosophers and physicians and a consistent theme in writing about melancholia through the Renaissance and the early modern period, this clustering of traits around the poles of sadness and fear has an obvious bearing on today's clinical picture and on the comorbidity of depressive and anxiety disorders. These states of fear and sadness were central, almost defining, features of melancholic subjectivity.

Second, recurrent reference is made to the unreasonable and apparently objectless nature of melancholy states. They were said to be states without or without sufficient "cause": seemingly pervasive and nebulous moods, not merely cognitive emotions or attitudes. As early as 150–200 AD, for example, Aretaeus of Cappadocia notes that those suffering melancholia and mania are "dull or stern; dejected or unreasonably torpid, *without any manifest cause*" (1856:299–300; my emphasis) And "fear and sadness without cause" become a hallmark of melancholy until the eighteenth century, noted in almost all accounts.

Third, self-centeredness, self-consciousness, and oversensitivity are emphasized. We find these traits described in the *Anatomy of Melancholy* by Robert Burton (1577–1640), for example. The melancholic man, Burton says, "dare not come in company for feare hee should be misused, disgraced, overshoot himselfe in gesture or speeches, or bee sicke, he thinkes every man observes him" (Burton [1621] 2001:395).

Fourth, recurring references link melancholia and states such as exaltation, grandiosity, and energy. This association arises in Greek writing and occurs, sporadically, until the beginning of the modern period (by the middle of the nineteenth century circular or bipolar diseases are identified with manic and melancholic or depressive manifestations). It is vividly illustrated by Pinel (1745–1826), for example, who comments in *A Treatise on Insanity* ([1801] 2000:205–6) that there are many instances of melancholics: "remarkable for their ardent enthusiasm, sublime conceptions, and other great and magnanimous qualities." Others "charm society by the ardour of their affections, and give energy to its movements by their own impassioned turbulence and restlessness."

Today, *depression* is associated with something close to each of these four characteristics. Its symptoms include fear, anxiety, and apprehension as well as sad, dejected, and despairing frames of mind. These moods are often nebulous, pervasive, and "objectless" or unwarranted by the apparent situation. Its psychological signs include self-centeredness, self-consciousness, and oversensitivity. Finally, depression is associated with moods and states of manic exaltation, restless energy, and grandiosity.

As well as these more subjective and psychological features of melancholy, there can be found some suggestion of shared behavioral features. These examples, however, most strongly illustrate the marked continuity both among early accounts of melancholia and between those early accounts and today's depressive subjectivity and symptoms.

One explanation for these similarities is that such descriptions of melancholia captured a condition as constant and unchanging as gallstones or heart disease, which did not alter in any fundamental way between these different eras or between these eras and our own time. This equation is frequently assumed in medical writing today, which accepts some variant on the view that, until the nineteenth century, in the words of one commentator, "melancholia was the term usually used to refer to the depressive syndrome" (Andreason 1982:24). The leading historical authority on melancholy and depression similarly comments on the remarkable consistency among descriptions of these conditions (Jackson 1986:27).

The conclusion that there is but one unchanging condition identified as *melancholia* in the past and renamed *depression* in our own era represents a troubling oversimplification, however. For example, commonalities found throughout the canon on melancholia may be explained more by the reiteration of certain neo-Galenic doctrine than by the observed recurrence of similar signs and symptoms. Until well into the modern period, medical writing on melancholia derived to a great extent from the study of the canonical writing, particularly works from the Galenic tradition (Berrios and Porter 1995; Jackson 1986). Some of the consistency in past accounts seems almost certainly due to diagnostic conceptions and expectations that affected, and limited, observation.

Moreover, many dissimilarities distinguish earlier accounts of melancholia from today's descriptions of depression, and three of these are particularly striking. First, the melancholia of past eras encompassed much more than modern conceptions of depression. For example, melancholia included what were known as disorders of the imagination (today's delusions and hallucinations): of melancholy men, as Burton says, some "have a corrupt eare, they think they heare musicke, or some hidious noise as theyir phantasie conceaves, corrupt eyes, some smelling: some one sense, some another" (Burton [1621] 2001:403). Together with various delusional states, these disturbances of perception are portrayed as standard features of melancholia. Modern depression can also give rise to psychotic symptoms, but such features are more commonly associated with schizophrenia. Because schizophrenia was not identified as such until well into the nineteenth century, we can guess that *melancholia* encompassed other forms of psychosis, such as schizophrenia.

Additional symptoms today associated with other syndromes were included in descriptions of melancholia. Melancholia appears to have covered the *scruples*— obsessions and compulsions today identified as *obsessive-compulsive disorder*. With the greater prominence given to fear (anxiety, apprehension) symptoms, it arguably encompassed not only today's mood disorders but today's anxiety disorders as well. Melancholic symptoms also included mistrustful attitudes toward others and suspicion of being the object of others' malice, which define today's persecutory paranoia. Thus, the earlier category of melancholia was considerably broader than the later one of depression.

Second, for hundreds of years, influenced by Aristotle and almost every subsequent thinker until the eighteenth century, melancholia also carried glamorous associations of intellectual brilliance and later even genius, associations absent from today's conception of depression (Klibansky, Panofsky, and Saxl 1964).[2] It was the disease of the man of learning, the disposition and occupational hazard of the intellectual and of any man of reflective and contemplative tendencies. Such desirable associations are almost entriely absent from today's conception of depression.

Next, melancholia was the disorder of the man of genius, sensitivity, intellect, and creativity, whereas today's depression is apparently both linked with women in epidemiological fact and associated with the feminine in cultural ideas. Depression's gender link is the reverse of the masculine and male associations of melancholia.

These last two are, of course, connected. Because genius, creativity, and intellectual prowess were themselves "gendered" traits associated with men and the masculine, the perceived link between women and depression, a product of the nineteenth century, inevitably expunged these more glamorous associations (Enterline 1995; Lunbeck 1994; Radden 1987, 2000a; Schiesari 1992).

There are two additional dissimilarities, each attaching only to twentieth-century depressive subjectivity and each, in my view, attributable to their statement in Freud's influential essay on mourning and melancholia (Freud 1917). The first is an attribution of states of loss to depressive states. Freud portrays the twentieth-century disorder as one in which the early loss of the object is relived. The second, related, trait is that of self-critical and self-hating attitudes. Following Freud, these attitudes have come to characterize twentieth-century depressive subjectivity. Arguably, neither an emphasis on loss nor such self-critical and self-loathing attitudes attached with any consistency to the melancholic states of pre-nineteenth-century eras (Radden 2000a, 2000b). Thus, to the extent that today's depression is a disorder of loss and self-loathing, it is dissimilar to the melancholia of other times.

Some of these differences between melancholia and depression are undeniably soft, culturally-dependent traits. We should be surprised if the connotations of disorders like these remained unaltered between one cultural and historical period and another. Indeed, melancholia and depression are obvious cases of what Hacking has called *interactive kinds*, categories—and conditions—affected not only by other cultural changes but by their sufferers' awareness of themselves as so classified (Hacking 1999). But any attempt to establish the respective similarities and differences between melancholia and depression by avoiding such apparently cultural associations would unacceptably beg ontological questions.[3] Thus, before undertaking any further comparative or contrastive analysis, we need to take a closer look at the methodology it presupposes.

Ontological Descriptivism

A determination about the alleged equation between the melancholia of other times and today's depression employing the compare/contrast approach introduced seems to invite a deeper, ontological question: What kind of entities are these conditions of melancholia and depression? And, in turn, this question sends us back to the methodological debates within psychiatry over descriptivism and the basis for classifying and characterizing mental disorders.

At least by that name, descriptivism is best known today as the epistemological approach adopted by the compilers of the *Diagnostic and Statistical Manual of Mental Disorders* (DSM)-III (1980) and subsequent editions (American Psychiatric Association [APA] 1980, 1987, 1994).[4] In their words, this approach to classification provides definitions of disorders consisting of "descriptions of the clinical features of the disorders...features...described at the lowest order of inference necessary to describe the characteristic features of the disorder" (APA 1980:7). This descriptivist approach serves the purpose of establishing a shared discourse in the presence of competing and incompatible theoretical and etiological assumptions about mental disorder: "clinicians can agree on the identification of mental disorders on the basis of their clinical manifestations without agreeing on how the disturbances come about," as the introduction points out (APA 1980:7). Employing a descriptive classificatory system like DSM-III, psychiatric categories such as *depression* are identified and arranged into sets of psychological, bodily, and behavioral traits that form observable sign and symptom clusters, or syndromes.[5] (For clinical understanding, the importance of these descriptions goes without saying, and the contribution of phenomenological psychiatry lies in its recognition of the value of close, subjective descriptions in identifying meaningful connections.)

Descriptivism comes in several guises, however, of which the purely epistemological classificatory principle defined above is merely one: *ontological descriptivism* is the view that categories such as the depression so identified refer solely to those observable sign/symptom clusters and not to any underlying causal framework. This is not to assert that such signs and symptoms are uncaused or—although this will perhaps be true—that their causes are unknown, but merely that they are not part of the meaning, or reference, of *depression*.[6]

In contrast to descriptivism, *extradescriptive* or *causal classifications* and ontologies allude to underlying causal (etiological) states believed to give rise to the more readily observable signs and symptoms of a disease. On such a causal analysis, *depression* refers not only to the observable features of the condition but also to these underlying structures. Since the second half of the nineteenth century and despite Carl Hempel's 1965 prediction that descriptive classifications would quickly give way to more theoretical ones, Western classifications have remained descriptive (Hempel 1965). But to the ontological question of what *melancholia* and *depression* are, both descriptivist and causal answers have been offered.

The causal models of depression since the early 1900s have come in two forms: the psychological model and that associated with biological psychiatry, which has recently seemed to eclipse the former. In biological, neo-Kraepelinian psychiatry, the notion of a discrete disease entity is central. This entity comprises the underlying biological state causing those symptoms and/or (because diseases may be asymptomatic) signs, together with those signs and symptoms; the totality comprises what has been called a *syndrome with unity* (Poland, Von Eckardt, and Spaulding 1994). With psychological theorizing, in contrast, the underlying structures causing the signs and symptoms of disorder are psychic rather than biological, although they may be understood to be grounded in biological states. (At first sight anomalous because its primary or originating cause is located in neither the psyche nor the brain of its sufferer, a condition such as posttraumatic stress disorder, whose proximate cause is the psychological state of trauma or stress, finds a place in the psychological category.)

The last decades of the nineteenth century saw the first use of the term *depression* as a noun and, arguably, the birth of the modern disorder of depression (Berrios and Porter 1995; Jackson 1986). Since then, each type of causal account (psychological and biological) has been applied to depression. And, before depression came to replace melancholia as the preeminent category within affective disorder, melancholia was similarly subject to biological and psychological causal analysis. The earlier humoral theory derived from Greek medicine and current chemical imbalance theories illustrate pre-twentieth-century and twentieth-century types of biological causal accounts, respectively. Freud's influential theorizing about loss in "*Mourning and Melancholia*" and the mid-twentieth-century learned helplessness hypotheses illustrate psychological accounts that were causal (Freud 1917; Seligman 1975).

Whether melancholia is to be equated with depression will apparently depend on whether we adhere to a descriptivist or a causal ontology—a methodological, but also a metaphysical, decision. To adopt descriptivism is to allow the similarities and differences between the respective descriptions of melancholy and depression to determine whether an unchanging condition, once named melancholia, was later renamed depression. If we adopt descriptivism, the compare/contrast method can be the only one available to us in making this determination. And to the extent that the pattern of similarities and differences presents an ambiguous picture, a decision will be reached based on the balance of the descriptive similarity or difference. (Were similarities to outweigh dissimilarities, we would accept the equation; were dissimilarities to outweigh similarities, we would deny it.) Embracing a causal ontology, in contrast, we might set aside these superficial measures and insist that despite differences in appearances, *melancholia* and *depression* are alternative names for the same underlying condition.[7] (If the causes of melancholia and depression were known, and known to be different, then there may be less temptation to equate the two conditions. But because the cause or causes are unknown, the hypothesis of a single unifying cause remains viable.)

To identify these models as ontologies is to make the determination over melancholia and depression on grounds that are more than merely pragmatic. A pragmatic approach, in contrast, would require us to consult our own interests and purposes in deciding whether melancholia and depression ought to be equated.[8]

If our goal is to determine what *melancholia* and *depression* are, we must consider the merits of each of these descriptivist and causal models in application to melancholia and depression. Before comparing descriptive and causal models, however, some clarifications are required, because there are several closely allied distinctions and contrasts from which the contrast between descriptivism and causal, extradescriptivism must be desegregated.

First, the distinction between *descriptive* and *causal models* is not be confused with the distinction between *categorical* and *dimensional* approaches to melancholia and depression. Disorders are dimensional if they lie on a continuum uniting abnormal with normal traits. A categorical approach treats mental disorders as discrete entities, different not merely in degree but in kind from the norm. Twentieth-century theorizing about mental disorder has often blurred the contrasts between descriptive and extradescriptive causal analyses and dimensional and categorical approaches, in part because of the powerful influence of Kraepelinian and neo-Kraepelinian thinking, which treats mental disorders as both causal and categorical. Nonetheless, these two distinctions are conceptually distinct: a descriptive account of depression (or any mental disorder) may be either categorical or dimensional, as may a causal account of depression.

The categorical approach construes diseases as discretely occurring trait clusters present in nature—that is, as natural kinds. (*Natural kinds* have been defined as bounded categories that have necessary and sufficient internal conditions for their identification or, in medicine, their diagnosis [Zachar 2000:168].) Only if there are natural kinds, a claim now debated, and if mental disorders are natural kinds, does the categorical approach make sense. Recent critics have been thoroughgoing and convincing in their rejection of the idea that mental disorders are, or are like, natural kinds (Hacking 1999; Haslam 2000; Healy 1997; Horwitz 2002; Luhrmann 2000; Radden 2000a; Zachar 2000). Nonetheless, the view that mental disorders are natural kinds is still widely held within today's biologically oriented neo-Kraepelinian psychiatry (Horwitz 2002; Luhrmann 2000).[9]

A second preliminary concerns the distinction between *meaning* and *reference*. A term's meaning and reference are distinguishable, and it might be supposed that the contrast between descriptive and causal analyses is more apparent than real inasmuch as the descriptivists allude to the meaning or intension of terms like *depression* whereas causal analyses capture reference, the extension of the term (Kripke 1980; Putnam 1975; Spitzer 1990). This is a conceivable interpretation of some descriptivist analyses of depression; in other accounts, however, terms like *depression* not only mean but refer to signs and symptoms only, not to underlying causal states.

Third, the distinction between descriptive and causal models also partially maps onto the distinction between illness and disease. Although this distinction has been challenged, illnesses have long been characterized, following Christopher Boorse, as self-identified, negatively valued, subjectively troubling symptom clusters; diseases, in contrast, are biologically based, objectively identified, and value-neutrally described conditions (Boorse 1974). The emphasis on the value neutrality of characterizations of disease in the disease/illness distinction would prevent our conflating the distinction between descriptive and causal categories with that between illness and disease. Descriptive analyses can purport to be as value neutral as causal ones, the DSMs illustrate. There are other dissimilarities between these two contrasts as well. The notion of disease is also restricted to biological, not psychic, underlying entities, thus excluding psychological versions of the causal model. Moreover, because *illness* is focused on symptoms, the category of illness denotes fewer features than may be captured in a descriptive analysis, which portrays signs as well.

Nor, finally, is the descriptivist analysis to be equated with the view that mental disorder is (merely) a social construction. The claim that mental disorders are social constructions is often stated in such ways as to render it trivially and uninterestingly true or probably false (Boghossian 1996; Devitt 1991; Gillett 1998; Hacking 1999). However, except in the trivially true sense, descriptivist analyses will be compatible with, but not reducible to, the view that no mind-independent reality (or natural kinds of kind) corresponds to categories such as *depression*. Whether epistemological or ontological, descriptivism doubts some of medical psychiatry's claims as to the meaning and reference of terms like *depression*—and/or the causal hypotheses implicit in medical psychiatry's account of it—without doubting the mind-independence of the signs and symptoms such terms name.

Traditionally, ontological questions about mental disorder have been answered in terms that are either descriptivist or causal, and it is these that are the focus of the following discussion. That said, it must be added that recent theorizing using Darwinian concepts of malfunction promises an ontology that can avoid some of the troubling theoretical consequences attaching to descriptivist and causal accounts (Murphy and Stich 2000; Nesse and Williams 1994; Stevens and Price 1996) although admittedly, such analyses bring some vexing problems of their own (Greenspan 2001; Roberts 2001; Woolfolk 1999).

Masked "Depression"

Back pain, dizziness, headache, and other somatic symptoms are said to be indicative of depression in China and Africa; acting out, substance abuse, and antisocial behavior supposedly reflect "masked" depression in American men. These conclusions about the presence of depression in non-Western cultures, and any claims about masked depressions, as urgently require analysis of their methodological and ontological implications as does the identification of melancholia with depression. Such analysis will also provide additional perspectives on the historical comparison between melancholia and depression (Fabrega 1989; Karp 1996; Kleinman 1986, 1988, 1995; Kleinman and Good 1985; Mezzich and Cranach 1988; Real 1997; Sartorius et al. 1990).

On a descriptivist analysis, these claims stretch the sign and symptom picture of depression beyond coherence. There is no apparent commonality between Western, Chinese, and African depression symptoms or, indeed, between Western (unmasked) women's and (masked) men's symptoms. Only a causal analysis, which posits common underlying states serving to unify and anchor these disparate traits, permits us to maintain that these are all cases of depression. (If fleeting, conscious states of subjective distress were experienced alike by those whose depression finds expression in somatic or acting out, antisocial behavior, and other masked symptoms, then such states might provide the unifying commonality required to extend *depression* to all cases. Neither theory, phenomenology, nor other empirical evidence supports this hypothesis, however.)

In accounting for the cross-cultural variation noted, adherents of causal analyses today sometimes are expressed in what Kleinman has named a *pathogenicity/ pathoplasticity model*. In this analysis, biology determines the cause and structure of particular mental disorders—what McHugh and Slavney call their *form*—whereas cultural and social factors influence the idiom in which they are expressed, their *content* (Kleinman 1988; McHugh and Slavney 1990). Thus, the underlying commonality in depression is biological and stable; the psychological and subjective symptom expression varies. In Kleinman's words, "Depression experienced entirely as low back pain and depression experienced entirely as guilt-ridden existential despair are such substantially different forms of illness behavior with distinctive symptoms, patterns of help seeking, and treatment responses that although diseases in each instance may be the same, the illness, not the disease becomes the determinative factor" (1988, 25).

Kleinman is uncommitted over whether depression is to be construed descriptively or causally in this passage. (In subsequent writing, Kleinman has somewhat shifted ground [1995]; however, the present discussion is focused on his analyses written in the 1980s.) His concerns are antithetical to classification, generalization, and this kind of ontology. Caring for these various ills, not reducing them to diseases, he believes, should be the central, perhaps even the sole, purpose of psychiatry. Nonetheless, depending on the treatment models adopted, even treatment may require a resolution on these ontological issues. If it does, only the unifying role of a causal ontology will protect from incoherence Kleinman's account of these varying forms of suffering as depression. To adopt descriptivism, in the case of cross-cultural comparisons, must be to conclude that depression is culture bound. Any suggestion that, although distinct illnesses, Western depression and Chinese depression may represent a single disease presupposes an extradescriptivist, causal ontology.

Drug Cartography

Recently, rapid developments in psychotropic drugs have stimulated a remapping of psychiatric categories based on psychopharmacological effects, and these also are pertinent to the discussion of cross-cultural depression (Healy 1997; Kramer 1993; Luhrmann 2000; Sobo 2002). By organizing disorders around these psychopharmacological effects, such a classification diverges from our present, symptom-based descriptivist classification not only in methodology but also in the classificatory landscape that results.[10] A variety of problems with impulse control, including overeating, gambling, paraphilias, and various patterns of alcohol and drug abuse, for example, are increasingly regarded as obsessive-compulsive spectrum disorders because selective serotonin reuptake inhibitors are effective in their treatment. In contrast to descriptive or causal classificatory principles, the principle of drug taxonomy, originally introduced by Peter Kramer, would classify as depression any condition alleviated by so-called antidepressant drugs (Kramer 1993).

At first glance, such an approach might also help us decide whether to equate Chinese or African somatized depression with Western depression, or to compare masked with regular depression. If each of the disparate symptom clusters (somatic symptoms in China, acting-out symptoms in American men, and felt sadness in American women) were effectively treated with the same psychopharmacological agent, then by employing drug cartography, we might suppose that these disparate conditions were all rightly known by the name *depression*.

No such psychopharmacological test would be available to us in trying to ascertain whether the melancholia of past times is to be equated with present-day depression, of course; such drugs were not invented in those times. But drug cartography may also be less useful in present-day comparisons, for two important reasons. First, because diseases involve both relational and inherent properties, it has been pointed out, even in prototypical medical conditions such as infectious diseases, response to the same drug may be different in two different patients suffering the same condition and the same in two different microorganismic infections (Zachar 2000:172). So caution will be in order if similarity of response to a drug is used to draw or redraw the classificatory boundaries.

Second, contrary to a seemingly widespread presumption, the presence of an effective drug X for a psychological state Y proves neither that the cause of Y was a deficiency of X nor even that the cause of Y was a brain state of any kind. A bad day at work may cause brain state Y, and X may be two beers at 6 PM. The brain correlate of Y (call it Y') on which X acts is no more the cause of the psychological state Y than it is an alcohol deficiency. This argument is flawed only if we accept some form of dualism. For the reductionist, the bad day at work reduces to or is identical with brain states, allowing that the earlier occurring brain state identical with the initiating psychological state(s) may be regarded as the initiating cause of some subsequent brain state Y. Such radically materialistic theories, where all causes are physical states, remain vulnerable to another problem, however. Controversy and seemingly intractable metaphysical disagreement over dualism will hinder efforts at an agreed-upon language for describing one state as the cause of another. This problem is outlined below, in a more general discussion of the drawbacks of accepting a causal ontology.

In summary, comparisons between Western depression and other cultures' depressions, as between depression and masked depression, seem to depend on the same unresolved issues over descriptivism encountered in our attempted cross-historical comparison between melancholia and depression. *Depression* cannot be equated with these other depressions on a descriptivist ontology, although it can with the adoption of a causal ontology; moreover, despite its apparent promise, the new drug cartography by which depression could be defined as any condition alleviated by antidepressant drugs may not be sufficient to allay or resolve these concerns.

Like the equation between depression and non-western "depression," the alleged equation between depression and melancholia can be maintained with the adoption of an extradescriptivist, causal ontology. But the metaphysical decision to go beyond descriptivism requires closer examination.

Evaluating the Merits of Descriptivism

Even in its relatively brief history, psychiatry has seen disagreement over how to resolve the ontological issue explored here, and diagnostic classification and theorizing have swung between contrasting descriptivist and causal analyses, or ontologies.[11] Some of these reversals have resulted from the pursuit of such unscientific ends as power, prestige, and money (Healy 1997). A recent analysis contends, for example, that the emphasis on diagnosis in the extradescriptive, causal diagnostic psychiatry of the second half of the twentieth century emerged "in order to raise the prestige of psychiatry, to guarantee reimbursement from third parties, to allow medications to be marketed, and to protect the interests of mental health researchers and professionals" (Horwitz 2002, 81).

Such social and political explanations for psychiatry's swing between descriptivist and causal ontologies are important for a full understanding of the tumultuous history of psychiatry's first century. Such explanations have tended to obscure the powerful, and surprisingly evenly matched theoretical considerations in support of and against, descriptivism, however. They must not be permitted to do so. Regardless of the social and political forces affecting psychiatry, the contrast between descriptivist and causal ontologies will remain a contested, polarizing issue because of the theoretical considerations at stake; these theoretical considerations need to be more clearly understood, and their importance needs to be recognized.

Given the complexity of mental disorder and the relative youth of the science that seeks to understand it, the dilemma between adopting descriptivist or causal analyses is to be expected. Surprising, however, is the extent to which the broad outlines have remained unaltered in the years since such issues were first discussed.

These outlines are captured by Henry Maudsley (1835–1918), writing well over a century ago: "The old [descriptive] classification...is as good as far as it goes, but it by no means goes to the root of the matter: whereas the [causal] classifications which pretend to go to the root of the matter go beyond what knowledge warrants (Maudsley 1867:268)".

In the same paradoxical way identified by Maudsley, descriptivism's strengths still appear to contain its weaknesses. Supporting a more descriptive analysis, two points are noteworthy (in addition to the apparent gain in understanding of meaningful connections emphasized by phenomenological psychiatry). First, such an analysis is etiologically agnostic and compatible with a range of explanations—biological, social, or psychological. This agnosticism offers a significant advantage. How to characterize the causes of mental disorder remains a deeply controversial issue. In studies of depression, recent research on parts of the limbic system, the prefrontal lobes, and the role played by dynorphin, for example, has entirely unseated previous orthodoxy implicating serotonin as the central causal factor.

A second strong advantage is that descriptivism avoids or at least reduces the vulnerabilities associated with theorizing. In today's empiricist climate of "evidence-based" medicine, with its emphasis on empirically established findings, unverified hypotheses are viewed with some suspicion (Horwitz 2002; Pincus and McQueen 2002). And descriptive approaches have achieved remarkable empirical advances by establishing statistically significant connections between symptoms and generalizations that, although short of causal explanations, permit certain forms of probabilistic prediction.

The primary drawback of descriptivism, however, lies in just those characteristics noted. Although not without predictive power, an account that is descriptive is not, as such, explanatory. It merely describes. In spite of the commonplace and seemingly irresistible tendency to see explanatory advantage in the assertion that the symptoms of depression are caused by depression, if we accept descriptivism, there is none. Certainly, descriptive symptom-defined categories permit probabilistic predictions that lend themselves to evidence-based treatment protocols. But in contrast to the possibilities that will accompany an understanding of etiology, such approaches offer limited and arguably misleading information (Graham 2002; Kendell 1989; Sobo 2002). As Kendell has put it: "the most aeteologically based classifications are more useful—*because they embody a wider range of implications*—than purely clinical classifications" (1989:46; my emphasis). With its explanatory vitality and promise, a causal approach introduces research possibilities, further hypotheses, and even hope of prevention or cure.

A glance at the drawbacks of a causal analysis must immediately temper this glimpse of the exciting prospects in store when we move beyond descriptivism, however. An extensive literature attests to the complexity, and problems, attendant on causal explanation in psychiatry (Glymour 1986; McLaren 1998; Schaffner 1993, 2002). Without appealing to this critical literature, I briefly note three factors seemingly sufficient to dissuade us from moving beyond descriptivism.

First, even with the great advances in brain science of the last decades, these etiological claims remain, thus far, no more than a promise for the functional disorders such as depression. It is acknowledged to be an article not of fact but of "faith" that the psychological disorders described in the DSM "will ultimately be anchored in specific etiological factors" (Zuckerman 1999:26).

Second, there is an additional vulnerability incumbent in any model positing underlying causes of mental disorder in the brain. It seems to require a resolution to long-debated issues about dualism. The standard causal analysis that correlates a psychological symptom such as a mood state (C) with an underlying brain state (B) cannot at the same time attribute a causal relationship between these two entities. Only by accepting some version of dualism would that attribution be possible. The allegiance of the modern-day brain scientist is often to some form of reductionism (Kandel 1998, 1999); thus the cause of mood state (C) must be some other brain state, occurring earlier in the causal chain, state (A). This is not problematic in itself, but it is troublesome at the level of explanatory discourse, where ambiguity attaches to the identification and description of the cause of this symptom (What is the cause of C, B, or A?). Were there no controversy over dualism, a decision could be reached as to whether the cause of C should be described as B or A. But hundreds of years of argument and analysis have left the mind–body problem unresolved. No early or easy resolution to the matter of dualism is likely, so no easily agreed-on decision over which is to be called the cause of C seems, presently, possible.

Third, Zachar has identified disease categories as "practical" rather than natural kinds: as he puts it, they cannot be fully defined with respect to inherent properties (Zachar 2000). To the extent that diagnostic classification is a normative and pragmatic practice and we classify to serve certain purposes, there is no reason to expect the underlying causes to have structural dimorphism with categories such as depression. In the words of Poland and colleagues: "Human interests and saliencies tend to carve out an unnatural domain from the point of view of nomological structure." And there is "simply no reason to suppose that the features of clinical phenomenology that catch our attention are the source of great human distress are also features upon which a science of psychopathology should directly focus when searching for regularities and natural kinds" (Poland et al. 1994:254). This is hardly a new observation. It has been made by those critical of psychiatric nosology since the middle of the twentieth century (Szasz 1963). Perhaps surprisingly, however, it appears to have remained largely unaddressed.

This review of the theoretical considerations for going beyond ontological descriptivism to determine whether to equate melancholia with depression reveals the difficulty of the decision involved here (and explains, perhaps, the failure of Hempel's prediction that more theoretically encumbered classifications would soon supersede descriptive ones). Despite its explanatory paucity, the limited nature of surface psychiatry permits it to avoid dangers and errors arising from overreaching. Although overreaching without conceptual warrant, only causal ontologies seem to promise the goals we all desire.

Conclusion

This discussion has explored some theoretical complexities inherent in the cross-historical comparison between melancholia and depression in the course of which an analysis and evaluation was offered of descriptive psychiatry, and of some recent trends in psychiatric classification. Only by adopting an extradescriptivist, causal ontology do we have theoretical warrant for maintaining the identity between melancholy and depression. Yet the causal analysis has serious vulnerabilities; moreover, apparently compelling reasons seem to support the adoption of descriptivism.

Ontological descriptivism leaves us free—and, indeed, required—to employ the simple compare/contrast method outlined at the start of this essay. If, on balance, today's depression resembles the melancholia of old, then the equation between the two conditions is warranted. Comparing non-Western with Western evidence of depression, Kleinman cites symptoms that are consistently distinct and dissimilar: as long as we comply with a refusal to reduce the illness to the disease and adopt, as we saw he must, a causal ontology, there is no difficulty insisting that although (perhaps) an identical disease, Western depression is a different illness from Chinese depression. But comparing melancholia and depression is a more difficult project because of the mixed pattern of similarities and differences between the symptoms of melancholia and depression sketched. Clearly, this is not an easy or conclusive answer. But my inclination is to rank the differences more persuasive than the similarities and judge that *melancholia* and *depression* are not to be understood as one and the same. Is this dame melancholy? My answer is, probably not.

Acknowledgments

Versions of this chapter were presented at the International Conference of Philosophy and Mental Health in Florence, Italy (2000); the Philosophy Department at the University of Louisville, Kentucky (2000); and the American Psychiatric Association Annual Meeting in Philadelphia (2002). I am grateful to audiences from those three meetings for valuable suggestions and corrections. Also, I wish to acknowledge the critical reading of members of PHAEDRA—Jane Roland Martin, Ann Diller, Barbara Houston, Janet Farrell Smith, and Susan Fransoza; and of George Graham, John Sadler, and Bill Fulford. My gratitude finally goes to two anonymous readers who contributed important suggestions.

Notes

1. In this discussion, *depression* refers to the condition known as Major Depressive Disorder and its variants, including that disorder when accompanied by the anhedonic *melancholic* features (APA 1994:383–84).

2. Arguably, these still attach to manic depression, particularly since a late-twentieth-century revival of some Romantic associations with that disorder (Jamison 1993).

3. Social constructionist accounts of mental disorder would reject the distinction between, and the implicit ontological commitment underlying, this characterization into soft and harder attributes, for example (Hacking 1999; Zachar 2000).

4. Ascribed to disorders, *functional* used to be distinguished from *organic* to indicate this focus on what is known and readily observable; dysfunction is a descriptive category in this contrast (APA 1980).

5. *Descriptivism* is also applied to the claim that value-free descriptions of medical conditions are possible (Boorse 1974; Fulford 1989; Thornton 2000). Although an important concept in psychiatric classification, the latter sense of *descriptivism* is not to be confused with and bears no relation to the *descriptivism* discussed here.

6. Rather, it is to adopt something closer to the analysis accepted for certain primarily observable dispositions, such as cheerfulness or untidiness. Although they are not uncaused, and their causes may well be unknown, the *cheerful* and *untidy* refer primarily, if not solely, to the recognizable clusters of responses we deem manifestations of cheerfulness and untidiness, respectively.

7. The contrast between descriptivist and causal analyses has been portrayed as a difference in kind not degree, yet it is likely that allegedly descriptive accounts actually contain certain assumptions and theoretical fragments which are an unavoidable aspect of any observation—an inadvertent leaching evident in the DSMs (Margolis 1994).

8. What might those interests and purposes be? Some late-twentieth-century preference for *melancholia* to describe *depression* has seemed to attempt to reinvest these states with some of the glamorous associations from the past (Butler 1990, 1993; Jamison 1993, 1995; Kramer 2000; Kristeva 1989; Solomon 2001). If such a trend alters the devastating stigma attaching to depression and its sufferer and offers some consolation or compensation for the suffering, then in pragmatic terms this may be judged reason enough to decide that *melancholy* and *depression* should be equated. (Moreover, those skeptical of the power of such cultural associations to alleviate suffering might read in the literary history of melancholy, where much suggests that this condition was courted, sought, and even cherished, not unlike the way states of hypomania are today. A line from Milton illustrates. After enumerating the intellectual and spiritual satisfactions, he anticipates for his later years, Milton for one concludes by striking a bargain with their source, Melancholy: "These pleasures, Melancholy, give. And I with thee will choose to live" (Milton 1890:319). A pragmatic approach is not adopted here, however.

9. The historical relationship between the dimensional and categorical approaches has recently been explored by sociologist Allan Horwitz, who shows that, rather paradoxically, the dimensional thinking of early-twentieth-century psychiatry hastened later adoption of the categorical Kraepelinian model (Horwitz 2002).

10. The effects of drug cartography are likely to be far reaching and are a subject of growing concern. As Healy puts it, the role of a drug company is not "to find the key that fits a predetermined lock or the bullet that will hit an objective target"; rather, we are at present in a state where "companies can not only seek to find the key to the lock but *can dictate a great deal of the shape* of the lock to which a key must fit" (1997:212; my emphasis).

11. In Germany, by the middle of the nineteenth century, polarized camps within the nascent field of psychiatry represented the psychicists, who applied mentalistic (not to say religious and poetic) language and presuppositions to mental disorder, and the somaticists with materialistic metaphors and an extreme reductionism, which viewed all mental disorder as caused by as yet unidentified lesions or other organic damage in the brain (Martin 2002; Pichot 1983; Shorter 1997). Somatism did not invite baldly etiological classifications of the kind derived from humoral theory, wherein melancholia was classed with other disorders such as epilepsy, quartan fever, headache, and paralysis precisely because they were each believed diseases of the black bile. Nonetheless, somatist assumptions produced classifications whose functional and symptom-based (and course-based) categories presupposed that lesions or malfunction affected underlying parts of the brain corresponding to the mental faculties. Faculty psychology ostensibly identified nothing more than functional categories. But the reification of the units it "carved" was an evident temptation in this era when the localization of diseases had proven such a successful hypothesis in other fields of medicine: "diseases"

of particular faculties were often understood to be localized pathophysiology (Radden 1996). Thus, whereas Kraepelin's classification was descriptivist (in contrast to the causal classification of Wernicke [1848–1905]), his ontology was not. In the early psychiatry that preceded Kraepelin, two other thinkers employed such a causal ontology while insisting on a descriptivist epistemology. An important influence on Kraepelin, Wilhelm Griesinger (1817–1868) accepted somatist ontology but asserted that, until underlying brain lesions could be identified, psychiatry must classify according to psychological function. Writing in England a little later, Maudsley adopted a similar position, at the same time emphasizing the biological basis for all mental disorders yet calling for a descriptively based classification for psychiatry. Like Griesinger, Maudsley insisted that until we know more about the brain, we cannot guess at the relationship between symptoms and their underlying causes. The more thoroughgoing descriptivism of the influential early-twentieth-century classifier Adolph Meyer rejected the suggestion that the symptoms of mental disorder were organically caused, a rejection echoed by many antipsychiatry thinkers in the mid-twentieth century such as Thomas Szasz (1965). This resulted in a descriptivism that are not just epistemological but ontological. Mental disorders were for Meyer reactions to social and psychological stressors. (This view, with its accompanying dimensionalism, is believed by some to have contributed to American psychiatry's drift toward what became a kind of diagnostic nihilism [Healy 1997:41].) Mid-twentieth-century classifiers such as the authors of DSM-III and Erwin Stengel, influential in the formation of the *Manual of the International Statistical Classification of Diseases, Injuries and Causes of Death (ICD-8)* (World Health Organization 1967), eschewed theory and etiological hypotheses. But this also appears to have been an epistemological descriptivism, consistent with and sometimes accompanied by, an explicitly causal ontology.

References

American Psychiatric Association (APA). 1980. *Diagnostic and statistical manual of mental disorders* (3rd ed.). Washington, D.C.: Author.

———. 1987. *Diagnostic and statistical manual of mental disorders* (revised 3rd ed.). Washington, D.C.: Author.

———. 1994. *Diagnostic and statistical manual of mental disorders*, 4th ed. Washington, D.C.: Author.

Andreason, N. 1982. Concepts, diagnosis and classification. In *Handbook of affective disorders* (pp. 24–44), ed. E. S. Paykel. New York: Guilford Press.

Aretaeus of Cappadocia. 1856. On the causes and symptoms of chronic diseases. In *The extant works of Aretaeus, the Cappadocian*, ed. Francis Adams; trans. F. Adams. London: Sydenham Society.

Berrios, G. E., and R. Porter, eds. 1995. *A history of clinical psychiatry: The origin and history of psychiatric disorders*. New York: New York University Press.

Boghossian, P. 1996. What the Sokal hoax ought to teach us. *Times Literary Supplement*, 13 December: 14–15.

Boorse, C. 1974. On the distinction between disease and illness. *Philosophy and Public Affairs* 5:49–69.

Bright, T. [1569] 2000. A treatise of melancholy. In *The nature of melancholy*, ed. J. Radden. Oxford: Oxford University Press.

Burton, R. [1621] 2001. *The Anatomy of melancholy*, ed. H. Jackson, New York: New York Review of Books.

Butler, J. 1990. *The psychic life of power: Theories in subjection*. Stanford, Calif.: Stanford University Press.

———. 1993. *Bodies that matter*. New York: Routledge.

Devitt, M. 1991. *Realism and truth*. 2d ed. Cambridge, Mass.: Blackwell.

Enterline, L. 1995. *The tears of Narcissus: Melancholia and masculinity in early modern writing*. Stanford, Calif.: Stanford University Press.

Fabrega, H. 1989. Cultural relativism and psychiatric illness. *Journal of Nervous and Mental Disorders* 177:415–25.

Freud, S. 1917. Mourning and melancholia. Vol. 4 of *Collected Papers*. London: Hogarth Press.

Fulford, K. W. M. 1989. *Moral theory and medical practice*. Cambridge: Cambridge University Press.

Gillett, E. 1998. Relativism and the social-constructionist paradigm. *Philosophy, Psychiatry, and Psychology* 5(1):37–48.

Glymour, C. 1986. Comment: Statistics and metaphysics. *Journal of the American Statistical Association* 81:964–66

Graham, G. 2002. Recent work in philosophical psychopathology. *American Philosophical Quarterly* 39(2):109–34.

Greenspan, P. 2001. Good evolutionary reasons: Darwinian psychiatry and women's depression. *Philosophical Psychology* 14:327–38.

Griesinger, W. 1867/1965. *Mental pathology and therapeutics*. A facsimile of the English edition of 1867. New York: Hafner.

Hacking, I. 1999. *The social construction of what?* Cambridge: Harvard University Press.

Haslam, N. 2000. Psychiatric categories as natural kinds: Essentialist thinking about mental disorders. *Social Research* 67:1031–58.

Healy, D. 1997. *The antidepressant era*. Cambridge: Harvard University Press.

Hempel, C. 1965. Fundamentals of taxonomy. In *Aspects of scientific explanation*, ed. C. Hempel (pp. 137–54). New York: Free Press.

Horwitz, A. 2002. *Creating mental illness*. Chicago: University of Chicago Press.

Hunter, R., and I. Macalpine, eds. 1982. *Three hundred years of psychiatry 1535–1860*. New York: Oxford University Press.

Jackson, S. 1986. *Melancholia and depression*. New Haven, Conn.: Yale University Press.

Jamison, K. 1993. *Touched with fire: Manic-depressive illness and the artistic temperament*. New York: Simon and Schuster.

———. 1995. *An unquiet mind*. New York: Knopf.

Kandel, E. 1998. A new intellectual framework for psychiatry. *American Journal of Psychiatry* 155:457–69.

———. 1999. Biology and the future of psychoanalysis: A new intellectual framework for psychiatry revisited. *American Journal of Psychiatry* 156:505–24.

Karp, D. 1996. *Speaking of sadness*. New York: Oxford University Press.

Kendell, R. E. 1989. Clinical validity. *Psychological Medicine* 19:45–55.

Kleinman, A. 1986. *Social origins of distress and diseases: Depression, neurasthenia and pain in modern China*. New Haven, Conn.: Yale University Press.

———. 1988. *Rethinking psychiatry: From cultural category to personal experience*. New York: Free Press.

———. 1995. *Writing in the margin*. Cambridge.: Harvard University Press.

Kleinman, A., and B. Good, eds. 1985. *Culture and depression: Studies in the anthropology and cross-cultural psychiatry of affect and disorder*. Berkeley: University of California Press.

Klibansky, R., E. Panofsky, and F. Saxl. 1964. *Saturn and melancholy: Studies in the history of natural philosophy, history and art*. New York: Basic Books.

Kramer, P. 1993. *Listening to Prozac: A psychiatrist explores antidepressant drugs and the remaking of the self*. New York: Viking.

——. 2000. The valorization of sadness: Alienation and the melancholic temperament. *Hastings Center Report* 30(2):13–18.

Kripke, S. 1980. *Naming and necessity*. Cambridge: Harvard University Press.

Kristeva, J. 1989. *Black sun: Depression and melancholy*. Trans. L. Roudiez. New York: Columbia University Press.

Luhrmann, T. 2000. *Of two minds: The growing disorder in American psychiatry*. New York: Knopf.

Lunbeck, E. 1994. *The psychiatric persuasion: Knowledge, gender, and power in modern America*. Princeton, N.J.: Princeton University Press.

Margolis, J. 1994. Taxonomic puzzles. In *Philosophical perspectives on psychiatric diagnostic classification*, ed. J. Sadler, O. Wiggins, and M. Schwartz. Baltimore: Johns Hopkins University Press.

Martin, J. B. 2002. The integration of neurology, psychiatry, and neuroscience in the 21st century. *American Journal of Psychiatry* 159:695–704.

Maudsley, H. 1867. *The physiology and pathology of the mind*. New York: Appleton.

McHugh, P., and P. Slavney. 1990. *The perspectives of psychiatry*. Baltimore: Johns Hopkins University Press.

McLaren, N. 1998. A critical review of the biopsychosocial model. *Australian and New Zealand Journal of Psychiatry* 32(1):86–92.

Mezzich, J., and M. Cranach, eds. 1998. *International classification in psychiatry: Unity and diversity*. Cambridge: Cambridge University Press.

Milton, J. 1980. *Collected Poems*. Boston: Moxon.

Murphy, D., and S. Stich. 2000. Darwin in the madhouse: Evolutionary psychology and the classification of mental disorder. In *Evolution and the human mind: Modularity, language, and meta-cognition* (pp. 62–92). ed. P., Carruthers, and A. Chamberlin. Cambridge: Cambridge University Press.

Nesse, R., and G. Williams. 1994. *Why we get sick*. New York: Times Books.

Pichot, P. 1983. *A century of psychiatry*. Paris: Editions Roger Dacosta.

Pincus, H., and L. McQueen. 2002. The limits of evidence-based classification of mental disorder. In *Descriptions and prescriptions: Values, mental disorders and the DSMs*. ed. J.Z. Sadler, (pp. 9–24).

Pinel, P. [1801] 2000 *A treatise on insanity*. In *The nature of melancholy*, ed. J. Radden. Oxford: Oxford University Press.

Poland, J., B. Von Echardt, and W. Spaulding. 1994. Problems with the DSM approach to classifying psychopathology. In *Philosophical Psychopathology*, ed. G., Graham, and L. Stevens. Cambridge, Mass.: MIT Press.

Putnam, H. 1975. The meaning of 'meaning.' In *Mind, language and reality*, Vol 2 of *Philosophical papers*, ed. H. Putnam. Cambridge: Cambridge University Press.

Radden, J. 1987. Melancholy and melancholia. In *Pathologies of the modern self: Post modern studies in narcissism, schizophrenia and depression* (pp. 231–50), ed. D. Levin. New York: New York University Press.

——. 1996. Lumps and bumps: Kantian faculty psychology, phrenology, and twentieth-century psychiatric classification. *Philosophy, Psychiatry, and Psychology* 3:11–14.

——., ed. 2000a. *The nature of melancholy: From Aristotle to Kristeva*. New York: Oxford University Press.

——. 2000b. Love and loss in Freud's "Mourning and Melancholia": A rereading. In *The analytic Freud: Philosophy and psychoanalysis*, ed. M. Levine. New York: Oxford University Press.

Real, T. 1997. *I don't want to talk about it: Overcoming the secret legacy of male depression*. New York: Scribner.

Roberts, J. 2001. Mental illness, motivation, and moral commitment. *Philosophical Quarterly* 51:41–59.

Sartorius, N., A. Jablensky, D. Regier, J. Burke, and M. A. Hirschfeld, eds. 1990. *Sources and traditions of classification in psychiatry*. Toronto: Hogrefe and Huber.

Schaffner, K. 1993. *Discovery and explanation in biology and medicine*. Chicago: University of Chicago Press.

———. 2002. Clinical and etiological psychiatric diagnoses: Do causes count? In *Descriptions and prescriptions: Values, mental disorders and the DSMs*, ed. L. Sadler. Baltimore: Johns Hopkins University Press.

Schiesari, J. 1992. *The gendering of melancholia: Feminism, psychoanalysis, and the symbolics of loss in Renaissance literature*. Ithaca, NY: Cornell University Press.

Seligman, M. 1975. *Helplessness: On depression, development, and death*. New York: W. H. Freeman.

Shorter, E. 1997. *A history of psychiatry: From the era of the asylum to the age of Prozac*. New York: Wiley.

Sobo, S. 2002. A re-evaluation of the relationship between psychiatric diagnosis and chemical imbalances. Retrieved 10/10/2002 from http://home1.gte.net/engeseth/ssobo.htm.

Solomon, A. 2001. *The noonday demon: An atlas of depression*. New York: Scribner.

Spitzer, M. 1990. On defining delusions. *Comprehensive Psychiatry* 31(5):377–97.

Stevens, A., and J. Price. 1996. *Evolutionary psychiatry: A new beginning*. London: Routledge.

Szasz, T. 1963. Classification in psychiatry. In *Law, liberty and psychiatry*. New York: Collier.

Thornton, T. 2000. Mental illness and reductionism: Can functions be naturalized? *Philosophy, Psychiatry, and Psychology* 7:67–76.

Woolfolk, R. 1999. Malfunction and mental illness. *Monist* 82(4):658–71.

World Health Organization (WHO). 1967. *Manual of the international statistical classification of diseases, injuries and causes of death (ICD-8)*. Geneva: Author.

Zachar, P. 2000. Psychiatric disorders are not natural kinds. *Philosophy, Psychiatry, and Psychology* 7(3):167–82.

Zuckerman, M. 1999. *Vulnerability to psychopathology: A biomedical model*. Washington, D.C.: American Psychological Association.

5

The Psychiatry of Cross-Cultural Suffering

Jennifer Hansen's subtle interpretation of Kleinman's writing provides me a welcome opportunity to clarify my own interest in Kleinman's wonderfully rich and provocative claims. As Hansen interprets Kleinman, all human beings are capable of falling into "illness of distress," which have a common source although they exhibit culturally varied (sign and) symptom expression. The universality of the sources of these Kleinmanian illnesses of distress, and the social and political implications of their strongly gendered epidemiology, is a powerful and important reminder about the state of the world today. As well, it might be a reminder about human nature; as Burton remarks:

> From these Melancholy Dispositions, no man living is free, no stoicke, none so wise, none so happy, none so patient, so generous, so godly, so divine, that can vindicate himselfe, so well composed, but more or less some time or other, he feeles the smart of it. Melancholy in this sence is the Character of Mortalitie. (Burton [1621] 2000:131)

Hansen also points to Kleinman's fear that cross-cultural, descriptive (or, as she rightly adds, phenomenological) psychiatry has thus far been infected with Western normative assumptions. One application of this concern appears to have direct relevance to my analysis, although Hansen graciously refrains from spelling it out: the belief that felt sadness is an essential subjective accompaniment to depression, without which the description of "depression" should be withheld, on Kleinman's view, is an example of an unwarranted Eurocentrism. (It might be added that the account I have offered reflects the essentialism of a Western natural kinds disease model, perhaps equally inappropriate for this wider and looser cross-cultural analysis—a challenge that requires a longer response than I can offer here, however.)

First published in *Philosophy, Psychiatry & Psychology* Vol 10, No. 1 (March 2003): 64-66. Reprinted with permission from Johns Hopkins University Press.

I am stung by the suggestion that my commentary on Kleinman puts me into the disreputable camp of Eurocentrists. So let me revisit what I presented as a dilemma for Kleinman.

In the passage quoted by Hansen, I proposed that Kleinman must either accept that illnesses are culture bound and culture relative, in which case it makes no sense to see them all as forms of depression, or else to accept some universal and unifying causal ontology that explains the diversity of symptoms and serves to unite these conditions as instances of the same category. At least on Hansen's interpretation of Kleinman's later work, it has become clear that the commonality that results in these culture-bound illnesses is social events. As Hansen puts it, what Kleinman suggests is universal is not "depression" as defined by the DSM but, rather, that all human beings "suffer illnesses of distress due to stressful life events" (2003:61). And although this distress may cause similar neurochemical reactions, it *may* just "predictably trigger illnesses" (2003:61). Hansen points out that by looking for the cross-cultural covariants of such illnesses, we can learn about the significance of our illness; thus, "Kleinman's illness approach offers us greater freedom to understand depression as a worldwide human illness that reveals important truths about our relationship to political and economic structures in culture and...an opportunity for a global feminist dialogue [over the high rates cross-culturally of female depression] about culture and gender" (2003:61). Hansen concludes that descriptivism leads to a cultural relativist position, which, in turn, denies feminist analyses a powerful cultural critique.

This is a compelling interpretation. We want to be free to notice and use these commonalities—to highlight, confirm, and fight against avoidable suffering everywhere in the world and especially the oppression of women. At the same time, we want to avoid the charge of Eurocentrism by honoring the culture-bound expressions of this universal distress. We want Kleinman to be granted the power of a causal ontology without being trapped in an overly medical, and Western, disease model.

Can we have it all? I hope so, but I am not sure. By attributing these depression illnesses to universal forms of human suffering, we seem to have risked losing what is distinctively psychiatric in this cross-cultural "psychiatry." As Burton says, these may be human nature, not illness. (That passage comes where Burton is contrasting melancholy as disposition with melancholy as disease, it should be added.) If universal human suffering is the underlying cause here, why psychiatry as a response? Religions such as Buddhism, with its emphasis that all life is suffering, offer a time-honored spiritual, not psychiatric, consolation to meet this state of affairs, and we have no reason to doubt their appropriateness or efficacy. Moreover, as Hansen suggests, a response may better come from social action, public policy, or political movements working for universal human rights than from clinical psychiatry. By characterizing these depressive illnesses as disorders originating in the individual the way clinical psychiatry does, we may be missing the relational and structural features that allow us to best respond to them.

That said, there may yet a distinctively psychiatric element left in this analysis. In every culture, many people suffer and survive, or even prevail. Thus, the pan-cultural causes Kleinman seeks may not reside in the suffering itself, or in its causes, as much as in the vulnerabilities that, in certain individuals, transform that suffering into illness. Whether these factors can be identified in a way that avoids cultural relativism, and Eurocentric categories and presuppositions, remains to be seen. It is certainly a worthwhile inquiry and one that, as Hansen notes, will need anthropologists, political scientists, and philosophers, as well as psychiatrists, to achieve.

Hansen accuses me of cultural relativism. I am not too concerned because it seems I am, thus far, in good company. To his enduring credit, Kleinman has shown us the complexities and cultural sensitivities, which a "cross-cultural psychiatry" of the kind he envisions would require. What he has not yet shown us is whether this inquiry is pan-cultural or psychiatric.

References

Burton, R. [1621] 2000. The Anatomy of Melancholy. In *The Nature of Melancholy*, ed. J. Radden. Oxford: Oxford University Press.
Hansen, J. 2003. Listening to people or listening to Prozac? Another consideration of causal classifications. *Philosophy, Psychiatry, and Psychology* 10:57–62.

6

Epidemic Depression and Burtonian Melancholy

Data indicate the ubiquity and rapid increase of depression wherever war, want, and social upheaval are found. The goal of this essay is to clarify such claims and draw conceptual distinctions separating the depressive states that are pathological from those that are normal and normative responses to misfortune. I do so by appeal to early modern writing on melancholy by Robert Burton where, although the inchoate and boundless nature of melancholy symptoms are emphasized, universal suffering is separated from the disease states known as melancholy or melancholia, and normal temperamental variation is placed in contrast to such disease states.

The particular report prompting the following discussion described widespread use of medication for depression symptoms among adolescent girls in a refugee camp in Chad. More generally, though, I take as my starting point data citing the ubiquity and rapid increase of depression wherever war, want, and social upheaval are found: 120 million people worldwide suffer from depression, we are told; by 2020, depression will be the second leading cause of ill health worldwide; depression is the greatest source of disability as measured by years lived with disability; 9.5% of Mexican adults suffer depression; the greatest costs of Hurricane Katrina, the latest mudslide, tsunami, civil war, and earthquake will be in terms of depression; and so on.

Of the several aspects of today's apparent epidemic of depression deserving philosophical examination, my focus is on preliminaries. How is depression understood when claims such as these are made? What is its relation to more ordinary states of suffering and distress and to normal temperamental differences? What are the limits of the concept? In this essay, I attempt to clear conceptual spaces around the condition(s) alluded to in accounts citing data on the incidence of depression. I do

First published in *Philosophical Papers* Vol 36, No.3 (November 2007): 443-464.Reprinted with permission from *Philosophical Papers*.

so by appeal to early modern writing, particularly that found in Robert Burton's great *Anatomy of Melancholy*, published in 1621. The earlier notion of melancholia and that of depression as it is understood today cannot be simply equated. Yet Burton's era also saw melancholy and melancholia in what were believed to be "epidemical" proportions. And, there are significant parallels between the broad category of melancholic states employed by Burton and today's notion of depression that invite application of some of the same conceptual distinctions. In particular, early modern writing emphasizes the inchoate and boundless nature of melancholy symptoms; universal suffering is sometimes explicitly separated from the disease states known as melancholy or melancholia, and normal temperamental variation is placed in contrast to such disease states.

In Burton's time, the distinctions and characterizations just noted could be secured by the anchoring tenets of humoral theory. Without such humoral anchoring, and in light of the findings and assumptions of today's biological diagnostic psychiatry, we must revisit each of them. My goals in this brief discussion are to show the need for analytic foundations when claims are made about depression, such as those cited at the outset of this discussion, and to draw attention to some contemporary attempts that may help provide those foundations.

Before turning to Burton's claims, one terminological clarification is necessary. "Melancholy" and "melancholia" were terms not systematically distinguished until a later period, and during Burton's era their employment was inexact, covering passing normal states, severe medical conditions, and enduring, natural temperamental types. In common parlance today, rather similarly, the term "depression" covers a wide range of subclinical or normal responses, as well as the more severe, lasting conditions that are acknowledged to be disorders. Others have attempted to restrict "depression" to clinical conditions. But the present discussion follows the looser usage: states of distress that are normal responses as well as those that are pathological are each "depressive states," and their sufferers, at least temporarily, are "depressed."

Distinctions among these different depressives states are the focus of what follows. Other than social and cultural nostalgia for the wisdom enshrined in writing such as Burton's, it might be asked, why should we care to preserve these distinctions, especially in light of their likely deleterious social effects, such as exclusion? One answer to that question is perhaps an aesthetic and cultural preference only. The tendency to collapse distinctions such as that between normal suffering and depressive disorder comes at a cost in the richness of our experience and understanding. A world in which all suffering had been reduced to medical symptoms would be an impoverished one, despite the good brought by modern medicine. A second answer possesses real moral heft. Collapsing these distinctions seems all too likely to forestall social and political action not only more fitting but, in directing itself toward the causes of much of this suffering, more effective. The hapless inhabitants of refugee camps may suffer depression and may require medical intervention. But if that intervention comes at the cost of neglecting why they are there in the first place, and why they suffer — that is, the questions spurring social and political action — then it will be difficult to justify. The apparent collapse of the boundaries separating these kinds of human suffering and the importance of maintaining conceptual space around depressive disorder have been the subject of recent concerns (Horwitz and

Wakefield 2007). Moreover, such concerns may be seen as part of a broader whole. Erosion of distinctions at the boundary of our categories of disease and disorder occurs where forms of "enhancement" apply medical treatments to nonmedical conditions. Although it is not one dealt with here, this practice has rightly been recognized to jeopardize important moral distinctions. (For a discussion of some of the issues involved and far-reaching implications of losing sight of this allied distinction, see Elliott and Kramer 2003, Conrad 2007.)

Burton famously insisted that melancholy states were universal, the lot of humankind. Melancholy is nothing less than the "Character of Mortalitie." And "From Melancholy Dispositions...no man living is free." Melancholy dispositions are for Burton distinguishable from melancholy the "habit," however. Melancholy dispositions make us "dull, sad, sour, lumpish, ill-disposed, solitary, any way moved or displeased." As a habit, melancholy is "a chronic or continuate disease, a settled humour...not errant, but fixed." In some people, "these Dispositions become Habits." For Burton, it seems, no human can avoid melancholy states but only some will succumb to melancholy the disease, when disease is in this discussion indicated by the settled, or chronic, nature of those states.

Burton is clearly leaving a conceptual space for distress that is not pathological. Mistaken as we would now say he was in his humoral assumptions, moreover, he had in humoral theory a means of distinguishing the two kinds of melancholy state by appeal to underlying causation. The disease of melancholy was marked by adustion, when the black bile became heated and smoky vapors interfered with brain functioning, thereby causing the disturbances of imagination that, in turn, brought apprehensive and disspirited mood states of melancholy. These machinations are explained more fully, and embraced more literally, in some earlier works, such as Timothy Bright's *Treatise of Melancholy* (1586). And by the time of Burton's writing, references to the black bile had begun to take on something of the quality of metaphor. Nonetheless, humoral theory provided a full explanation: the chronicity of the disease of melancholy was the result of adustion.

This distinction between pathological and more normal suffering does not always receive stress in Burton's *Anatomy*. (In that rambling and inconsistent compendium, few distinctions are systematically employed.) Nor does it in the rest of the canon of writing on melancholy from that era. It does not need to. As products of natural and unnatural humoral arrangements, normal melancholy and pathological melancholy differ at most as variations on a unitary condition, and only in extreme cases or through long-term study will melancholy the disease be observably different from more normal melancholy states and temperaments. Rather than immediately observable, this is a distinction attributable to and theoretically provided for by the complex variations, normal and abnormal, in the black bile.

Melancholy's nature as inchoate and boundless was also able to be accommodated by humoral lore. "The tower of Babel never yielded such confusion of tongues as this Chaos of Melancholy doth variety of its symptoms," says Burton, in one of many efforts to emphasize the unbounded, open-ended nature of the symptomatology and subjectivity of melancholy. The force of this conviction of Burton's was not that the *concept* of melancholy could not be bounded but that the plethora of its symptoms in the world could not. That unboundedness made it hard, or even impossible, to provide a list of all melancholy's symptoms but not to define it. Because of the anchoring and unifying role played by humoral explanations, the diversity and unbounded variety of symptoms provided no reason to question whether melancholy was one thing or many. Again, it is arguable that Burton was drifting away from a literal reading of humoral theory and that remarks such as the above prefigure a Wittgensteinian "family resemblance" conception of the category of melancholy. Ostensibly, though, Burton accepted that such symptoms were united by their source in the endless variations of the humor.

Ideally, if we are to remain faithful to the parallel with Burton, an account of pathological depression will contain explanatory force, attributing pathological depression to the brain states, and or experiences, that caused it. And it is true that today's causal analyses sometimes postulate such antecedents. Compromising resilience to life's vicissitudes, preexisting genetic and other biological conditions of vulnerability such as reduced volume of the hippocampus and an absence of glial cells are thought by some to combine with adverse experiences to yield the depressive response (e.g., Kramer 2005). These are controversial interpretations of what are thus far ambiguous findings, however. (For a critique of such interpretations, see Horwitz and Wakefield 2007:175–77). Science may eventually confirm such hypotheses and secure conceptual space around depressive disorder with a causal definition. Meanwhile, though, we must at least insist on the difference and honor philosophical efforts to preserve it.

Without anchoring humoral theory, then, we face a conceptual problem: depressive states of despair, discouragement, numbness, dispiritedness, sadness, demoralization, anxiety, and grief result not just from biological and interpsychic causes but from the vicissitudes of life. And they are, as Burton says, the lot of humankind. The effects of ordinary love and loss affect us with what appear to be states indistinguishable from the symptoms of major depression and dysthymia. So, too, do experiences like painful social disruption, deprivation, and oppression. Because it no longer adheres to humoral *or other* causal analyses and is instead solely "descriptive" in its account of symptoms, contemporary diagnostic psychiatry appears without a way to secure the conceptual distinction between these different kinds of depression. (Horwitz and Wakefield make this point when they contrast the earlier "contextualized" approaches with the decontextualized one adopted with the descriptivist 1980 DSM-III [Horwitz and Wakefield 2007].)

The social and political origins of many depressive symptoms have been acknowledged and emphasized. Philosopher Jennifer Hansen speaks of "a worldwide human illness that reveals important truths about our relationship to political and economic structures in culture," which "says something about what pressures and freedoms culture offers individuals" (Hansen 2003:61). And a diagnosis of dysthymic disorder, it has been observed, will likely represent the *medicalization of social problems* in much of the world, where severe economic, political, and health constraints create "endemic feelings of hopelessness and helplessness, where demoralization and despair are responses to real conditions of chronic deprivation and persistent loss, where powerlessness is not a cognitive distortion but an accurate mapping of one's place in an oppressive social system." (This is medical anthropologist, Arthur Kleinman [1987:452].)

Preserving the conceptual space around depression understood as a real disorder rather than a more normal response—whether to oppressive conditions or to life's vicissitudes—is a goal with practical, as well as theoretical, interest and implications. The task is to justify and account for the presumption that states of pathological depression are importantly distinct from normal responses to life's vicissitudes and to explain why the disease or illness status of depression is not arbitrarily assigned. Practical implications include when and whether to treat; remedies and or preventive measures, and questions of resource allocation; how to understand the role of the sufferer; and so on.

The category of nonpathological depression is a heterogeneous one, as we have seen, including responses to experiences and states of affairs both avoidable and unavoidable, the results of human nature and the human condition, as well as of seemingly contingent and preventable forms of oppression and misfortune. No matter what their situation, humans have pride and suffer from slights; they form close attachments, so suffer when loved ones suffer, grieve when they die, and so on. Perhaps due to this heterogeneity, instances of nonpathological suffering will not permit ready characterization, and efforts at analytic definition have been focused on circumscribing pathological rather than normal suffering.

This is a challenge that has received considerable attention from philosophers and other theorists, and three approaches to defining pathological suffering are distinguishable among their efforts. One of these dismisses the distinction, not acknowledging any real difference between pathological depression and more normal depressive responses. This, we shall see, is the position adopted by Freud and, later, by Melanie Klein. In a second approach, the suffering resulting from more normal and normative causes is separated from pathological suffering by exclusion. This is the approach adopted by the authors of the DSMs, for instance (American Psychiatric Association 1994). Pathological depression is characterized as a syndrome or pattern that is not merely an "expectable or culturally sanctioned" response, such as grief and mourning. A third approach attempts to circumscribe pathological depression by providing an analytic definition of affective disorder, mental disorder, or disease, within which it can be seen to fall. Summed up, these three approaches offer the following prescriptions:

1. Deny there is any real difference between pathological and normal/normative suffering (Freud and Klein, for example)
2. Exclude normal and normative suffering by fiat (DSM approach)
3. Find a definition for pathological depression (affective or mental disorder, or disorder) that can be used to exclude other forms of suffering.

Before turning to (3), as the most promising of these approaches, one or two comments about (1) and (2) are required.

Seemingly recognizing the conceptual contrast we are concerned to preserve, Freud later spoke of psychoanalysis as transforming neurotic misery into ordinary unhappiness. Yet exploring the difference between normal mourning and pathological depression in his famous 1917 essay on mourning and melancholia, he concluded that normal and pathological responses were really *equally pathological*. Mourning does not seem to us as pathological, he states, only because "we know so well how to explain [it]" (Freud 1967:153). Klein also insists that "because this state of mind is common and seems so natural to us, we do not call mourning an illness" (Klein 1935:354). Stephen Wilkinson draws the same conclusion—although ironically as part of a *reductio* argument—when he identifies insufficiencies in each of the criteria proposed to distinguish normal grief from pathological depression (Wilkinson 2000). Because it simply denies the conceptual space between normal and pathological suffering, this position violates our intuitive sense that these forms of suffering are importantly different and of the reasoning provided at the outset of this essay. If preserving such conceptual space is a defensible goal, then the answer provided in (1) is question-begging.

The method of exclusion by fiat employed in (2), and reference to responses that are "expectable or culturally sanctioned" requires further clarification. First, not all expectable responses will be culturally sanctioned, and not all that are culturally sanctioned may be expected. In the present discussion, "normal" refers to responses that are expected and "normative" is reserved for those that are culturally sanctioned, with the understanding that many normal reactions are proscribed or treated with moral indifference, while responses that are normative reflect evaluations as to appropriateness, fittingness, or moral acceptability. Death of loved ones is not only expected to bring sadness and grief, such a response is judged appropriate and proper; the person who fails to feel it, is considered morally wanting. More generally, whether and how a person suffers in response to life's vissicitudes functions as a central indicator of moral character in our, and probably every, society.

Second, although many other experiences will bring comparable sadness and be both normal and normative, mourning is offered as a sole example of a culturally expected response by the authors of the DSM. In this respect, grief is thus positioned as a prototype of normal responses of sadness and distress.[1] Since whatever the variations their cultural expression may take, some such responses to the death of loved ones seem to be close to universal, the example of the depressed responses associated with grief and mourning is a compelling one. Even as an instance of distress that is incontestably normative, however, grief shades into a penumbra that is relative to particular cultures and even to particular individuals, where norms are controversial, unsettled, and contested. Within the scope of "mourning," we can encounter differing moral intuitions over the appropriateness of responding with grief to the loss of a pet, for example, an aborted or miscarried fetus, a romantic relationship, or a slowly eroded friendship. Norms surrounding these and many other responses to life experience seem to be less agreed upon, less stable, and less clear-cut.

Mourning the loss of a loved one, then, is in this respect an unusual case and, I now want to stress, a rather misleading one. In cultures more traditional than our own, reliance on the appropriateness of certain responses relative to cultural mores may serve to distinguish normal and normative suffering, even in these and other less clear-cut cases. But in nontraditional cultures such as that of the United States, questions of appropriateness, rationality, and proportionality are controversial and contested. Moreover, in today's nontraditional society, mental health norms are more often *appealed to as arbiters* than *framed by* other norms. They are also clubs in the increasingly fractious war over the applicability of medical presuppositions to cultural structures and strictures.

Under these circumstances and within nontraditional cultures such as the U.S. one, the method of exclusion employed in (2) leaves dangerously arbitrary and vulnerable the line between normal and pathological depression. Faced with this controversy, it seems sensible to turn to the remaining approach, (3), finding a definition of pathological suffering to distinguish it from depression that is more normal and normative.

Efforts to define disease or disorder often appeal to the concept of (harmful) dysfunction, and certainly a notion of *reduced functioning, disability*, or *incapacity* is central to lay conceptions of mental illness. Moreover, the usual facultative divisions into cognition, memory, motivation, perception, judgment, feeling, and so on provide us with a map of the kinds of psychological dysfunction associated with particular mental disorders. (It is the very facultative map, indeed, on which mental disorders were originally classified.)

But not only are normal and pathological depression indistinguishable in terms of their symptom expression, as we saw earlier—resulting in pain as intense, sadness as profound, and despair as overwhelming, for example—so they are in terms of an everyday sense of reduced functioning. Depression and suffering resulting from life's vicissitudes sometimes render their sufferer both *equally or more* apparently dysfunctional than those whose suffering is the symptom of disorder. Pathological depression, habituated despair and discouragement wrought of powerlessness, and genuine grief all have the effect of deadening responses, dampening motivation, and slowing and compromising cognition, for example; in this respect, they are equally likely to interfere with "getting on with things." So while it is a key to lay understanding of other forms of mental disorder, observable dysfunction cannot be interpreted as an attribute distinguishing pathological from more ordinary misery.

Dysfunction also enters into more formal definitions of disorder (APA 1994, Boorse 1975, Wakefield 1992, Megone 2000, Horwitz 2002). In the two best known of these types of definition, disease (or disorder) is defined as dysfunction relative to norms of functioning in some reference group (Boorse) and as dysfunction that is a maladaptive in the evolutionary sense (Wakefield). (Both accounts, it should be pointed out, accept the analogies between mental or psychological and organic conditions, and neither draws a significant difference between "disease" and "disorder.")

But both definitions have also been subject to extensive and damaging criticism. Critiques of Boorse's account of dysfunction relative to a reference group press on the difficulties of fixing on a *suitable* reference group (e.g., Cooper 2002:266–67). Additional difficulty is involved when this effort concerns normal and normative depression. The effects of life's vicissitudes on individual character are widely variable, depending as they do on idiosyncratic values, ideals, goals, and self-identity. Isolating the appropriate reference group against which one person's dysfunction could be judged abnormal will likely be even more difficult than settling on the appropriate reference norms for demarcating ordinary physical diseases. Consider, for example, a group comprising X who believes in an afterlife, Y who does not and instead accepts a tragic view of life, and Z who, having no fixed opinion on such matters, is convinced that value lies in a dignified approach to whatever comes. Or, consider R and S, an undertaker and a clown, respectively, each committed to the same worldview. With the latitude created by this sort of meaning-driven and idiosyncratic variability, the designation of an appropriate reference group must be an unacceptably arbitrary one.

Its unsubstantiated, empirical, essentialist assumptions about the way natural selection underlies natural functions have been widely noted as substantial and perhaps irreparable flaws in Wakefield's analysis. (See also Cooper 2002, Gert and Culver 2004, Murphy and Woolfolk 2000, Poland 2002, Lilienfeld and Marino 1995.)

Dissatisfied with accounts of disease as (harmful) dysfunction, whether defined statistically or by appeal to evolutionary psychology, Rachel Cooper has proposed a different approach, and I want to devote some attention to this alternative. Cooper introduces a set of conditions she believes necessary and sufficient for "disease," as understood within the medical paradigm: (1) diseases are bad things to have, (2) the afflicted person is unlucky, and (3) the affliction can potentially be medically treated (Cooper 2002).[2] This definition seems a promising one and, in light of the now well-rehearsed problems associated with both Boorsian and Wakefield accounts, deserves a closer look.

Although Cooper's criteria derive from ordinary nonpsychiatric disorder and disease, we can simplify her analysis for our purposes here (and reduce their vulnerability to counterexample) by limiting the scope of (1)–(3) in this definition — proposing them as definitive of *affective disorder or disease* only. Still, Cooper's criteria are not quite sufficient to exclude all normal and normative suffering. Normal responses are also sometimes bad luck, as Cooper accounts for it; vis., the sufferers "could reasonably have hoped it might have been otherwise" because, as she puts it, either (i) they feel worse compared with an earlier state, (ii) they consider themselves worse off than others, or (iii) they believe there is a good chance that everyone could be better off. The oppressed inhabitants of a refugee camp, or the AIDS orphan could be in each category described in (i)–(iii). Moreover, (i)–(iii) introduce another problem. As subjective assessments made by the patient, (i)–(iii) may not capture all conditions we would normally suppose to be affective disorders or diseases. The manic patient would be unlikely to assess her situation this way, for example; indeed, relying on subjective assessment with many mood-disordered patients will engender the same problem. As pathological states, both mania and depression very typically affect the capacity to make global comparisons of the kind captured in (i). This problem will require a reformulation of (i) in less-subjective language, so that the explication of "bad luck" now reads: either (i) they feel *or are* worse compared with an earlier state; (ii) they consider themselves worse off than others; or (iii) they believe there is a good chance that everyone could be better off.

Finally, Cooper's third condition seems naive, even Panglossian. Once a method of remedying a particular condition is developed and placed in the hands of a medical practitioner (and others able to exploit the situation for gain), as Carl Elliot has observed, that condition "tends to become reconceptualized as a medical problem"(2004:429). The rush to medicate all forms of depression in the present antidepressant era attests that normal and normative depressive responses can be, and (many think) too often are, medically treated. This point has been stressed in recent analyses noting the powerful forces aligned by a common interest in medicalizing, overdiagnosing and overtreating ordinary depressive states (Healy 1994, 2004; Horwitz and Wakefield 2007).

In light of these concerns, several qualifications can be added to Cooper's conditions. Ill fate is customarily distinguished from misfortunes resulting from injustice, when this is a morally significant difference. Employing this distinction, we can insist that those suffering diseases (disorders) believe themselves unlucky because — *not as the result of a violation of their human rights* — they feel *or are* worse compared with an earlier state, consider themselves worse off than others, or believe there is a good chance everybody could be better off. As stated, this qualification may be too stringent. For it will also serve to exclude some conditions we would intuitively judge to be genuine disorders or diseases, such as schizophrenia. (Arguably, for example, a failure to provide treatment for those with severe disorders such as schizophrenia might be regarded as a violation of their human rights.) A more complete qualification will define being unlucky as feeling worse, *not merely as the result of a violation of their human rights*. This adjustment should serve to exclude normal and normative suffering that results from injustice.

Cooper's third condition concerning medical treatment that we saw to be naive given the current climate of overtreatment, invites a second qualification. The affliction can be potentially medically treated and, we may add, *does not lend itself to more obvious, effective, socially sanctioned, remedies or preventive measures*.

The group of responses making up normal and normative suffering, it was pointed out earlier, is heterogeneous. Those resulting from bereavement are an apparently unavoidable aspect of being human, for example, while those resulting from forms of oppression, we like to think, are not. The two qualifications added to Cooper's definition serve to exclude two types of normal and normative responses: those arising from avoidable states of affairs and those that have alternative, socially sanctioned remedies. Depression resulting from unavoidable aspects of being human can be excluded by adding a qualification to the first part of Cooper's definition: diseases are bad things when they are *not apparently unavoidable aspects of being human*.

Suitably reduced so that it deals only with the affective disorders of concern here, and qualified in the way outlined above, Cooper's account reads:

> Affective disorders (diseases) are (1) bad things to have *that are not apparently unavoidable aspects of being human*; when (2) the afflicted persons are unlucky in the sense of feeling *or being* worse than previously, considering themselves worse off than others and or believing there is a good chance everybody could be better off, when this *is not merely as the result of a violation of their human rights*; and (3) the affliction can potentially be medically treated *and does not lend itself to more obvious, effective, socially sanctioned, remedies and or preventive measures*.

This definition has its own vulnerabilities: the nature of human nature is itself vague and contested; the scope of human rights is similarly open to challenge; and any determination that remedies are socially sanctioned will eventually require further refinement and clarification since it, too, seems to rely on unsettled and contested norms. This reformulation seems to move us some way toward the end we seek. It is still designed for "diseases" in the traditional sense, however. On the traditional model, affective diseases (or disorders) are understood as the manifestations and effects of an underlying pathological process originating in the individual (at least as a diathesis or risk factor) and characterized by an episodic course or career. Yet some disorders, if not diseases strictly so called, seem to elude this framing, either by not presupposing a particular originating cause within the person (posttraumatic stress disorder is an obvious example here) or by not giving evidence of an episodic course. Dysthymic personality may be one of these exceptions.

A trait-based depressive personality disorder, dysthymia is grouped with the family of depressive disorders. With its origins in the earlier trait-based category of neurotic depression, dysthymic disorder is the mildest of depressive disorders, whose diagnosis requires disturbances of mood and only two additional symptoms from a disjunctive set and whose trait-based and static nature is indicated by the requirement that these symptoms must have lasted for some time (at least two years for adults and one for adolescents and children). In terms of severity, dysthymia rests between major depressive disorder and the normal, passing sadness and suffering of everyday life, although it is in DSM-IV placed on a separate axis from other conditions in recognition of its status as an unchanging trait cluster.

In early modern writing about melancholy, the same humors that might culminate in a severe disease condition gave rise to normal temperamental variations as well. The melancholy man was not ill in any way. His was a fixed tendency to respond more gloomily and sourly than would, for example, the sanguine or choleric man. His traits, too, resulted from differences in the balance of humors within his body, but in a tradition harking back to classical times, humoral character ascriptions such as these were employed without medical connotations. This category of a person of melancholy disposition or temperament is orthogonal to Burton's contrast, introduced earlier, between melancholy as disposition and habit. The melancholy man was disposed to be "dull, sad, sour, lumpish, ill-disposed, and solitary" as, from time to time, humans all are. His fixed and long-term tendencies were not sufficiently marked to be evidence of the habituated disease state (melancholy the habit), however.

Typologies of this kind and trait-based accounts of personality may have less currency today, either in folk psychology and lore or in more formal analyses.[3] Yet, arguably, the category of a temperamentally depressive or melancholic personality is one we still recognize and want to avoid confusing with any disorder. It is widely accepted that, as Horwitz and Wakefield observe, there is "a normal distribution of intensities with which non-disordered people respond to stressors" (Horwitz and Wakefield 2007:117). And the basis of those differentiated responses, we can suppose, will include mildly depressive or melancholic temperaments.

It seems, then, that depressive personality styles and patterns that are relatively stable, and mild, may result either from normal temperamental variation or from whatever underlying states account for dysthymic personality disorder. However, remembering the description of what can seem to mimic the diagnosis of dysthymic personality—demoralization and despair as a habituated response to chronic deprivation and persistent loss—we must recognize a three-part distinction here. Some personality patterns will reflect habituated responses to stressful lives.

(Although employing a somewhat limited range of depressive symptoms, the so-called learned helplessness hypothesis apparently addresses this claim. Passivity and a failure to believe in oneself, it has been shown, seem to result from being deprived of opportunities for autonomous action [Seligman 1975].) The trait clusters making up depressive personality types may result from underlying states of disorder, from normal temperamental variation unrelated to setting, or from habituated responses to stressful lives. These types may *appear* indistinguishable. But conceptually they are separate, and there seems reason to maintain that separation.

In an attempt to demarcate disorders wrought by social stressors, appeal has been made to the notion of a separate "sustaining" (Gert and Culver) or "environmental maintaining" (Wakefield) cause, the presence of which betokens not genuine disorder but a normal response to stress. Such a cause is one whose effect will not outlast its continuing stimulus. Only when the suffering originally caused by trauma outlives the trauma (most notably in forms of posttraumatic stress disorder) are there grounds for attributing disorder, according to this view. Stephen Wilkinson has offered a neat definition of a sustaining cause: (a) x is a cause of c; (b) x is not part of (i.e., is distinct from) the person with c; (c) if x were removed, c would cease to exist almost immediately—that is, x is necessary for sustaining c (Wilkinson 200:301). Wilkinson's particular focus is the application of the notion of a sustaining cause to distinguish grief and mourning from pathological states, an effort he shows to be confounded by equivocation over the characterization of x. If what persists is the griever's sense of loss, he points out, then x is not distinct from the person with c. On the other hand, interpreting it as a fact (the fact of the loved one's death) the truth of which continues unchanged will lead to highly counterintuitive conclusions in other cases (Wilkinson 2000:302–3). Granted, this critique may apply with grief and mourning. But other external stressors do seem to function as sustaining causes so defined. In many instances, we should indeed expect that when depressive states result from stress, the habituated response to it would be no more than a sustaining cause—ceasing with the cessation of the stressor and thus seeming to confirm that here were no ordinary, or at least no lasting, states of disorder. Moreover, it might well be that recurrent stresses sometimes cause lasting pathological depressive states or dispositions, again conforming to the model in proving themselves to be more than mere sustaining causes.

In many cases then, the sustaining cause model will allow us to separate pathological from normal and normative depressive traits. Applied to our task of demarcating normal cases of a habituated numbness and dis-spiritedness resulting from external stressors, this criterion comports with our intuitions only incompletely, however. For we can also envision cases where, once habituated, even normal and normative responses might either outlast their stressors or result in a *lasting, but non-pathological*, alteration in the temperament of the sufferer. They might transform her from a sunny to a sourer person, for example, or from a light-hearted to a graver one. In this kind of case, the initiating cause is not a mere sustaining cause because its effects outlive it. But the resulting effect is not pathology or disorder; it is normal temperamental or character change.

Few permanent character changes probably engender the sadder, sourer, more reflective responses we would recognize as melancholic or depressed (and this, presumably, is fortunate). Yet, for example, those who have witnessed or participated in great human evil can seem so changed. Holocaust survivors sometimes speak this way about themselves or give evidence of such transformation, for example. Those who have come to sincerely repent great and irreparable harm they have wrought do also. And so sometimes do those whose belief in human or divine goodness has been permanently and shatteringly expunged. It may even be that mental disorder itself sometimes leaves a residue of normal long-term effects on character. Speaking of earlier episodes of melancholia in the lives of John Bunyan and Leo Tolstoy, Williams James remarks that "the iron of melancholy left a permanent imprint," and he does not imply that the illness lingered but rather that it was profound enough to permanently change the character of these two men (James 1961:143). The difference between normal and normative responses is evident here: extreme and life-changing experiences such as these are too rare for us to speak with any confidence of the resulting character effects as *expectable*. But we certainly regard them as normative—they are fitting and appropriate in light of the experience or experiences undergone. Certain experiences, when sufficiently profound, ought to permanently mark the person and show in that person's outlook and responses, it is generally believed. And the person unaffected by such experiences is widely deemed shallow, or callow, or morally wanting.

The melancholy or depressive type of character or personality may or may not reflect innate temperamental differences, as thinkers from classical to early modern times believed. But these examples seem to require us to acknowledge normal change that results in such character types. Thus, corresponding with the temporary suffering that is recognized to be a normal or normative response to certain sorts of external stressor is permanent personality transformation—also the result of such stressors—that is equally normal and normative. It will be possible to add to Cooper's amended definition of affective disorders (diseases) to exclude the case of normal temperamental variation and these permanent transformations by adapting (1) as follows:

> Affective disorders (diseases) are (1) bad things to have that are (i) not apparently unavoidable aspects of being human or the results of (ii) normal temperamental variation or (iii) character change wrought by extreme experiences.

Conclusion

There seem reasons to maintain separations found in some early modern writing, I have argued here. Attributions of depression can and should be distinguished from (i) universal suffering in response to life's vicissitudes, from (ii) normal temperamental variation, and from (iii) habituated responses and even permanent, nonpathological changes in temperament resultant from painful and oppressive lives. Until such time as fully causal accounts of pathological depression allow us to separate those from depressive states that are more normal and normative, we must look toward philosophical definitions that attempt to circumscribe those states that reflect pathology, of which Cooper's is one of the most helpful.

Notes

1. Horwitz and Wakefield similarly position grief as the paradigm. They do so with the explanation that all forms of normal and even adaptive sadness are instances of "loss," on analogy with the loss suffered upon the death of a loved one. I have commented elsewhere on the risk of trivialization incumbent in sweeping "loss" analyses such as these (Radden 2000a, 2000b:222–26).

2. This last condition finds its origins in work on disease by Reznek (1987).

3. Powerful critiques of the presuppositions underlying trait theories include those of Mischel 1968 and Ross and Nisbett 1991.

References

American Psychiatric Association. 1994. *Diagnostic and Statistical Manual of Mental Disorders*, 4th ed. Washington, DC: American Psychiatric Press.

Bright, T. 1586. *A Treatise of Melancholy*. London: John Windet.

Boorse, C. 1975. On the Distinction between Disease and Illness. *Philosophy and Public Affairs* 5:49–68

Burton, R. [1621] 2000. The Anatomy of Melancholy. In *The Nature of Melancholy*, ed. Jennifer Radden. Oxford: Oxford University Press.

Conrad, P. 2007. *The Medicalization of Society: On the Transformation of Human Conditions into Treatable Disorders*. Baltimore: Johns Hopkins University Press.

Cooper, R. 2002. Disease. *Studies in the History and Philosophy of Biological and Biomedical Sciences* 33:263–82.

Elliott, Carl. 2004. Mental Health and Its Limits. In *The Philosophy of Psychiatry: A Companion*, ed. Jennifer Radden. New York: Oxford University Press 415–35.

Elliott, C., and Kramer, P. 2003. *Better Than Well: American Medicine Meets the American Dream*. New York: Norton.

Freud, S. [1917] 1957. Mourning and Melancholia. In *Collected Papers*, Vol. 4:152–70, authorized translation under the supervision of Joan Rivière. London: Hogarth.

Gert, B., and Culver C.M. 2004. Defining Mental Disorder. In *The Philosophy of Psychiatry: A Companion*, ed. Jennifer Radden. New York: Oxford University Press 415–35

Hansen, J. 2003. Listening to People or Listening to Prozac? Another Consideration of Causal Classifications. *Philosophy, Psychiatry, & Psychology* 10(1):57–62.

Healy, D. 1997. *The Antidepressant Era*. Cambridge, Mass: Harvard University Press.

———. 2004. *Let Them Eat Prozac: The Unhealthy Relationship between the Pharmaceutical Industry and Depression*. New York: New York University Press.

Horwitz, Allan. 2002. *Creating Mental Illness*. Chicago: Chicago University Press.

Horwitz, Allan, and Wakefield, Jerome 2007. *The Loss of Sadness: How Psychiatry Tranformed Normal Sorrow into Depressive Disorder*. New York: Oxford University Press.

James, William. 1961. *The Varieties of Religious Experience*. New York: Macmillan.

Klein, M. 1975. *Love, Guilt and Reparation and Other Works*. London: Hogarth.

Kleinman, A. 1987. Anthropology and Psychiatry: The Role of Culture in Cross-cultural Research on Illness. *British Journal of Psychiatry* 151:447–54.

Kramer, Peter. 2005. *Against Depression*. New York: Viking.

Lilienfeld, S., and L. Marino. 1995. Mental Disorder as Roschian Concept: A Critique of Wakefield's "Harmful Dysfunction" Analysis. *Journal of Abnormal Psychology* 104:411–20.

Megone, C. 2000. Mental Illness, Human Function, and Values. *Philosophy, Psychiatry, & Psychology* 7(1):45–65.

Mischel, W. 1968. *Personality and Assessment*. New York: Wiley.

Murphy, D., and Woolfolk, R. 2000. The Harmful Dysfunction Analysis of Mental Disorder. *Philosophy, Psychiatry, & Psychology* 7:241–93.

Poland, Jeffrey. 2002. 'Whither Mental Disorder?' Unpublished manuscript.

Radden, Jennifer. 2000a. Introduction to *The Nature of Melancholy*, ed. Jennifer Radden. New York: Oxford University Press.

———. 2000b. Love and Loss in Freud's "Mourning and Melancholia": A Rereading. In *The Analytic Freud: Philosophy and Psychoanalysis*, ed. Michael P. Levine. London: Routledge; 211–30.

Reznek, L. 1987. *The Philosophical Defense of Psychiatry*. London: Routledge.

Ross, L., and Nisbett, R. E. 1991. *The Person and the Situation*. Philadelphia: Temple University Press.

Seligman, M. 1975. *Helplessness: On Depression, Development and Death*. New York: Freeman.

Wakefield, J. 1992. Disorder as Harmful Dysfunction: A Conceptual Critique of DSM-III-R's Definition of Mental Disorder. *Psychological Review* 99:232–47.

Wilkinson, S. 2000. Is "Normal Grief" a Mental Disorder? *Philosophical Quarterly* 50(200):289–304.

7

Emotional Pain
and Psychiatry

All pain involves affect. Studies have confirmed that affective elements and higher cognitive states of expectation and memory frame and interpret even the most ordinary pain sensations. Yet pain comes in varied forms. Some is experienced as an emotion, or a mood, rather than a localized sensation. These features of pain experience raise a host of conceptual questions. Is it important to distinguish localized painful sensations from the pain, suffering, and hurt that come to us in the form of emotional states? Does our pain language admit of more and less literal usage, if so? Is its abhorrence intrinsic to all pain experience? The following essay explores questions such as these in light of contemporary neuroscientific and philosophical research about painful sensations. Although alert to the affective elements tempering painful sensations, that research has almost entirely ignored pain and suffering that is nonlocalized and nonsensory. An older philosophical literature deals with more obviously emotional pain and suffering, but it, too, is incomplete. These omissions, it seems likely, limit our understanding of all pain experiences.

The nature of the relation between different pain experiences has particular urgency because of the central part played by emotional pain within clinical and diagnostic psychiatry. There, as integral to a standard definition of mental disorder, as a common symptom of several disorders of mood and affect such as depression, and as central to diagnostic categories involving psychogenic or somataform "pain disorders," such pain requires clarification and analysis.

In Section 1, the centrality of emotional pain to psychiatric definitions and lore is illustrated using examples from the current Diagnostic and Statistical Manual (APA 1994). The introduction to DSM-IV employs a definition of "mental disorder"

Adapted from "Sensory and Affective Components of Pain, Suffering and Hurt" in *Fact and Value in Emotion* (2007), edited by Louis Charland and Peter Zachar (Consciousness and Emotion Book Series). Amsterdam: John Benjamins, 2008. Published with permission from John Benjamins Publishing Company, Amsterdam.

that includes reference to what appears to be emotional pain; excessive pain of an emotional kind is also noted as a defining symptom of several different mood disorders such as depression; and finally, the diagnostic category of "pain disorder" includes a definition that maintains ambiguity over whether the pain that is the basis for the diagnosis is a painful sensation or emotional pain, when it appears to require both kinds.

Section 2 provides conceptual clarification in this complex and important area, with the ultimate goal of avoiding confusion over pain, suffering, and distress as they appear in psychiatric theorizing and lore. Particular points of emphasis are selected based on common ambiguities and misunderstandings over what have sometimes, misleadingly, been termed "physical" (or bodily) and "mental" (or psychological) pain and suffering.

Emotional Pain as a Symptom and Indicator of Mental Disorder

In the introduction to DSM-IV, we find a definition of mental disorder. It is to be conceptualized, we are told, as "a clinically significant behavioral or psychological syndrome or pattern that occurs in an individual and that is associated with *present distress (e.g., a painful symptom)* or disability (i.e., impairment in one or more important areas of functioning) with a significantly increased risk of suffering death, pain, disability, or an important loss of freedom" (APA 1994:xxi; my emphasis). A general concern with this passage (and especially with the use of the parenthetical example) is its ambiguity: we are left unclear whether something like the distinction between emotional pain and painful sensations is recognized, and the "present distress" and "painful" symptom referred to describes the former. That passage seems to be an offspring of one in the revised previous edition where each mental disorder is said to be "associated with present distress (a painful symptom)" (DSMIII-R 1987:xxiii). The parenthetical paraphrase here apparently serves to indicate that the distress is equated with, rather than merely exemplified in, a painful symptom, but this formulation, too, remains ambiguous. In so central a definition, the relation between present "distress" and the pain of a painful symptom require more thorough and careful analysis.[1]

The second place we find reliance on the category of what at least appears to be emotional pain is in definitions of affective or mood disorder. References are to "depressed mood," as a symptom of a range of conditions; and the "symptoms" of a major depressive episode are said to include "feelings of worthlessness or guilt," "recurrent thoughts of death," "[reports of feeling] depressed, sad, hopeless, discouraged, or "down in the dumps" and "clinically significant distress" (APA 1994:320). Other "symptoms," some psychological and some not, are also cited as diagnostic for these sorts of disorder, but I have selected the group of states and reports quite clearly bespeaking emotionally painful phenomenology. Because there is no effort to otherwise explain and define the central category of "depressed mood," it is arguable that the states listed here are more privileged than some others. Be that as it may, these states appear to be instances of emotional pain rather than painful sensations, and this status requires some additional acknowledgement.

The final ambiguity is found in the definition of "pain disorder." In DSM-IV this condition is said to be "characterized by pain as the predominant focus of clinical attention" (APA 1994:445). Left unclear is what kind of pain. Pain disorder comes under the broader category of somatoform disorders (including somatization disorder, undifferentiated somatoform disorder, conversion disorder, hypochondriasis, body dysmorphic disorder, and somatoform disorder not otherwise specified), all said to share "the presence of physical symptoms that suggest a general medical condition" and that "cause clinically significant *distress*" (APA 1994:445; my emphasis). Physical symptoms of the kind identified here need not be painful sensations. (Rashes, for example, may be prickly without being painful.) So while they are believed to have psychogenic causes, in *order to warrant this diagnosis* the symptoms of pain disorder (and other somatoform disorders) must be accompanied by distress over or about them—hence, emotional pain. Again, we have a confusion of pains: the "pain" of pain disorder that is the focus of clinical attention seems likely both painful sensations and painful emotions.

The goal of the following discussion is to untangle passages such as these. With some preparatory acknowledgement of the complexities involved, and the use of consistent language and clearer examples, the ambiguities and confusions identified here could be remedied. As the architects of future diagnostic and statistical manuals prepare for a revised edition, they should aim for such conceptual clarification.

Conceptual Complexities and Clarifications

Pain is subjective: whatever its origin and status, it enters our lives as a mental state, experienced directly by its subject, and known to others through phenomenological report. Its negative valence is consistent, strong, and seemingly intrinsic. We may adopt additional attitudes toward it (relief, dread, gratitude, or equanimity, for example), but normal pain is immediately abhorrent and undesirable. It comes in varied forms, and only some is experienced as localized sensations, akin in many respects to bodily sensations like itches, throbs, or giddiness. But always, it is a cultural as well as a private state and a social as much as a biological one.

In this section, focus is on the scientific findings, together with some philosophical analyses, that might guide us toward a better understanding of the relation between the affectively framed painful sensations (s-pain) resulting from real or imagined tissue damage and the more straightforwardly emotional pain (e-pain) associated with disorders such as depression. Strong analogies unite these states, undeniably. But there are also phenomenological and conceptual contrasts distinguishing s-pain and e-pain that might discourage us from conflating the two. Here I lay out some of what is at stake in the way we depict pain with the hope of avoiding terminological confusion when, in the context of psychiatric analyses, these central states are described and defined.

A much-quoted definition of pain from the International Association for the Study of Pain is a good place to begin. It is a problematic definition, yet worth looking at, not only because it has been so influential in the past few decades of pain research but because its ambiguities and inconsistencies are emblematic of the seeming confusions in this area. Pain is "an unpleasant sensory and emotional experience associated with actual or potential tissue damage, or described in terms of such damage." This brief definition is followed by a controversial note insisting that "pain is always subjective.... Activity induced in the nociceptor and nociceptive pathways by a noxious stimulus is not pain, which is always a psychological state, even though we may well appreciate that pain most often has a proximate physical cause" (IASP 1986:250).

Most immediately pertinent for us, the IASP account resists treating pain as *reducible to* the stimulation of pain receptors. In this respect, the note following the definition confirms conclusions drawn in several philosophical analyses of painful sensations (Edwards 1979, Grahak 2001, Kripke 1980, De Grazia 1991, Sullivan 1995, Radden 2002, Aydede and Gizeldere 2002). Without painful sensation, the activation of physiological pain centers (the nociceptive pathways) would not be considered an instance of pain, for pain itself "is an experience, not a stimulus or a response" (Sullivan 1995:278).

This fundamental point is confirmed by appeal to our use of the term "pain" in everyday language. And, in a recent article, Murat Aydede and Guven Gizeldere also pointed out that the whole conceptual apparatus of the scientific study of pain is built on subjective report and on the separation of first-person accounts of pain sensations from investigation into biological events. If painful sensations were reducible to nociceptive stimulation, this research would have been impossible. Thus, of scientific findings about pain sufferers, these researchers point out, "No objective observations of the causes of their condition, non-verbal behavior, and/or the brain damage involved, would all by themselves be strong enough to force scientists to seek functionally and anatomically separate brain mechanisms.... The accumulation of this sort of (mostly) subjectively obtained abnormal data...led to the identification of the neural substrates through brain imaging studies: the phenomenology strongly guided what to look for, and where" (Aydede and Guzeldere 2002:10). The findings of these studies are only conceptually coherent in the context where the separation between the phenomenology and the brain states is acknowledged. (With this established, these authors actually propose a nomenclature that acknowledges the dual contribution of neuroscience and phenomenology in the term "neurophenomenology.")

Summing up this recognition that pain is more than the stimulation of pain receptors, we might use an old philosophers' tag and say that, in the case of pain, to be is to be experienced or perceived (*esse est percipi*).

Another aspect of the IASP account is worth attention. The brief definition concerns itself with painful sensations to the exclusion of more emotionally toned pain and suffering, apparently accepting, as many seem to do, that when "pain" is used of suffering not involving actual or potential tissue damage, it is employed in some extended or secondary sense. This position is adjusted—or even reversed—in the note following the definition, where it is acknowledged that reported pain in the absence of tissue damage "or any likely pathological cause" should nonetheless be "accepted as pain." The inconsistencies between the initial definition and subsequent note are of course confusing. But though rather begrudgingly (and only granting "pathological causes" originating from within the person rather than from, say, external events), the note does appear to allow the pain of depression the status of real pain, appropriately so described.

Pain Is Not Merely an Episode of Simple, Localized Sensory Experience

Focused as it has been on the painful sensations associated with tissue damage (real or imagined), pain research has nevertheless come to recognize that all pain is less simple, more cognitively mediated, and thus more *like an emotion* than had previously been supposed. The unsurprising bit of this that could hardly escape even preconceptual insight is that painful sensations comprise distinguishable phenomenal strands, some more sensory, and others—in particular, the feeling of abhorrence or displeasure pain brings—more akin to other affective states. Then the surprising aspect: every part of pain experience is extensively "cognitively mediated." Such psychic elements as memory, personal and social attitudes, role expectations, and life experience, as well as mental and emotional health and bodily traits, affect how pain feels.

A range of sources, including the subjective reports of patients having undergone brain surgery (prefrontal lobotomy and cingulotomy), brain imaging, and anatomical studies, have confirmed the first, unsurprising, distinction between "sensory-discriminative" awareness of *what the pain is like in terms of quality and severity,* and motivational-affective awareness of *how intolerable it is* (Melzack 1961, Melzack and Wall 1983, Fernandez and Turk 1992, Fernandez and Milburn 1994, Treede et al. 1999, Price 2002). Interestingly, the term "painful" retains the ambiguity between these two traits in everyday, preconceptual usage. Research subjects must be guided to distinguish and report a pain's intensity separately from its unpleasantness.

Now, to the surprises. Pain experiences are mediated by elements that are complex and unpredictably idiosyncratic, revealing the extensive influence of higher-order cognitive states. Efforts have been made to distinguish within motivational-affective awareness. H. L. Fields, for example, separates the "stimulus bound (primary) unpleasantness" from the "secondary unpleasantness" he identifies as a "higher level process" with a "highly variable relationship to stimulus intensity...largely determined by memories and contextual features" (Fields 1999:S61). Yet primary forms of unpleasantness are also mediated by motivational-affective factors, so not even primary unpleasantness is consistently coupled with stimulus intensity. Voluntarily accepting a painful experience versus being forced to undergo it alters, and lessens, even the degree of ("primary") unpleasantness of the experience, it has been shown (quoted by Hall 1989:654). And other studies have demonstrated that the perceived intensity of pain, as well as its ("secondary") unpleasantness, are both mediated by expectations, beliefs, and other cognitive states (Montgomery and Kirsch 1996). At best, then, Fields can maintain that the affective influence on secondary unpleasantness will be relatively greater than that on primary unpleasantness.

Common sense confirms the general point, now regularly noted by researchers, that pain is cognitively mediated this way. The pain of (natural) childbirth for the mother will likely be as stimulus intense and ("primary") unpleasant as any she has endured, yet relatively bearable, on the dimension of "secondary unpleasantness," because of what it portends, folk wisdom insists.[2] It goes without saying that pain may be worth enduring *for some greater good*.[3] And the fact that pain judged natural, healthy, ennobling, or otherwise instrumentally valuable will be not only less abhorrent but also less intense is widely acknowledged, along with lore about human suggestibility. The parent's kiss and touch, children and adults believe, lessen the pain of children's minor injuries—an assumption confirmed in recent research, where imaging has shown that even placebo "analgysics" activate the brain's natural opiate-producers that serve to reduce the stimulus intensity and unpleasantness of nociceptive stimulation (Zubieta et al. 2005).

The basic neuroscience of these observations is also quite well understood. Rather than a simple sensation, pain is modulated by influences from several parts of the brain, including the prefrontal cortex that exercises executive control over all other cortical centers. More specifically:

> [There are] serial interactions between pain sensation intensity, pain unpleasantness, and secondary affect associated with reflection and future implications (i.e., suffering). These pain dimensions and their interactions relate to ascending spinal pathways and a central network of brain structures that process nociceptive information both in series and in parallel. Spinal pathways to amygdala, hypothalamus, reticular formation, medial thalamic nuclei, and limbic cortical structures provide direct inputs to brain areas involved in arousal, bodily regulation, and hence affect. Another major input to these same structures is from spinal pathways to somatosensory thalamic (VPL, VPM) and cortical areas (S-1, S-2, posterior parietal cortex) and from these areas to cortical limbic structures (insular cortex, anterior cingulate cortex). This cortico-limbic pathway integrates nociceptive input with information about overall status of the body and self to provide cognitive mediation of pain affect. Both direct and cortico-limbic pathways converge on the same anterior cingulate cortical and subcortical structures whose function may be to establish emotional valence and response priorities. This entire brain network is under dynamic top-down modulation by brain mechanisms that are associated with anticipation, expectation, and other cognitive factors. (Price 2002:392)

As well as aches and pains, sensations (or what are sometimes known as "bodily sensations") include such things as itches, tickles, muscle spasms, throbbings, giddiness, and dizziness. They have often been depicted as episodes of localized sensory experience that are simple, immediate responses to stimuli. In light of the above findings about the cognitive complexity of pain, we can conclude that even painful sensations are not *merely* sensations thus understood. (And it seems likely that many other sensations are equally complex—those comprising orgasm, for example.)

As the above-quoted passage shows, pain is a composite whose separate sensory and affective elements have been identified. Moreover, in rare instances, these elements even detach from one another phenomenally. Cases of "reactive dissociation," for example, are those in which subjects report feeling the pain sensation without any accompanying affective component of unpleasantness.[4] But these are abnormalities. In the normal case, the sensory and affective aspects of painful sensations are inextricably linked: phenomenologically, they present themselves as a single, unified experience.[5]

*Painful Sensations, Like "Merely Psychological" Pain
and Suffering, May Be Psychogenically Caused*

Some of the strongest support for the conclusion that pain is not merely an unmediated sensory response comes from the evidence that pain sensations often occur in the absence of any identifiable tissue damage. They are "psychosomatic," as it is sometimes put. Apparent instances of painful sensations, caused not by tissue damage but by psychic states, are frequently documented in the psychiatric literature where, until the term was expunged for its political connotations, they were known as "hysterical" symptoms. Apart from the more-controversial diagnoses such as fibromyalgia, whose psychogenic status remains contested, there is the pain-related diagnostic category of "pain disorder," introduced earlier, which exhibits presumed psychogenic underpinnings. Pain disorder is defined as the occurrence of pain in one or more anatomical sites when "psychological factors are judged to have the major role in the onset, severity, exacerbation, or maintenance of the pain" (APA 1994:461–42).

It is a given that psychogenic factors account for painful psychic states that are not sensations. What is at issue here, then, is not whether such psychogenically caused states occur but how they should be described. As it pertains to terminology, the question becomes whether the pain and suffering brought about, at least in part, by psychological states, is actually—and literally—"pain."

Emotional Pain Is Not a Metaphor

The anguish often wrought by depression is as unpleasant as any painful sensation its sufferers experience. But is it pain? Its almost exclusive attention to painful sensations has allowed most recent pain research to avoid this initial matter of terminology. And psychiatric writing often appears to regard the depression sufferer's pain as "pain" in an extended or metaphorical sense, as noted above, or to restrict the term "pain" to painful sensations and employ "suffering" to cover experiences like the depressive's anguish.

Among philosophers, the terms "mental pain" and "physical pain" have sometimes been assigned to these two kinds of experience (for instance, Trigg 1970). Others have spoken of "psychological" and "bodily" pain (Scarry 1985). But this usage is misleading and problematic on at least two counts. To begin with, the sensation of pain is as quintessentially phenomenal (and hence, in the sense intended, "mental" or "psychological") as are painful and distressing emotions. No less or more real than the pain from a blow on the head, and long allied to such pain, depressive anguish is as literally "painful" as, and no more "mental" or "psychological" than, pain from that blow.

Interesting here are recent remarks made by Helen Mayberg, professor of psychiatry and neurology at Emory University, who has pioneered surgical depression treatment focused on area 25 in the brain. She begins pointing out that although a common understanding of depression equates it with a form of *deficit*, her work suggests the reverse. Talk to a depressed person, she remarks, "and you have this bizarre combination of numbness and what William James called 'an active anguish.' 'A sort of psychical neuralgia,' he said, 'wholly unknown to healthy life.' You're numb but you hurt. You can't think, but you are in pain. *Now, how does your psyche hurt? What a weird choice of words. But it is not an arbitrary choice. It's there. These people are feeling a particular, indescribable kind of pain*" (quoted by Dobbs 2006:55; my emphasis). Mayberg is a specialist in the pain of depression, and she here goes to considerable lengths to emphasize that she speaks advisedly and literally when she describes the pain of depression this way. And she follows a long tradition. The suggestion that of two uses one is primary and the other secondary or metaphorical seems unsustainable.

Jamie Mayerfield proposes to use the term "suffering" to refer to pain such as that experienced in depression (see also De Grazia 1998). Despite the considerable disanalogies, however, there are also strong analogies between different forms of pain. And neither "pain" nor "suffering" better fits one than another. Moreover, we speak of hurting, and being in discomfort and anguish with reference to each kind of experience. Thus preserving the term "suffering" for states that are not sensations seems arbitrary and confusing. It may be true that, as Mayerfield points out, the Greek *lupé* was rather distortedly translated as "pain" by the Utilitarians, when the then-broader "suffering" would have been more accurate (Mayerfield 1999). But the word "pain" stuck, and it applies today in the broad way that "suffering" also does. (As Rem Edwards has remarked, "Nonlocalized discomforts have been called "pain" time and time again in the discourse of both philosophers and plain men" [Edwards 1979:36].) Moreover it is instructive, if *lupé* spans both states, suggesting that the Greeks, too, were alive to the analogies encouraging us to use one word for both kinds of suffering.

Edwards's solution to this terminological matter is to employ the terms "pain 1" and "pain 2" for distinguishing painful emotions and sensations. But the terms emotion pain (e-pain) and sensation pain (s-pain), that have been used to mark the same contrast, enjoy some descriptive advantage, so " e-pain" and "s-pain" for these two sorts of pain will be employed to allow us to keep track of these two kinds of experience in what follows.

Although Analogous, S-Pain and E-Pain Differ

As discussed, the affective, phenomenal element of its unpleasantness is characteristic of each kind of pain, and that element is moreover mediated by higher-order cognitive states such as memory and expectation. What must be emphasized, then, is that s-pain is so named not because it is without any phenomenal affective elements but because it alone involves sensations. In the normal case, s-pain comprises sensation and affective phenomenal attributes, and, in this respect, it appears to differ from e-pain, which is experienced as an emotional state only. S-pain is named for the sensation it includes.

Indicative of the analogies between s-pain and e-pain is the fact that not just the term "pain," but a broad range of others—such as "hurt," "suffering," "discomfort," "anguish," and "distress"—span these two kinds of unpleasant state. And important forms of behavioral expression are common to them both: gasps, cries, moans, grimaces, and tears, for example. Indeed, a characterization of s-pain provided by

Mayerfield could be read as applicable to both kinds of experience (although it was not so intended). Speaking of painful sensations, he remarks, "pain is a particularly useful model":

> Everyone at one time or another has experienced it. . . . We recognize it instantly, and name it unerringly, when it strikes us. There are certain things known to cause it in virtually all people; and even when it has invisible or unlikely causes, we can recognize its occurrence in other people by characteristic cries, grimaces, and recoiling movements. In our own case we can specify with considerable precision when it comes and goes, when it grows more intense, and we are unlikely to confuse it with other bad things that may happen to us. There is something "real" about pain." (Mayerfield 1999:24)

To the commonalities such as these that pertain to the way pain experience affects its sufferers must be added another: pain is a cultural phenomenon. Framed, understood, and interpreted by social and cultural values and meanings, painful sensations as much as painful emotions reflect their sufferer's place in the social world they find themselves in.

Confronted with these many similarities, it is tempting to presume that the category of "pain" is a unitary one. Yet, despite these commonalities, s-pain must not be too hastily equated with e-pain, nor e-pain reduced to s-pain. There are systematic differences between these two sorts of painful experience. Each must be acknowledged and explored before we reach any final conclusion as to the best way to understand and portray the relationship between these two groups of experiences.

Eight conceptual and phenomenological differences will be dealt with in turn. Summarizing, we can say that in contrast to e-pains, s-pains (i) are spatially localized; (ii) are more temporally localized; (iii) are closer to being felt states by their nature; (iv) contain (in the normal case) elements of stimulus intensity and unpleasantness, not mere unpleasantness; (v) enjoy a stronger reportorial authority (while not immune from error); (vi) are subject to a particular set of metaphorical descriptions; (vii) are always intentional though not as fully intentional; and (viii) are not subject to appraisal in light of social norms.

Some of these differences are matters of degree rather than kind, and not all of (i)–(viii) are uncontroversial. Taken together though, (i)–(viii) constitute a set of differences that are sufficiently formidable to regard s-pain and e-pain as distinguishable. These may encourage us to speak of the term "pain" as having two senses, as some philosophers have wanted to do. Or, "pain" may be a looser (family resemblance) type of category of which s-pain and e-pain represent recognizable variants.

(i) Most obviously, sensations are spatially localized while emotions are not.[6] Several of the differences described in (ii)–(viii) are little more than implications of (i), and, indeed, its localization has sometimes been treated as alone sufficient to mark the distinction between s-pains and e-pains (for example, Edwards 1979:44). We may be inaccurate in our belief as to where we feel the pain, but with the awareness of a painful sensation comes awareness of *where it feels to be*. (This feature of pain has given rise to an account of pain as "an emotion at a place" [Blum 1996].) And this remains true even when, as after a fall, or suffering influenza, we might insist that the painful feeling is located *everywhere in our body*. "Nonlocalized feeling" is not the same thing as "universally localized feeling," as it has been put, and: "The former has no definite bodily locus at all, whereas the latter seems to be present 'all over' (Edwards 1979:39–40).

Emotional pain is not similarly tied to location. It is true that emotions have sometimes been assigned bodily parts in our Western cultural traditions, as the term "heartache" vividly illustrates. But modern anatomical knowledge has relegated such associations to the status of lingering and weak metaphors. And when accompanied by somatic sensations—the lump in the throat that comes with a poignant sight, the sinking feeling in the stomach with apprehension—these sensations are regarded as distinct, occasional *accompaniments* of emotions.

(ii) Sensations are also more closely localized in time: they are particular episodes or occurrences with identifiable beginnings and endings. Emotions, in contrast, although their onset can often be timed to a particular occasion, are then frequently less like episodes or occurrences and more like dispositions to act or feel. We readily ascribe emotions to those who are evidently not experiencing them at that time. "She is sleeping, but I know she is still pained by her father's rejection" is an unexceptional and fairly commonplace way of speaking. "She is sleeping, and she is in great pain in her lower back," is more problematic. If back pain cannot as readily be attributed to the sleeper as can emotional pain, one way to explain this is to say that back pain is localized temporally as well as spatially.

Another, and more common way to explain the difference between "She is sleeping, but I know she is still pained by her father's rejection" and "She is sleeping, and she is in great pain in her lower back" is to insist that there cannot be unfelt back pains. So we get to:

(iii) s-pains bear a closer relation than do e-pains to *being felt*. This view, encapsulated in Gilbert Ryle's remark (about s-pain) that "'unnoticed pain' is an absurd expression" (Ryle 1949:203), is widely accepted still (for example, Turski 1996:26).

The impossibility of unfelt (s-)pain has been recently challenged in the philosophical literature. The case of an s-pain that arouses a sleeper seems to contradict the view that there cannot be unfelt (s-)pains and has been raised as a philosophical puzzle or problem for the customary analysis of (s-)pain as a state that must be felt. Attempting to account for such cases of seemingly unfelt pains, Terry Dartnall separates *what is* from *what is known*, concluding: "the feeling of the pain didn't spring into existence when you woke up, but got gradually worse until it woke you up." What sprang into existence was "your awareness of it" (Dartnall 2001:99). Others have questioned this analysis, however. Decrying what he takes to be Dartnall's misguided "problematizing" of (s-)pain, J. L.Garfield speaks of a mistaken account of introspective knowledge, according to which "introspection gives us inner episodes veridically and *in their totality*" (Garfield 2001:1; my emphasis). Necessary but not sufficient for the sensation of pain, stimulation of the nociceptive pathways would at best have been the prompt for the pain that occurred on awakening. In that respect, Garfield's use of "totality" implies, it was a part, but *not the whole*, of the pain involved.

Without engaging with every aspect of the exchange over unfelt or unconscious s-pain (and other sensations), I would point out that the apparent puzzles around the case of s-pain that wakes the sleeper are not comparably worrisome when sleep is interfered with by e-pain. We toss and turn, apparently fretting while half, or fully, asleep; we reach consciousness with unaccountable ("objectless") feelings of apprehension or gloom; our e-pains enter our dreams and nightmares, sometimes serving to wake us. And, although this account itself has been questioned, these states seem to be remembered on waking, not experienced de novo. Which if any of these experiences rank as unfelt e-pains, or even parallel the case of allegedly unfelt s-pains, may be debated. But at the least we can conclude that such unfelt, or partially felt, e-pains are commonplace and do not seem to merit the status of philosophical puzzles or problems.

So while the possibility of unfelt s-pains is debatable, and debated, that of unfelt e-pains is not, or is less so. As we saw in the case of the sleeping woman pained by her father's rejection, e-pains are often ascribed (by others) in the absence of conscious awareness of e-pain by their subject. In addition, a kind of "unfelt e-pain" is presupposed in the important concept of masked depression.

Masked depression is frequently attributed within psychiatric theorizing and lore. It is introduced in several ways: where there is an attitude of manic insouciance or one of apathy rather than the depressed mood deemed appropriate or predictable; where certain behaviors "substitute" for the feeling (as when substance abuse is said to be an expression of underlying depression, for example); where such a substitution or conversion transfers the feeling into somatic symptoms; and where mechanisms such as denial, repression, or dissociation are said to conceal the underlying e-pain.[7] We do not need to accept every account of masked depression (many are dependent on dubious or arguable theoretical posits) to recognize that no comparable attribution seems to be made in respect to sensation pain. Arguably, we may be the recipients of stimulation to our pain centers that is prevented from entering consciousness. But, as was emphasized earlier, the stimulation of pain centers is not the same as pain. The term "pain" is reserved, so that only when it enters conscious awareness as an experience does it become actual "pain."

(iv) The elements of stimulus intensity and unpleasantness, respectively, are each present and phenomenologically identifiable in s-pain. This follows, of course, from the fact that s-pain is a felt sensation and stimulus intensity is a sensory measure. Because e-pain is not a sensation, and at most has somatic accompaniments, stimulus intensity and unpleasantness are indistinguishable in the experience of e-pain. (Even in William James's theory of emotion, which allows that emotions are responses to felt somatic states, the relationship between these separate elements is a causal one: the affect and its sensory cause are only contingently connected [James 1884]).

(v) Also related to the localized nature of s-pains is a further apparent difference, if not of kind then at least of degree, concerning the reportorial authority accorded the subject. Reports on one's own sensations generally go unchallenged. They are not deemed immune from error—to the contrary. But sufferers are treated as authorities about their own s-pains, as the case of phantom limb pain attests. We have no hesitation in speaking of pain here, even while acknowledging that reports of phantom limb pain must be, and must be known to their subject to be, inaccurate as to the location assigned to the pain. Our first-person reports—as to whether s-pains are present, their degree of intensity, their location in space and time, their degree of unpleasantness, and their other sensory attributes—are immune from *correction*, yet not from *error*. This feature of our everyday concept of (s-)pain, and pain reports, as Aydede has pointed out, distinguishes (s-)pain reports from perceptual reports, for example.

Despite superficial grammatical similarities, Aydede argues, different truth conditions govern visual reports such as "I see a dark discoloration on the back of my hand" (1) and pain statements such as "I feel a jabbing pain in the back of my hand" (2). By uttering the latter (2), he notes:

> I am saying something like "I am undergoing an experience which tells me that some sort of physical disturbance is occurring in the back of my hand." If so, that there is no physical disturbance occurring in my hand...doesn't make (2) false. The fact that I can still correctly point to where it really hurts in my hand after hearing from my doctor that nothing is wrong with my hand is explained by reinterpreting what I say and do with that gesture: I am still undergoing an experience which represents my hand as having something physically wrong with it. (Aydede 2006:5)

As references to masked depression seem to indicate, we do not generally enjoy the same reportorial authority when it comes to e-pain. (See, for instance, the remark that "introspection of emotional states is so much less reliable than that of other states of consciousness" [Seager 2002:666].) The truth conditions for "I am pained by my father's rejection" are not the same as those for the visual claim in (1) above ("I see a dark discoloration on the back of my hand"). But neither are they as immune from revision and correction as (2) ("I feel a jabbing pain in the back of my hand"). E-pain statements apparently fall somewhere between s-pain statements and ordinary perceptual claims with respect to this epistemic dimension of reportorial authority. Two factors likely account for this status. E-pain, as we have seen, is often best understood not as episodic suffering but as longer-term states and dispositions; moreover, it is more complex than s-pain because it usually comes embedded in a more-extensive network of consciously held cognitive states. These differences can explain why we are treated as more prone to error, to exaggeration, and to distortion in our reports of e-pain.

(vi) S-pain resists literal description. In Elaine Scarry's words, it "has no voice" and "shatters language" (Scarry 1985:3, 5).[8] Recognizing that the conventional medical scale of mild to severe captured only one aspect of the phenomenology of s-pain experience, researchers have sorted and classified the metaphors employed by patients into three groups: those referring to "temporal" aspects of the experience ("quivering" "throbbing," and "pulsing," for example); to the "thermal" (such as "burning," "scalding," "searing"); and to the "constrictive" ("pinching," "crushing," and "cramping") (Melzack and Wall 1983). In their appeal to metaphor, and their reference to sensory attributes, these descriptions are distinctive to our efforts to convey the experience of s-pains and are without parallel in descriptions of e-pains.

(vii) A related aspect of s-pain apparently distinguishes it from e-pain: as sensations, s-pains are not about or of anything beyond themselves. This is sometimes what is meant when they are described as "intransitive."[9] In contrast, emotions and so e-pains are intentional: that is, they are usually about, over, or directed toward intentional objects that are, or may be, beyond themselves (Gordon 1987).

These questions of intentionality are complex and contested. In what follows, it will be shown that while s-pains are always intentional, they differ from e-pains in being only minimally so. They are over or about themselves: that is, they are intransitive. E-pains, in contrast, may be transitive or intransitive. When they are intentional, they are fully and richly intentional. Their objects include other inner states, things, states of affairs, propositions—or themselves.

As this conclusion suggests, the notion of an intentional object—that toward which the e-pain is said to be directed, over, or about—requires refinement. It may be either a situation or a state of affairs captured propositionally (such as the proposition that my friend has died) or a concrete existent in the world, such as a (living) person, a bodily state, or, indeed, a psychic state such as, and including, itself.[10] When I anguish over the effects of my debilitating depression, for example, my own pain and suffering may be the object of my anguish. My depression depresses me.

The differences just noted may seem attributable to the fact that an adverbial rather than an act-object analysis fits the experience of pain. Understanding (s-)pain on an act-object model, it has been claimed, involves a misapprehension. If all pain is better understood adverbially, then any disparities between e-pain's and s-pain's respective transitivity and intransitivity will be beside the point. On this view, pain— and, it is often asserted, pleasure—are properly understood in adverbial terms: they are ways of experiencing something, rather than something we experience. "(S-)pain" now becomes an adverb describing the way we feel, not the thing we feel. In the reasoning of a recent such account, "When we describe a pain, we are . . . qualifying a verb rather than a noun. . . . 'I feel a sharp pain' is an answer to the question 'How do you feel?' not to the question 'What do you feel?'" (Douglas 1998:129).

Precisely because, as we saw earlier, e-pains are not intransitive and take a range of objects that typically go beyond themselves, the act-object account seems the more obviously applicable. But even in the case of s-pains, an adverbial analysis encounters difficulties. At least on its surface grammar, "I feel a sharp (s-)pain" does exhibit an act-object structure—my feeling is over or about the felt (s-)pain. (Indeed, since if s-pain were a kind of perception, it would also invite an act-object analysis, some have found a way to accommodate s-pain within a representational theory of consciousness by proposing that s-pain is an object of experience [Langsam 1995, Bryne 2001].) "I feel a sharp pain" may sometimes also be an answer to "How do you feel?" But depending on the context, "I feel a sharp pain" answers "What do you feel?"—just as, colloquially, "Despair." may be an answer to both "How do you feel?" and "What do you feel?" Applying an adverbial analysis to e-pains would seem to involve similar, context-dependent ambiguities.

The adverbial account is incomplete, then. And concerns over it such as these encourage us to explore where we might stop short of adopting such a position, in order to maintain, as I wish to do, that "I feel a sharp pain" might as equally be the answer to the question "What do you feel?" as "How do you feel?" Thus Trigg, looking at disanalogies between e-pain and s-pain (in his terminology "mental pain" and "physical pain") finds another feature, not noted thus far. The main difference between the experiences Trigg names mental and physical pain, he proposes, may be "the type of 'object' which each has. 'Mental pain' could be distress at situations, while 'physical pain' would be distress at sensations." In that case, he goes on, it need not be at all surprising that "it is logically necessary for someone suffering 'physical pain' to feel something. *If the sensation were absent, there would be no 'object'* . . . and hence no pain" (Trigg 1970:7; my emphasis).

The difference between e-pains and s-pains, Trigg is asserting here, does not lie in the presence or absence of intentional objects, as long as we remember that these may be either propositions or concrete things in the world. Both kinds of pain have objects and conform to the basic act-object model. But the sole object of s-pain (and any sensation) is the sensation itself. Sensations may also sometimes be the objects of e-pain, but the considerably richer intentionality of emotions allows that e-pain's objects include (propositions about) situations and states of affairs, not merely sensations.

In a recent review and sorting of intentionality theses, Alex Byrne distinguishes theories according to scope and arranges them into "unrestricted" and "restricted." Unrestricted intentionalists hold, while restricted intentionalists deny, he says, that intentionalism also applies to bodily sensations (such as s-pains) (Byrne 2001:205). Trigg's account, then, is unrestricted. Unrestricted intentionalism for bodily sensations is the position favored by Byrne himself, on the grounds that bodily sensations possess intentional content related to their phenomenally displayed location in the form of a proposition. Whenever the experience or sensation is endured, as he puts it, "the world seems a certain way, namely, that there is a twinge in the knee" (Byrne 2001:229). While also maintaining an unrestricted theory, Trigg's account diverges here: for him, the intentional object is the sensation itself, whereas for Byrne it is a proposition about the sensation. Setting aside these close differences, however, it is possible to recognize that in either variant of the unrestricted intentionality that allows sensations to be intentional objects, the objects of sensations can only be the sensations or the propositions about them. And in this respect, at least, s-pains differ from e-pains, whose intentionality has a broader reach.

Only clear and unequivocal examples of s-pain and e-pain have been described thus far in this discussion. But before we leave this question of intentionality, attention must be drawn to e-pains that are ostensibly without objects or whose objects are so vaguely defined and pervasive as to be all-encompassing. States such as "uneasiness," "fearfulness," "jitteriness," and "dispiritedness" arguably lie somewhere in between emotions and sensations and so might fall under some third, hybrid category.

Certainly, aspects of these states can be pointed to that would account for our inclination to regard them as hybrids. First, these are each apparently objectless emotions, detached from the framing intentional structure that makes them about or over something in particular that is beyond themselves. Unlike many emotions, these may present themselves as "intransitive" and closer, in that respect, to sensations. Moreover, each is associated with a well-defined set of sensations that often accompany them. The descriptive terms themselves ("uneasiness," etc.), we can thus suppose, have come to connote their sensory accompaniments. When we think of dispiritedness, we are reminded of the felt bodily slump and drooping posture associated with it, and so on. That the terms used to describe these states carry sensory and emotional connotations is undeniable. Yet while the ways we describe them are genuinely ambiguous—"dispiritedness" may allude to either the sagging sensation or to the disheartened frame of mind, for example—the sensations and emotions associated with them remain separable states.

Rather than preventing us from distinguishing e-pain from s-pain by appeal to Trigg's characterization of the respective nature and scope of their objects, these moods that are sometimes deemed "objectless" reveal the importance of the stress I have placed on the passage from Trigg quoted above: "It is logically necessary for someone suffering 'physical pain' to feel something. *If the sensation were absent, there would be no 'object'*...and hence no pain." S-pains *must have objects*, in the minimal sense involved with intransitive sensations; e-pains need not have them, although when they do, their objects may be sensations or any other inner states, things, situations, or states of affairs—or propositions about any of these. It is not intentionality as such that separates e-pains from s-pains on this analysis, as restricted intentionalism asserts, but rather the type and complexity of that intentionality.

Summing up: the difference between e-pains and s-pains vis à vis intentionality comes to this: s-pains are never "objectless," as e-pains sometimes appear to be; instead, s-pains are always, but only, minimally intentional, over or about themselves—that is, they are intransitive. When they are intentional, e-pains are fully and richly intentional: they may be over or about inner states, things, states of affairs, propositions—or themselves.

(viii) Unlike s-pain, e-pain is subject to appraisal—whether appropriate to its circumstances, proper, understandable, even reasonable, or not. This is an implication of its intentionality: such appraisal is based on the aptness of a relation, that between the feeling itself and its object or occasion. This particular characteristic of e-pain has been proposed as the basis, or part of the basis, for distinguishing pathological states of depression and sadness from more normal and appropriate sadness. Thus, Alan Horwitz and Jerome Wakefield speak of "contextuality" as an inherent, normal aspect of many psychological mechanisms. By this, they mean "they are designed to activate in particular contexts and not to activate in others...innate mechanisms regulate reactions of sadness, despair, and withdrawal naturally come into play after humans suffer particular kinds of losses" (Horwitz and Wakefield 2007:15). When they reflect pathology, on this account, loss responses "emerge in situations for which they are not designed, they can be of disproportionate intensity and duration to the situations that evoke them, and...they can occur spontaneously with no trigger at all" (Horwitz and Wakefield 2007:17).

Separate E-Pain May Accompany S-Pain

S-pain has several affective components, but not all are *phenomenal* qualities of the experience. We are aware of the feeling of displeasure, while the affectively toned beliefs, expectations, memories, and other states forming these additional ingredients occur beneath—or before—conscious awareness. (They are "subdoxastic" or "subpersonal" states, inaccessible to consciousness [Stich 1978].)

Independent of the other affective elements framing and shaping our experience of s-pain beneath the surface of conscious awareness, it is also true that separate e-pain sometimes accompanies the experience of s-pain. I may be distressed that the (s-)painful sensation is so unpleasant, for example. (Consider this case:

my daughter and I are both to have a medical procedure. I go first. I had persuaded my daughter it would not be painful. It is painful, more than I expected. The s-pain I experience might here be the object over which, because of a sense of having violated my daughter's trust, I experience (mild) e-pain.) But the unpleasantness of s-pain is a basic phenomenal experience intrinsic to the normal experience of s-pain, and such e-pain is at most a contingent accompaniment.

There Can Be Comorbidity between S-Pain and E-Pain

Just as s-pain normally involves the affective, phenomenal element of its unpleasantness, conditions such as depression may be similarly accompanied by painful sensations. Empirical data attest to the apparent "comorbidity" of chronic pain (s-pain) and psychiatric disorder (e-pain); moreover, some studies have also been taken to demonstrate a particular link between chronic pain and depression. Neither alleged link has gone unchallenged (Hardcastle 1999). But whether or not they are commonly present alongside depression, these pain sensations (s-pain) do not prevent us from describing the experience of depression as e-pain.[11] For such sensations are portrayed as *accompanying* the e-pain of depression rather than being identified with it. As the term "comorbidity" implies, the sufferers of chronic pain (s-pain) alongside depression (e-pain) suffer (when they do) two disorders, not one with two distinct, pain-related symptoms.

Conclusion

By offering conceptual clarification in a complex area, the preceding analysis aims to ameliorate some of the present confusion over pain, suffering, and distress as they are understood in psychiatric theorizing and lore. Focus is on common ambiguities and misunderstandings over what have sometimes, misleadingly, been termed "physical" (or bodily) and "mental" (or psychological) pain and suffering. I show that pain is not merely the stimulation of pain receptors; that pain is not merely a localized episode of sensory experience; that painful sensations may have psychogenic causes; that "emotional pain" is not a metaphor; that although analogous, s-pain and e-pain differ; that separate e-pain may accompany s-pain; and that there can be comorbidity between s-pain and e-pain. Because strong analogies also link these two kinds of pain experience, the purpose here is merely to lay out and acknowledge similarities and differences such as these rather than to insist, as some have, that "pain" possesses two senses.

More generally, the method and epistemological presuppositions employed here have influenced these conclusions in the sense that some of them derive from phenomenological reports only available to conscious awareness. That suggests no new brain science will alone serve to unseat these findings, which are conceptual rather than empirical. While it might encourage us to reconsider the weight we accord the disanalogies outlined here, even the discovery that apparently identical neurons fire, in identical fashion, when e-pain and s-pain occur, would not require us to disregard the distinction between e-pain and s-pain pointed to in this discussion.[12]

Notes

1. There are several other critiques of this passage, the most telling of which is by Russell, who points out that its employment of the medical term "symptom" involves both a failure to apply and a misapplication of the medical model (Russell 1994:247).

2. Whether all mothers remember it that way—they do not—is another matter.

3. The mortification of the flesh in medieval asceticism highlights and exemplifies cultural differences in relation to such assessments (Kroll and Bachrach 2005).

4. Hall 1989; Fernandez, Clark, and Rudick-Davis 1999; Ploner, Freund, and Schnitzler 1999.

5. There is "phenomenal unity" as Michael Tye defines it: a matter of simultaneously experiencing perceptual qualities entering into the same phenomenal content (Tye 2003:36).

6. It has been questioned whether this trait holds for all sensations (Armstrong 1968). But no one challenges the claim at least as it is made for pain.

7. Following the lead of Arthur Kleinman, cross-cultural studies have been taken to suggest that depression in non-Western cultures is almost always "somatized"—that is, experienced in the form of bodily ills rather than the conscious states of (e-)pain and distress that are its central characteristics in our culture (Kleinman 1988, Gaw 1993, Kirmayer and Young 1998, Moerman 2002). Rather than a marginal case, it is suggested, masked depression may be the paradigm and misleadingly named.

8. Although beyond the scope of this discussion, the political and power implications of this feature of pain's inexpressibility are explored and developed in Scarry's important work (Scarry 1985).

9. Armstrong uses the term "intransitive" in a rather different way. He distinguishes (transitive) sensations such as touch and inner (intransitive) sensations such as pains. But because of his perceptual theory of sensation, Armstrong goes on to attribute a "concealed transitivity" to pains as well (Armstrong 1968:309).

10. For a careful discussion of this point, see DeLancey 2002, chapter 5.

11. Interestingly, some of the newer classes of antidepressants and second-generation antiepileptic drugs have proven effective in the treatment of chronic pain. This finding results from the analgesic effect of these drugs, however, not their antidepressant effect, and is believed to modulate pain transmission by interacting with specific neurotransmitters and ion channels.

12. I am grateful to Professors Lawrence Kaye and Murat Aydede, each of whom read and offered suggestions on earlier drafts of this essay. In addition, I have benefited from comments when this material was presented at the James Martin Advanced Research Seminar, at the Philosophy Faculty, Oxford University, in November 2006, with a commentary by Guy Kahane, and by incisive help from Frank Keefe.

References

American Psychiatric Association (1994). *Diagnostic and statistical manual.* 4th ed. Washington, DC: American Psychiatric Press.
Armstrong, D. (1968). *A materialist theory of mind.* London: Routledge and Kegan Paul.
Aydede, M. (2000) An analysis of pleasure vis à vis pain. *Philosophy and Phenomenological Research* 61(3):537–70.
Aydede, M., and Guzeldere, G. (2002). Some foundational problems in the scientific study of pain. *Philosophy of Science* 69(Supp):S265–83.
Blum, A. (1996). The agony of pain. *Philosophical Inquiry* 18(3/4):117–20.

Byrne, A. (2001). Intentionalism defended. *Philosophical Review* 110(2):199–240.

Dartnall, T. (2001). The pain problem. *Philosophical Psychology* 14(1):95–102.

De Grazia, D. (1991). Pain, suffering, and anxiety in animals and humans. *Theoretical Medicine* 193–211.

———. (1998). Suffering. In E. Craig (ed.), *Routledge Encyclopedia of Philosophy*. London: Routledge.

DeLancey, C. (2002). *Passionate engines: What emotions reveal about mind and artificial intelligence*. New York: Oxford University Press.

Dobbs, D. (2006). A depression switch. *New York Times Magazine*, April 2, 2006:50–55.

Douglas, G. (1998). Why pains are not mental objects. *Philosophical Studies* 91(2):127–48.

Edwards, R. B. (1979). *Pleasures and pains: A theory of qualitative hedonism*. Ithaca: Cornell University Press.

Fernandez, E., and D. C. Turk (1992). Sensory and affective components of pain: Separation and synthesis. *Psychological Bulletin* 112(2):000–000.

Fernandez, E., and T. W. Milburn (1994). Sensory and affective predictors of overall pain and emotions associated with affective pain. *Clinical Journal of Pain* 10(1):000–000.

Fernandez, E., T. S. Clark, and D. Rudick-Davis (1999). A framework for conceptualization and assessment of affective disturbance in pain. In *Handbook of pain syndromes: Biopsychosocial perspectives*.

Fields, H.L. (1999). Pain: An unpleasant topic. *Pain* 6(Suppl.):61–69.

Garfield, J. L. (2001). Pain deproblematized. *Philosophical Psychology* 14(1):103–7.

Gaw, A. (1993). *Culture, ethnicity, and mental illness*. Washington, DC: American Psychiatric Press.

Gordon, R. (1987). *The structure of emotions*. Cambridge: Cambridge University Press.

Grahek, N. (2001). *Feeling pain and being in pain*. Oldenburg, Denmark: BIS-Verlag, University of Oldengurg.

Hall, R. J. (1989). Are pains necessarily unpleasant? *Philosophy and Phenomenological Research* 49(4):643–59.

Hardcastle, V. (1999). *The myth of pain*. Cambridge, MA: MIT Press.

Horwitz, A., and Wakefield, J. (2007). *The loss of sadness: How psychiatry transformed normal sorrow into depressive disorder*. New York: Oxford University Press.

IASP (1986). Pain terms: A list with definitions and notes on pain. *Pain* 3(Suppl):216–21.

James, W. (1884). What is an emotion? *Mind* 9:188–205.

Kirmayer, L. J., and Young, A. (1998). Culture and somatization: Clinical, epidemiological, and ethnographic perspectives. *Psychosomatic Medicine* 60(4):420–30.

Kleinman, A. (1988). *Rethinking psychiatry: From cultural category to personal experience*. New York: Free Press.

Kripke, S. (1980). *Naming and necessity*. Cambridge: Harvard University Press.

Kroll, J., and Bachrach, B. (2005). *The mystic mind: The psychology of medieval mystics and ascetics*. New York: Routledge.

Langsam, H. (1995). Why pains are mental objects. *Journal of Philosophy* 92(6):303–13.

Leighton, S. R. (1986). Unfelt feelings in pain and emotion. *Southern Journal of Philosophy* 24:69–79.

Mayerfield, J. (1999). *Suffering and moral responsibility*. New York: Oxford University Press.

Melzack, R. (1961). The perception of pain. *Scientific American* 204(2):41–49.

Melzack, R., and Wall, P. D. (1965). Pain mechanisms: A new theory. *Science* 150(3699):971–79.

———. (1983). *The challenge of pain*. New York: Basic Books.

Moerman, D. (2002). *Meaning, medicine and the "placebo effect"*. Cambridge: Cambridge University Press.

Montgomery, G., and Kirsch, I. (1996). Mechanisms of placebo pain reduction: An empirical investigation. *Psychological Science* 7(3):174–76.

Nelkin, N. (1994). Reconsidering pain. *Philosophical Psychology* 7(3):325–43.

Noordhof, P. (2001). In pain. *Analysis* 61(2):95–97.

Ploner, M., H. J. Freund, and A. Schnitzler (1999). Pain affect without pain sensation in a patient with a postcentral lesion. *Pain* 81(1/2):000–000.

Price, D. D. (2002). Central neural mechanisms that interrelate sensory and affective dimensions of pain. *Molecular Interventions* 2:392–403.

Radden, J. (2002). Some implications of an embrace: The DSMs, happiness and capability. In John Z. Sadler, ed., *Values and psychiatric classification*. Baltimore: Johns Hopkins University Press.

Russell, D. (1994). Psychiatric diagnosis and the interests of women. In J. Sadler, O. A. Wiggins, and M. Schwartz, eds., *Philosophical perspectives on psychiatric diagnostic classification*. Baltimore: Johns Hopkins University Press.

Ryle, G. (1949). *The concept of mind*. London: Penguin.

Scarry, E. (1985). *The body in pain: The making and unmaking of the world*. New York: Oxford University Press.

Seager, W. (2002). Emotional introspection. *Consciousness and Cognition* 11(4):666–87.

Stich, S. (1978). Beliefs and subdoxastic states. *Philosophy of Science* 45(4):499–518.

Sufka, K. J. (2000). Chronic pain explained. *Brain and Mind* 1:155–79.

Sullivan, M. (1995). Key concepts: Pain. *Philosophy, Psychiatry, and psychology* 2(3):277–80.

Treede, R.-D., D. R. Kenshalo, R. H. Gracely, and A. K. P. Jones (1999). The cortical representation of pain. *Pain* 79:105–11.

Trigg, R. (1970). *Pain and emotion*. Oxford: Clarendon.

Turski, W. G. (1994). *Toward a rationality of emotions: An essay in the philosophy of mind*. Athens: Ohio University Press.

Tye, M. (2002). On the location of pain. *Analysis* 62(2):150–53.

———. (2003). *Consciousness and Persons: Unity and Identity*. Cambridge, MA: MIT Press.

Zubieta, J. K., Bueller, J. A., Jackson, L. R., Scott, D. J., and Xu, Y. (2005). Placebo effects mediated by endogenous opioid activity on μ-opioid receptors. *Journal of Neuroscience* 25(34):7754–62.

8

Lumps and Bumps

Kantian Faculty Psychology, Phrenology, and Twentieth-Century Psychiatric Classification

INFLUENCED BY THE GREAT psychiatric classifiers of the past, Western twentieth-century nosological maps reveal a notable division among the severe conditions known as either disorders (DSM) or psychoses (ICD). The forms of dysfunction associated with mood or affect are separated from those associated with schizophrenia. We may suppose we understand why this is so. Yet many psychological concepts, we know, are a reflection of culture. And it is not only that other cultures mark aspects of the self, personality, disposition, and behavior in terms and categories distinguishable from ours and adhere to contrary mental health norms. In addition, the very broadest categories and divisions by which different mental disorders are classified are in other cultures and traditions radically different from ours, as a recent survey (1990) by Wig has illustrated. Based on an analysis of medical classifications in Asian, African, and Islamic traditions, Wig concludes of the current division of psychoses separating mood or affective disorder from schizophrenia that "such concepts *do not find a recognition* in traditional Third World classifications" (195; my emphasis).

Perhaps not a great deal need be made of this. Any one of several possibilities would permit us to avoid the conclusion that our Western division is arbitrary, misleading, or unacceptably culturebound. Other taxonomies might be wrong, inaccurate, or based on bad science. Or they may be culture-relative: intelligible within the guiding conceptual schemas of the settings that have given rise to them but "untranslatable." Finally, other taxonomies might be a reflection of cultural variation in epidemiology. Yet whatever they are taken to mean, such findings as Wig's disturb; they seem to invite at least an exploration into the historical and theoretical bases for the late-nineteenth-century classification in which our present-day division is rooted. They alert us to the possibility of historical contingencies that might mean

First published in *Philosophy, Psychiatry & Psychology* Vol. 3, No.1 (March 1996) 1-14. Reprinted with permission from Johns Hopkins University Press.

our taxonomy is less than universally applicable, arbitrary, or, worse, reflective of some ideological or normative bias.

That is the impetus for the present essay. We need to trace these divisions to their source in the theories of faculty psychology from the eighteenth century in Europe and America, through whose lens early classifiers such as Kraepelin saw the world. Doing so, we shall discover how the separation of affection from cognition looks to be Eurocentric, as Wig's findings suggest, rather than a natural division, and "modernist," a creation of seventeenth- and eighteenth-century thinking. And we shall see how recognition of this feature of the division was obscured—on the one hand by its transparent familiarity, and on the other by its complex emergence through and relation to faculty psychology, whose own dubious association with phrenology in the nineteenth century led to faculty psychology's ostensible demise.

Diseases of the Intellect and Diseases of the Passions

In the literature on psychiatric classification, classifiers themselves have come to be classified. There are "splitters" who elaborate the differences between disorders and symptom clusters, and "lumpers," who stress the similarities. (Whether these types—splitters and lumpers—reflect styles or fashions of classification linked to a particular era, rather than personal idiosyncracy, is an interesting question but not one explored here.) Kraepelin was a lumper par excellence, and his lumps are reflected in the broad division between manic-depressive disease and dementia praecox. Earlier divisions and "splittings" were brought together by Kraepelin in two categories of psychosis: one for mental disease primarily affecting mood or affect; another for dysfunction or disease primarily affecting cognition and perception. The former, which included hebephrenia, introduced by Hecker in 1871, catatonia (Kahlbaum 1874), dementia simplex (Diem 1905), and dementia paranoides (Ferrarino 1905) became, after a series of revisions to his taxonomy in the several editions of Kraepelin's textbook, "dementia praecox"; later, using Bleuler's term, this was to become the schizophrenias. The latter of the two categories became manic-depressive illness and subsumed under that head both *folie circulaire* (Falgret 1851) and *folie à double forme* (Baillarger 1853), as well as some of the melancholias, the manias, and the milder, single or multiphasic affective disorders. (Involutional melancholia retained its own, distinct category with other conditions of late onset such as the pre-senile and senile dementias.)

This "lumping" effect occurred over several years, only reaching its final shape with the sixth edition of Kraepelin's textbook in 1896. Kraepelin was influenced by disease theory in other fields of medicine and in the analogy between mental conditions and brain diseases, such as general paresis, whose organic basis was recognized and understood. Thus, Kraepelin's "lumps" were not mere classificatory constructs; they named, he believed, disease entities. Dementia praecox and manic-depressive illness were natural kinds, syndromal clusters each with distinct, if as yet undetermined, organic aetiology, and each with a distinctive course and prognosis. Dementia praecox was chronic and unremitting; those suffering manic-depressive illness had more hope for cure, or at least remission. (These are not generalizations supported by late-twentieth-century clinical observation, as has been noted [Bleuler 1978; Angst 1992]).

DSM-I (1918) reflected these divisions between affective and more cognitive defects, and whatever their other advances, in this respect subsequent editions have altered little substantively. They have, however, in nomenclature. First, DSM-IV distinguishes as "mood disorders" major depressive disorder, dysthymic disorder, and bipolar disorder. It is this group that Kraepelin subsumed under the category of "manic-depressive illness," and to which I shall refer as disorders of mood or affect throughout this essay. Kraepelin's dementia praecox became "schizophrenia," and is so classified in DSM-IV; it was also regarded, as we shall see, as a form of nonaffective, and thus of primarily cognitive disorder, and I shall maintain that convention. (Confusingly, "cognitive disorder" in DSM-IV is a classification restricted to deficits of thought or memory whose etiology is known to reside in brain structure or function.) Second, under Adolph Meyer's influence in U.S. psychiatry, the term "reaction" replaced "disease" in DSM-I (and later editions), for Meyer saw mental disorder as psychological or personality reaction to both psychosocial and biological factors. (Interestingly, Jaspers's influential alternative classification extends the term "disease" to schizophrenic and manic-depressive conditions, though withholding it from other "psychopathies" such as obsessional neuroses and what we would classify as personality disorder—and qualifying its use as a merely regulative one, in the Kantian sense [Jaspers 1963].)[1]

The distinction between affective and more cognitive disorders mirrors one of the entrenched—we would now say "modernist"—philosophical classifications that dominated seventeenth-, eighteenth-, and nineteenth-century thought in the West—in particular, the contrast between passion (or emotion) and reason (or cognition). In Kantian theory and subsequent "Kantianism," this duality is associated with—and often reified through—a pervasive faculty psychology. The distinct categories of affect and cognition were understood to reflect distinct, independent functions. Increasingly, these came to be regarded as distinct parts of the human mind; later, they were identified with distinct areas of the brain.

It is plausible to point to Kant as one philosophical source of Kraepelin's lumps. Certainly many others before and after Kant have contributed to the philosophical tradition that relies on these categories, including David Hume. But Kant's work appears likely to have had a special part to play in German nosological development. Not only did Kant develop and explore the fundamental duality between feeling and reason, but also he relied on, formalized, and perpetuated the particular version of faculty psychology on which Kraepelin's analysis of mental diseases seems to have rested. Although Kant's influence on the development of psychology in the nineteenth century is widely acknowledged, as is the influence of faculty psychology on psychiatric thinking in general, the particular aspect of his legacy on abnormal psychology and psychiatric classification explored here has been overlooked.

Before we investigate this Kantian genealogy of psychiatric nosology, a word of explanation about the expression "faculty psychology." Faculty psychology has been around—and has been kicked around—for as long as psychology has existed as an institutional domain. Its history is spectacular, checkered, and confusing: it has been overtly decried but implicitly embraced; it has been attacked as a logical fallacy; it has been allied to a wildly disreputable theory about bumps on the head; it has been eclipsed (rather than refuted) by associationism and experimentalism; it has been redefined and reinvented. Most recently, faculty psychology has made a comeback—albeit chastened definitionally—in some ways less ambitious, in other ways more, but very much alive within the doctrine of functionalism associated with Fodor and his school.

Part of the confusion has arisen over words and meanings. If by faculty psychology we mean knowledge structures—the informational (and perhaps ultimately causal) specification that explains how we acquire knowledge—then many would be glad to endorse faculty psychology. And within the boundaries of that definition—though not always so named—faculty psychology has never disappeared. If, on the other hand, we build more into our definition, insisting as some have, that faculties are associated with particular, independently functioning parts or modules of the brain corresponding in some way to the typology of our psychological abilities, or even that they are localized organs, then we might lose some adherents to the doctrine.[2] If we extended the concept beyond the sphere of cognitive abilities to our emotional and volitional categories, we would lose even more adherents. If we designated "faculty psychology" as not the analysis of how knowledge is "possible," as Kant argues, but as the positing of an additional entity which explains that process, then like most twentieth-century Kant scholars, we should find faculty psychology otiose at best (Wolf 1963; Bennett 1966; Strawson 1966). So the task of uncovering the eighteenth-century and particularly Kantian faculty psychology underlying Kraepelin's nosological schema, and then questioning the legitimacy of its divisions, will require care—care over what is there, and *what is acknowledged to be there*, and over how the expression "faculty psychology" is understood.

The distinction between reason and passion, and the cognitive and affective, was marked in some philosophical traditions which appeared considerably earlier than Kant's. Yet the distinction gained salience and force during the seventeenth and eighteenth centuries and the time when Kant completed his major works. In an earlier era, Blakey (1850) claimed, a more common division existed between understanding and will; in contrast, Jackson (1986) documents an eighteenth-century division of the faculties into imagination, intellect, and memory. With the emergence of modern scientific method came an attempt to distinguish nature from human subjectivity and value; reason was increasingly regarded as the means of discovering the value-free reality of the objective world, and its links with human preferences, values, and feelings were understated. Emotions, too, were recast—as passions, as noncognitive forces beyond their sufferer's control and eluding rational understanding. Moreover, the distinction between reason and passion is now recognized to have been a reflection of genderized thinking: reason was allied to maleness, passion to femaleness.[3] Male and female roles were systematically organized around and understood in terms of this contrast. For example, by the time of Hegel, reason had come to be associated with the public realm, passion with the private and domestic. In addition, this dualism was normative, as reason and the capacities of the cognitive faculties were traits valued beyond passion and the affective faculties.[4]

Of course, neither the duality between reason and passion nor the concept of mental faculties were Kant's exclusive preserve, even in his era. Much of Kant's faculty psychology was derived, for example, from his teacher Christian Wolff (1679–1754). Nonetheless, although Kant only gave voice to the assumptions of an entrenched and pervasive tradition in the one case and an inherited psychological framework in the other, he developed and uniquely enunciated the fundamental duality between feeling and reason (and, later, between the triad of reason, feeling, and volition) through his reliance on faculty psychological thinking. By so doing he succeeded in formalizing, concretizing, and perpetuating the division and unintentionally reifying the affective and cognitive faculties (and volitional or conative faculties) in ways that were to be felt throughout the nineteenth century.

Because of the interactionist view of the relationship between the faculties adopted by Kant, it is at least arguable, and it has been argued, that his analysis avoids this reification (Leary 1982). However, whether or not Kant himself was guilty of reifying the mental faculties and viewing them as isolated, independent entities, it remains true that the subsequent nosological tradition influenced by Kant was guilty of such reification, and so were subsequent forms of "Kantianism."

Kant had an active interest in mental disorder and later wrote about it himself using faculty psychological distinctions.[5] But his earlier, "critical" epistemological writing (dating from the first edition of the *Critique of Pure Reason* in 1781) reveals the categories likely to have influenced early nosology. In the first *Critique*, Kant took on the issues of knowledge, attempting to reconcile two traditions — innate ideas and empiricism — by showing that both sensory and conceptual elements were required to yield an understanding of the world. But to produce that synthesis, he postulated several cognitive faculties. Knowledge was a marriage of the faculties of sensibility and understanding, mediated by the faculty of imagination. In the second — the *Critique of Practical Reason*, where Kant is concerned to explain the moral life — we find him relying on the much-worked set of contrasts pitting reason and the cognitive, a higher part of the self, against a lower part; for Kant, these were the passions, particularly inclination and feeling. The moral life is portrayed as a transcending of the passions by reason in a struggle for domination. This conception, too, has echoes as far back as Plato's model of the divided psyche, although in Greek thinking, for example, emotion was not excluded from the realm of reason in the way it subsequently came to be (Lloyd 1979, 1984; Jagger 1989; Turski 1994). Reason and the cognitive, with their emphasis on generality rather than on particularity and on objectivity rather than on subjectivity, must control and master.

In addition to the duality between reason and passion, Kant also included a third factor: will. Particularly in the *Critique of Judgement* (1790), and most explicitly in the lectures on psychology and in his *Anthropologie* (1800), we find the triad composed first of the faculty of reason (or cognition), next, of passion (or affectivity), and finally, of will, or volition (or conation). Again, Kant was not the first to introduce this tripartite division of faculties — Tetans and several others preceded him (Leary 1982).

The faculty psychological underpinnings associated with the notion of will have already received some attention in work about psychiatric nosology. Twentieth-century philosophy and psychology have each questioned earlier presuppositions about the faculty of volition or will, revealing how the mechanistic models and metaphors of that theory have stood in the way of a useful understanding of the complexities of voluntary action (Ryle 1949; Frankfurt 1971). And in recent writing on psychiatric classification, Berrios and others have shown the same misapprehensions, revealing how the volitional faculty or faculties have influenced thinking about, and particularly classification of, personality disorder to yield the notion of a diseased faculty of will and diseases of the volitional faculty (Werlinder 1978; Smith 1979; Berrios 1993). Our concern here, however, is not the triad distinguishing will from affection and cognition but rather, the duality between passion (or affection) and reason (or cognition), a division that is built more deeply into twentieth-century systems and is more consistently mirrored in Kraepelin's own taxonomy. Kraepelin organized his system in two ways: "general symptomatology" and "forms of mental disease." In the former, we do find the tripartite division or something like it: disturbances of perception and mental elaboration are distinguished from disturbances of emotion, and each of those from disturbances of volition and action. In the latter, however, we can only discern the influence of the division between affection and cognition.

That the intellect and the emotions (and the will) were inevitable, natural provinces in which the world was seen to divide apparently came to be unchallenged. This was as true in England, Scotland, and America as it was on the Continent. Examples of the distinction abound in works of fiction and nonfiction alike, and in sermons and stories, poems and prose. The distinction also appears in the classifications of normal psychology, where we find it in the very titles of texts, such as Bain's *The Senses and the Intellect*, published in England in 1855, and in his *The Emotions and the Will* (1859). Sometimes these references convey the reifying implication, or assumption, that the terms "intellect" and "emotions" refer not merely to theoretical constructs but to independent, localized entities identifiable in the world; sometimes they do not. Often ambiguity remains: we are left in doubt about how far the author intends us to understand the intellect and the emotions to be organic entities as distinct from functional constructs. We also find such divisions, and such ambiguity, within writing on abnormal psychology. At least the *distinction* between cognition and affection appears with the early French psychiatric nosologists Pinel and Esquirol (Pinel 1809; Esquirol 1838). And it appears in the classification of Griesinger, Kraepelin's predecessor, who distinguished disturbances of cognition and thinking from those of mood (and those of will) (Griesinger 1867). Griesinger, however, was not apparently proposing that impairment of the affective, cognitive or volitional functions constituted evidence of separate diseases, afflicting one or the another organic and localized faculty.

Griesinger's view differed from that of his famous pupil in another respect: he believed that these distinguishable forms of impairment indicated different stages of a single illness. This, together with his failure to embrace the strong disease model adopted by Kraepelin, seemed to prevent him from taking the additional, reifying step we find in Kraepelin's work, whereby disease of affective function meant a diseased organ of affect. Whatever their similarities, this contrast between Griesinger's and Kraepelin's use of the faculty psychological categories is noteworthy. Griesinger merely relied on the familiar division between the affective and intellectual to distinguish the kinds of defect found in different phases of mental disease. Kraepelin, too, relied on the division when he undertook the analysis of mental diseases in terms of their general symptomatology, a preparatory exercise that took the first hundred pages of each edition of the textbook. But Kraepelin moved considerably farther toward the notion of diseased affective and intellectual faculties as he went on to identify and classify the syndromal clusters he titled the "Forms of Mental Diseases." These were, for him, natural entities with specific and localized organic features. Like many others in the emerging clinical medicine of the second half of the nineteenth century, Kraepelin appears to have been influenced by Virchow's notion of disease entities. "There are no general, only local, diseases" was Virchow's credo (Virchow 1858).

There are suggestions that the nineteenth-century practice of dividing psychiatric conditions into diseases of affect and diseases of cognition required changes and restrictions in the definition of that hitherto embracing category of "melancholia," which the conditions had begun to receive earlier in the century. Jackson documents a move away from the (cognitive) delusional features previously emphasized in accounts of melancholia toward emphasis on affective symptoms (Jackson 1986).[6] Correspondingly, emphasis on the more cognitive symptoms of delusions, hallucination, and thought disorder came to mark the emergence of the cluster of newly identified dementia praecox symptoms by the end of the century, even though that cluster also included certain deficits or disorders of an affective kind.[7]

The meaning of these restrictions and lumpings into affective and cognitive disorder is made very clear in the writing of the English authority Maudsley (1835–1918), who proposes the presence or absence of delusions as a criterion to distinguish the two (affective and cognitive) varieties of insanity: those where the "mode of feeling or the affective life is chiefly or solely perverted" and those where "ideational or intellectual derangement" predominates (1868:344). But Maudsley, like Griesinger, stopped short of fully reifying the faculty psychological categories he relied on, warning that "the different forms of insanity are *not actual pathological entities*" (369; my emphasis).

Anticipating Maudsley, but equally explicit on this topic, was Rufus Wyman, an American alienist and MD, who was physician superintendent of McLean Asylum, Charlestown (a branch of the Massachusetts General Hospital), between 1818 and 1835. Writers on mental philosophy, Wyman observed, "arrange the mental operations or states under two heads, one of which regards our knowledge, the other our feelings. The former includes the functions of the intellect.... The latter includes the affections, emotions or passions, or the pathetical powers or states." Wyman continues: "This division of the mental states or functions has suggested a corresponding division of mental diseases of the intellect and diseases of the passions" (1830).

After offering a description of typical manifestations of each kind of disease, Wyman remarks that to exhibit clear and exact views of the insane mind, "it seemed necessary to consider separately diseases of the intellect, and diseases of the passions." Yet, he complains, "they are seldom so observed.... The most common form of insanity is a combination of disordered passions, and disordered intellect, in variety and gradations almost infinite" (Wyman 1830). It seemed "necessary," Wyman observes, to consider diseases of the intellect and diseases of the passions separately. He accepted unquestioningly the conceptual fabric of the times, it seems, yet chafed, as a clinician, within the constraints it imposed.

Kraepelin's failure to acknowledge the faculty psychological framework we can attribute to him is revealing in itself. That Kraepelin read Kant avidly while a medical student, he notes in his memoirs; that his system in these respects patterns itself on Griesinger's, which utilizes these divisions, we can readily observe; and that Kraepelin was deeply influenced by his teacher and mentor Wundt, who was an acknowledged Kantian on certain points, he admits.[8] But the rest we must infer.

Several factors explain the hidden and implicit nature of the Kantianism in Kraepelin's classification. One, introduced already, is that the distinction between the cognitive and the affective had become so much a part of the conceptual fabric that its theoretical and conventional nature was rendered invisible. Another is that, as he himself took pains to emphasize, Kraepelin resisted the introduction of theory in his work. He saw himself as engaged in empirical study and believed such study could and should be free of theoretical presuppositions. This was also the goal of much subsequent thinking about psychiatric classification, particularly that culminating in DSM-III and ICD-10 under the influence of Hempel (Sadler, Wiggins, and Schwartz 1994). With our late-twentieth-century understanding of the philosophy of science, we recognize Kraepelin and Hempel to have set a vain standard. But that Kraepelin set such a standard for himself explains a failure to examine or acknowledge the dualities and assumptions on which his taxonomy rested. Finally, by the last quarter of the nineteenth century, when Kraepelin wrote, faculty psychology was not a fashionable doctrine. To understand why, we need to look more closely at the fate of the mental faculties in the hundred years between the publication of Kant's third *Critique* (1790) and Kraepelin's monumental series of editions of *Kompendium der Psychiatrie*, which began in 1893. By tracing the history of faculty psychology this way, we shall also discover the kinds of argument that might address Rufus Wyman's claim that we must necessarily classify the world into diseases of the intellect and diseases of the passions.

Faculty Psychology and Phrenology in the Nineteenth Century

Exploring what happened to faculty psychology after Kant, we find first that it suffered not so much—or not merely—a refutation as an eclipse. Out of the earlier associationist theory grew a powerful movement, whose own genealogy can be traced to Locke, Hume, and other British empiricists: associationist theory and sensationalism combined with experimentalism. This combination left no room for faculty psychology. In addition, faculty psychology acquired a bad reputation. It had come to be associated with Gall, whose explorations into the mental faculties proved too abundant when, after his famous discovery in 1770 that those of his fellows who had good memories also had prominent eyes, he began to associate mental faculties with bumps on the head. Finally, some important conceptual arguments were adduced against faculty psychology—interestingly, and ironically, one of them by Gall himself.

Three sorts of critique to which faculty psychology has been subject will be introduced here, each voiced during this nineteenth-century period. Of these, the first two depend on implications behind the layered and complex notion of faculty psychology and so require further clarification of that term.

Faculty Psychology, Sense 1

Sometimes "faculty psychology" has been understood to imply that localized organs in the brain correspond to the divisions we use to classify human capabilities, as Kraepelin seems to have believed. As a result, critique has been directed toward showing either that no such localized organs are identifiable or that only an interaction between several parts or systems of the brain can account for the particular capabilities we observe in psychology and behavior.

Apart from the disrepute which it suffered through its association with and absurd reduction to phrenological bumps and head measurements, the "localized organs" thesis was challenged during the second half of the nineteenth century by some neurologists. Their observation of continuing capacity despite injury to the regions of the brain identified with particular psychological and behavioral functions seemed to belie the localization thesis (Dupuy 1873). Like the mind, and due to the unity of the mind it was believed to produce, the brain was portrayed not as a collection of parts with special functions but as a singly functioning whole. Disagreements over localization and specialization have endured; moreover, despite progress in understanding the brain's complex systems, room for speculation remains today.

Since it concerns emotional response, one present-day discussion of these faculty psychological claims is of particular pertinence and interest here. From the evidence of localized brain damage and subsequent impairment, Damasio concludes reason and emotion "intersect" in the ventromedial prefrontal cortices and also in the amygdala (Damasio 1994:70). But as the notion of intersection indicates, this is a thesis about neural systems of great interactive complexity; it is hardly faculty psychology in the sense of a localized organ of reason or emotion. A systems analysis and complex interactionism, then, considerably modify the localization interpretation of faculty psychology expressed in Sense 1.

Faculty Psychology, Sense 2

If faculty psychology asserts that separate capabilities correspond to different functional entities, then it confronts a long tradition that challenges faculty psychology as a way of describing and explaining human capabilities, insisting that spurious explanatory value has been attributed to psychological faculties. This sort of critique is linked with associationism, the doctrine which, while it might acknowledge that faculties exist, casts them as constructs out of some more fundamental entities. Associationism grew from the atomistic, sensation-based thinking of British empiricism — plus a scientific tendency toward parsimony. Why postulate mental faculties if we can understand human psychology as the product of accumulated experience, associationists asked? Whether we can so understand psychology remains dubious: the associationists seemed at least to have to postulate one "faculty" of their own, to effect the synthesis from the blooming, buzzing confusion of immediate sensation — the faculty enabling us to form associations. Maybe so, they replied, but at least we are not unnecessarily multiplying empty explanatory entities and propounding an extended form of pseudo-explanation. Although the decline of faculty psychology was based less on logical critique than on the power and popularity of the newer brands of psychology, this latter objection is thought by some to have been the most telling (this is Fodor's judgment, for example). It is a type of critique that is traceable to Molière, with his satires over *virtus dormativa* in the third quarter of the seventeenth century, but also to Locke and Hume.[9] The intricacies and misunderstandings associated with this old quarrel are many (King 1978), but they are not of immediate concern to us here.[10]

Final Critique

A final critique of faculty psychology rests not on the particular interpretation that term receives as much as on the arbitrariness of the divisions implied by particular faculty psychological analyses. And as we saw, it is less in their other faculty psychological implications—although these are important historically—as in the arbitrariness of Kraepelin's divisions where the danger to modern-day psychiatric taxonomy lies.

Within faculty psychology, different divisions were proposed throughout the eighteenth and nineteenth centuries. Alongside Kant and the German faculty psychologists who influenced him with their more widely adopted, classical division between reason and passion (or reason, passion, and will), were alternative schemas, several of which enumerated large numbers of separate divisions. There were the eighteenth-century Scottish faculty psychologists such as Thomas Reid and Dugald Stewart, who postulated two kinds of faculties or "powers": active and intellectual—the former affective and conative, the latter cognitive. The thirty-five active powers included such attributes as a sense of duty, a sense of the ridiculous, and a memory for colors; the thirteen intellectual powers included memory, attention, and moral taste. Most famously—or infamously—there was Gall (1758–1828), with his twenty-seven determinate faculties: Gall, whose misrepresentation by his followers and attachment to the theory of phrenology led subsequent generations of psychologists to denounce faculty psychology.[11] In part perhaps because of its use in medical thinking, to which Rufus Wyman alludes, and more generally because of the power and influence of Kantianism, the division adopted by Kraepelin and the late-nineteenth-century nosologists had come to prevail over competing schemas. But while they were in competition through the end of the eighteenth and the first third of the nineteenth centuries, such alternative schemas offered a challenge to the Kantian separation between reason and passion: perhaps, they suggested, such a division was misleadingly arbitrary and at odds with human experience.

A challenge to the division between affective and cognitive faculties on the basis of arbitrariness would argue that conceptually, emotions and other affective states are either not separable or not rightly divided from cognitive states. And strangely, given that history remembers him as the unabashed reifier of mental faculties, this argument appears to have been introduced into the discussion of mental faculties by Gall. Gall's objection to faculty psychology was not an objection to the model or principle of attributing mental faculties on the basis of recognizable psychological functions or traits as much as an objection to the way in which the divisions had hitherto been made.[12] The real faculties, Gall proposed, were twenty-seven "determinate" faculties modified by "general attributes" such as cognition and affection. These were faculties such as educability, verbal memory, poetry, memory for persons, cunning, and metaphysical depth, to name a few.[13]

Gall directed this conceptual challenge toward the classical, Kantian division between reason and affect; others later developed the same style of argument and directed it toward classifications into several separate cognitive faculties, such as understanding and imagination. Notable among these was Blakey, writing in 1850, whose rejection of mental faculties contained two of the three kinds of critique outlined above. He quoted with approval from Locke in emphasizing that faculty psychology has spurious explanatory value, and he challenged the division between separate cognitive faculties (understanding, imagination, memory, etc.) as arbitrary (Blakey 1850).

If we play on the notion of faculties most common today, associated with the universities, Gall's argument may be said to be "interdisciplinary," at least concerning affective states. The determinate faculties, he noted, were "neutral" with respect to affection, as they were to cognition and conation. That is, none of the determinate faculties belonged exclusively to one category; rather, each belonged to all three.

This kind of objection to the traditional faculty psychological division between affection and cognition was occasionally heard again during the nineteenth century, despite the wide and pervasive influence of the division splitting affection from cognition. In psychology, we find it in the work of Shand, who was an early influence on psychologists such as Stout and McDougall at the beginning of the twentieth century (Shand 1896:1920). Shand held that an emotion includes three elements: a cognitive attitude, a conative attitude, and a feeling attitude. He thus merged the traditional division separating the affective from the cognitive and conative. But Shand's voice was effectively drowned by others, particularly within psychology. Reflecting the influences of positivism, behaviorism, and empiricism on psychology, the more common view that prevailed for the greater part of the present century (the so-called dumb view of emotion [Spelman 1982]), identified emotions with involuntary, noncognitive states such as sensations.

Freudian theory, too, may be seen to forbid a sharp division between the cognitive and the affective. An emotion, for Freud, was intentional, and thus intrinsically cognitive, an affective state over or about its (cognitive) "object." Freud's and Shand's more "interdisciplinary" model, which resists this sharp, division between cognition and emotion, gained influence in both disciplines during the second half of the century. Applied to cognition and affection (and, although it is not our immediate concern here, conation), it is familiar from some late-twentieth-century thinking about emotions within clinical psychology, particularly the work of Beck and his followers. Beck insisted on the cognitive components in all affective states (Beck 1967, 1974, 1976, 1978). On Beck's cognitive theory of depression, the patient's negative view of the world and the future, in the form of cognitive states, causes the accompanying feelings of despair and hopelessness.

Within philosophy, a similar, although noncausal, understanding of emotions has been acknowledged and has acquired support in the second half of this century through the influence of philosophers such as Sartre, Solomon, and Calhoun.[14] Philosophical cognitivist theories of emotion also assert that feelings, emotions, and attitudes involve beliefs. This thesis has at least two distinguishable parts. First, emotions are intentional. It is not merely that these states are stimulated by and dependent on beliefs but that the cognitive states are constitutive of affective states. Affective states are, as philosophers say, intentional states. Second—it is in fact a corollary of the first—their cognitive elements serve to define and differentiate affective states. My response is identified as "regret" rather than "sadness," for example, wholly or in part by the cognitive specification of its object (as a past state of affairs).

The cognitivist account does not reduce affective states to cognitive states. Neither does it permit us to disengage their cognitive elements from affective states, as any classification based on the postulation of distinguishable affective and cognitive faculties would seem to require. Concerned to avoid analyses whereby emotions either (a) reduce to (their constituent) beliefs or (b) are seen to comprise separable belief and feeling elements, some theorists have gone further, recognizing the need to portray emotions in holistic terms. Rather than mere sets of beliefs, or belief-feeling conjuncts, for them, emotions are patterns of attention, perception, and judgment arising from a tacitly held interpretive scheme that encompasses and frames all experience (Rorty 1980; de Sousa 1980; Turski 1994). Like Merleau-Ponty, they recognize emotions to be "wholly bodily and wholly intelligent" (Merleau-Ponty 1962:188).

Recapitulating the links and associations we find in these strange eddies of eighteenth-, nineteenth-, and twentieth-century intellectual history, we see that ironies abound. Through the course of the nineteenth century, the Kantian division between reason and passion came to be reified through the faculty psychology of Kantianism and phrenology. Yet it was none other than Gall, intent on a reifying faculty psychology of his own, who introduced and emphasized the means for a conceptual mending of the reason-passion split.

Practical Corollaries

The challenge of arbitrariness occurs at different levels, including a very practical one. Recent research has implicated the faculty psychological legacy in mental status examinations, where a more holistic approach to psychological functioning would be desirable (Spitzer 1994). Our particular concern is clinical diagnosis, which has had its own quarrel with the arbitrariness of these divisions. After noting that mental diseases tend to be classified in conformity with the distinction between cognitive and affective faculties, Rufus Wyman disputes the difficulty of applying categories based on such a taxonomy, since, as he puts it, the most common form of insanity is a combination of disordered passions and disordered intellect, "in variety and gradations almost infinite." Mental disorder is not "jointed" in nature the way this sharp division between diseases of cognition and diseases of affect suggests. In other words, according to Wyman, we encounter more cases of mixed, schizo-affective conditions than we do the class of either purely cognitive or purely affective disorders.

Notice that this position is compatible with the faculty psychological view which recognizes the distinct faculties of cognition and affection. But it asserts that these faculties are more often each diseased together than diseased singly. Only if we accept conceptual arguments designed to entirely mend the affective-cognitive split, such as were offered by Gall and have been developed by cognitivists, are we required to see the prevalence of mixed, schizo-affective conditions as deeply incompatible with the faculty psychological legacy.

Kraepelin himself, at the practical level, admitted to these problems. No experienced diagnostician would deny, he asserts (1920 ed.), that cases where it seems impossible to arrive at a clear decision, despite extremely careful observation, are "unpleasantly frequent." Similar practical concerns are acknowledged on the part of Sir J. Batty Tuke, who is quoted by Thomas Johnstone in the preface to the English edition of Kraepelin's *Clinical Lectures*: "[A] large class exists in which it is impossible to say whether they are melancholic maniacs or maniacal melancholics" (1904:2).

This sort of challenge over arbitrariness has been reiterated in our own time. First with Gourley and later with Brockington, Kendell has used statistical analysis to challenge the reliability of the diagnostic indicators of the distinction between schizophrenia and mania (Kendell and Gourley 1970; Brockington and Kendell 1979, 1980). Second, using similar methods, and proposing a shared, genetic etiological source to explain the link between affective disorders and schizophrenia, Crow has proposed that we see a continuum extending from unipolar, through bipolar affective illness and schizo-affective psychosis, to typical schizophrenia, with increasing degrees of defect (Crow 1986, 1987). Finally, some interesting longitudinal studies by Jules Angst in Zurich (Angst 1992) reveal the prevalence—even preponderance—of schizo-affective conditions, mixed psychoses between schizophrenia and affective disorders. On the basis of his findings, Angst hypothesizes a continuum in the sense of transitional symptom clusters between schizophrenia and affective disorders—each one, he stresses, accompanied by depressive symptoms. In all, Angst distinguishes five such clusters. Two are affective clusters—one primarily depressive, and one with primarily manic-depressive symptoms. The third, a schizo-affective cluster, consists of manic, depressive, and hallucinatory-paranoid symptoms, and is followed by a fourth cluster consisting of primarily schizophrenic, paranoid hallucinatory syndromes. Angst's fifth cluster is composed of catatonic-hallucinatory symptoms.

Such clinically based analyses and studies as these may lend credence to other and perhaps more ambitious claims like the "unitary psychosis" thesis (Berrios and Beer 1994); at the least, these analyses seem to affirm that accepting the affective-cognitive division will prove as burdensome in diagnostic practice today as Wyman insisted it did for him in 1830.

Our Kantian and eighteenth-century European inheritance is inconvenient. We might doubt the wisdom of accepting it as a basis for a taxonomy of mental disorders and consider embracing a new division such as Angst's if only because, as Wyman found, there's more of a muddle out there than Kraepelin's Kantian schema is equipped to portray. But the Kantian inheritance also seems more deeply arbitrary. We might fear that it will sow conceptual confusion and thus color and distort what we see. Perhaps nothing short of a set of new, holistic categories can capture the fusion of affection and cognition which is human experience and response.

Conclusion

Rendered transparent, on the one hand, by its ubiquity and familiarity, and obscured, on the other hand, by its complex emergence through and relation to faculty psychology and phrenology, the seemingly Eurocentric, modernist and gendered division between affection and cognition was reified through and remains reflected in Kraepelin's influential nosological categories. On disclosure, we have seen it as likely to hinder as help our observation of mental disorder.

Acknowledgments

This essay was originally presented (as "The Kantian Genealogy of the DSMs") at the 1993 Annual Meeting of the Association for the Advancement of Philosophy and Psychiatry; it has been extensively revised in the light of generous and helpful comments from the audience at that meeting, from John Sadler, and from three anonymous readers for *Philosophy, Psychiatry, and Psychology*.

Notes

1. The history of how Kraepelin's great classification came to dominate thinking about mental disorders in the twentieth century is amply documented, and it will not be rehearsed here. See Alexander and Selesnick (1966), Altschule (1965) Ackerknecht (1986), Jackson (1986), Hoff (1992), and Wallace (1994). We know less about where Kraepelin acquired those ideas, beyond the obvious influences he himself has acknowledged, such as Griesinger and Wundt (Kraepelin 1987).

2. Many, for example, would reject Gall's principle that "the brain is composed of as many particular and independent organs as there are fundamental powers of the mind" (1835: VI 308).

3. In the light of twentieth-century epidemiological data about women and certain kinds of affective disorder, notably depression—and, indeed, of Kraepelin's own observation that more women than men suffered manic-depressive conditions—the recognition by feminist historians and philosophers that this is a gendered division seems a particularly unsettling one. While not an argument against the division between reason and passion, or against Kraepelin's division of disease entities, it suggests that the gender and value associations identified here would likely affect, and distort, clinical observation.

4. For a full discussion of the extent to which reason and its contrary passion are gendered concepts, see Lloyd (1979, 1980); an account of the full range of clustered associations that can attach to the dichotomy between emotion and thought is found in Lutz (1989), who documents and deconstructs "emotion" as estrangement, irrational, unintended and uncontrolled act, danger and vulnerability, physicality, natural fact, subjectivity, female, and as value.

5. Kant believed that mental illness could be understood as various cognitive deficiencies—the improper workings of the rational mind. Disorders of the cognitive faculties included madness, which was the inability "to bring ideas into mere coherence necessary for the possibility of experience"; insanity due to a "falsely inventive imagination"; delirium, where a disordered faculty of judgment let the mind be deceived by analogies; and, finally, lunacy, where the patient "disregards all the facts of experience and aspires to principles which can be entirely exempted from the test of experience" (1800: 112–13).

6. The anomalous case of involutional melancholia in Kraepelin's schema remains an exception; it is a condition defined primarily in terms of delusion.

7. That these "cognitive" symptoms may have come to have a prominence in our understanding of schizophrenia at odds with clinical findings has been noted and demonstrated in quite recent studies (Andreason 1987).

8. Wundt accepted a Kantian notion of the faculty of apperception, the psychological function of which connects sensory data to yield knowledge of the external world. Without apperception, Wundt insisted, there could be no knowledge of science at all (Hoff 1992).

9. Thus Hume wryly remarks of philosophers' "invention" of the words "faculty" and "occult quality": "they only need say that any phaenomenon, which puzzles them, arises from a faculty or an occult quality, and there is an end of all dispute and enquiry upon the matter" (Hume 1739:224).

10. Interestingly, modern-day functionalists believe there is a perfectly adequate answer to this challenge. As represented by Fodor (1983), functionalism welcomes the suggestion that mental faculties are to be functionally individuated and avoids ontological commitment for its (primarily cognitive) faculties precisely by defining them in terms of their causal role: thus, in Fodor's words "the language faculty is whatever is the normal cause of one's ability to speak" (26).

11. After its emergence as the most promising psychological and physiological science of its day, respected and acknowledged in medical and academic circles throughout Europe and America, phrenology suffered a decline so extreme as to take the reputation of its founder, Gall, with it. This was in great part due to its popularity, and, particularly, the popularized version of its principles expounded by Gall's pupil Spurzheim (1776–1832). For an account of the fate of Gall and his ideas in the hands of Spurzheim, see de Giustino (1975).

12. This was in part because he had changed the model or conception of mental faculties. Gall was looking at psychological, particularly personality, traits as the starting point for his postulation of psychological faculties, whereas the faculty psychology we associate with Wolff and Kant, for example, looked at immediately observable psychological capacities and functions.

13. This distinction of Gall's between general attributes and mental faculties corresponds to Fodor's between "vertical" and "horizontal" faculties, respectively (Fodor 1983).

14. See Sartre (1948); Solomon (1977 [a], [b]); Rorty (1980); de Sousa (1980, 1987); Calhoun (1980, 1984); and Gordon (1986).

References

Ackerknecht, E. 1986. *Short history of psychiatry.* New York: Hafner.

Alexander, F., and S. Selesnick. 1966. *The history of psychiatry.* London: Allen and Unwin.

Altschule, M. 1965. *Roots of modern psychiatry: Essays in the history of psychiatry.* 2nd ed. New York: Grune and Stratton.

Andreasen, N. C. 1987. Schizophrenia and schizophreniform disorders. In *Diagnosis and classification in psychiatry: A critical appraisal of DSM-III,* ed. G. L. Tischler. Cambridge: Cambridge University Press.

Angst, J. 1993. Today's perspective on Kraepelin's nosology of endogenous psychoses. *European Archives of Psychiatry and Clinical Neuroscience* 2243:164–70.

Beck, A. 1967. *Depression: Clinical, experimental and theoretical aspects.* New York: Hoeber.

———. 1974. The development of depression: A cognitive model. In *The Psychology of depression: Contemporary theory and research,* ed R. J. Friedman and M. M. Katz. Washington, DC: Winston.

———. 1976. *Cognitive therapy and the emotional disorders.* New York: International Universities Press.

———. 1978. *Cognitive theories of depression.* Philadelphia: University of Pennsylvania Press.

Bennett, J. 1966. *Kant's analytic.* Cambridge: Cambridge University Press.

Berrios, G. E. 1984. Descriptive psychopathology: Conceptual and historical aspects. *Psychological Medicine* 14:303–33.

———. 1993. European views on personality disorders: a conceptual history. *Comprehensive Psychiatry* 43:14–30.

Berrios, G. E., and D. Beer. 1994. The notion of unitary psychosis: A conceptual history. *History of Psychiatry* 5:13–36.

Blakey, R. 1850. *History of the philosophy of mind*. London: Longman.

Bleuler, E. 1978. *The schizophrenic disorders: Long-term patient and family studies*. Trans. S. M. Clemens. New Haven: Yale University Press.

Brockington, I. F., and R. E. Kendell. 1979. The distinction between the affective psychoses and schizophrenia. *British Journal of Psychiatry* 135:243–48.

Calhoun, C. 1980. The Humean moral sentiment: A unique feeling. *Southwestern Journal of Philosophy* 11:69–78.

———. 1984. Cognitive emotions? In *What is an emotion?*, ed. C. Calhoun and R. Solomon. Oxford: Oxford University Press.

Crow, T. J. 1986. The continuum of psychosis and its implication for the structure of the gene. *British Journal of Psychiatry* 144:419–29.

———. 1987. Psychosis as a continuum and the virogene concept. *British Medical Bulletin* 43:754–67.

de Guistino, D. 1975. *Conquest of mind: Phrenology and Victorian social thought*. London: Croom Helm.

Esquirol, J. E. D. 1838. *Des malades mentales*. Paris: Balliere.

Fodor, Jerry. 1983. *The modularity of the mind*. Cambridge: MIT Press.

Frankfurt, H. 1971. Freedom of the will and the concept of a person. *Journal of Philosophy* 14:5–20.

Gall, F. J. 1835. *On the functions of the brain and of each of its parts*. Ed. Nahum Capen. Trans. Winslow Lewis Jr. Boston, n.p.

Griesinger, W. 1965 [1867]. *Mental pathology and therapeutics*. A facsimile of the English edition of 1867. New York: Hafner.

Hoff, P. 1992. Emil Kraepelin and philosophy. In *Phenomenology, language and schizophrenia*, ed. M. Spritzer et al. New York: Springer-Verlag.

Hume, D. 1739. *A treatise of human nature*. Oxford: Oxford University Press.

Jackendoff, R. 1987. *Consciousness and the computational mind*. Cambridge: MIT Press.

Jackson, S. W. 1986. *Melancholia and depression: From Hippocratic times to modern times*. New Haven; Yale University Press.

Jagger, A. 1992. Love and knowledge: Emotion in feminist epistemology. In *Women, knowledge, and reality: Explorations in feminist philosophy*, ed. A. Garry and M. Pearsall. New York: Routledge.

Jaspers, K. 1963 [1913]. *General psychopathology*. Trans. from the 7th German edition by J. Hoenig and M. W. Hamilton. Chicago: University of Chicago Press.

Kant, I. 1952 [1790]. *Critique of the faculty of judgement*. Trans. J. C. Meredith. Oxford: Oxford University Press.

———. 1964 [1781]. *Critique of pure reason*. Trans. Norman Kemp Smith. London: Macmillan.

———. 1978 [1798]. *Anthropologie*. 2nd ed. Konigsberg: F. Nicolovius.

———. 1993 [1788]. *Critique of practical reason*. 3rd ed. Trans. Lewis White Beck. New York: Macmillan.

Kendell, R. E., and I. F. Brockington. 1980. The identification of disease entities and the relationship between schizophrenic and affective psychoses. *British Journal of Psychiatry* 3:24–31.

Kendell, R. E., and J. Gourlay. 1970. The distinction between the affective psychoses and schizophrenia. *British Journal of Psychiatry* 117:261–70.

King, L. 1978. *The philosophy of medicine: The early eighteenth century*. Cambridge: Harvard University Press.

Kraepelin, E. 1883. *Compendium der psychiatrie*. Leipzig: Abel. First edition of what later became *Lehrbuch der psychiatrie*.

——. 1899. *Lehrbuch der psychiatrie*. Leipzig: Abel.

——. 1904. *Lectures on clinical psychiatry*. Authorized Translation. Rev. and ed. Thomas Johnstone. New York: Hafner.

——. 1987. *Memoirs*. Edited by H. Hippius, G. Peters, and D. Ploog. Berlin: Springer-Verlag.

Leary, D. 1982. Immanuel Kant and the development of modern psychiatry. In *The problematic science: Psychology in nineteenth-century throught*, ed. W. R. Woodward and M. G. Ash. New York: Praeger.

Lloyd, G. 1979. The man of reason. *Metaphilosophy* 10:18–37.

——. 1984. The man of reason: "Male" and "female." In *Western philosophy*. Minneapolis: University of Minnesota Press.

Lutz, C. 1986. Emotion, thought, and estrangement: Emotion as cultural category. *Cultural Anthropology* 1:287–309.

Merleau-Ponty, M. 1962 [1945]. *Phenomenology of perception*. Trans. C. Smith. London: Routledge.

Pinel, P. 1809. *Traite medico-philosophique sur l'alienation mentale*. 2nd ed. Paris: J. A. Brosson.

Ryle, G. 1949. *The concept of mind*. London: Hutchinson.

Sadler, J., O. Wiggins, and M. Schwartz, eds. 1994. *Philosophical perspectives on psychiatric diagnostic classification*. Baltimore: Johns Hopkins University Press.

Sartre, J-P. 1948 [1939]. *The Emotions: Outline of a theory*. Trans. B. Frechtman. New York: Philosophical Library.

Shand, A. 1896. Character and the emotions. *Mind* 5(n.s.): 218.

——. 1920. *The foundations of character*. London: Macmillan.

Solomon, R. 1977(a). The logic of emotion. *Nous* 11:41–49.

——. 1977(b). *The passions*. New York: Doubleday.

Smith, R. 1979. Mental disorder, criminal responsibility and the social history of theories of volition. *Psychological Medicine* 9:13–19.

Spelman, E. V. 1992. Anger and insubordination. In *Women, knowledge, and reality: Explorations in feminist philosophy*, ed. A. Garry and M. Pearsall. New York: Routledge.

Spitzer, M. 1994. The basis of psychiatric diagnosis. In *Philosophical perspectives on psychiatric diagnostic classification*, ed. J. Sadler, O. Wiggins, and M. Schwartz. Baltimore: Johns Hopkins University Press.

Strawson, P. 1966. *The bounds of sense*. London: Methuen.

Virchow, R. 1971 [1858]. *Cellular pathology as based upon physiological and pathological histology*. Trans. F. Chance. New York: Dover.

Wallace, E. 1994. Psychiatry and its nosology: A historico-philosophical overview. In *Philosophical perspectives on psychiatric diagnostic classification*, ed. J. Sadler, O. Wiggins, and M. Schwartz. Baltimore: Johns Hopkins University Press.

Werlinder, H. 1978. *Psychopathy: A history of the concepts—Analysis of the origin and development of a family of concepts in psychopathology*. Stockholm: Almqust and Wiksell International.

Wig, N. 1990. The Third World perspective on psychiatric diagnosis and classification. In *Sources and traditions of classification in psychiatry*, ed. N. Sartorius et al. Toronto: Hogrefe and Huber.

Wolf, C. 1732. *Psychologica empirica methodo scientifica pertractata*. Frankfurt, n.p.

Wolff, R. P. 1967. *Kant's theory of mental activity*. Cambridge: Harvard University Press.

Wyman, R. 1830. A discourse on mental philosophy as connected with mental disease. Delivered before the Massachusetts Medical Society, Boston. Reprinted in R. Hunter and I. Macalpine. *Three hundred years of psychiatry 1535–1860*. (New York: Oxford University Press, 1970), 810–11.

9

Love and Loss in Freud's "Mourning and Melancholia"

A Rereading

"Mourning and Melancholia" is one of Freud's most revered works. Yet it is deeply ambiguous and opaque. In particular, we leave it unsure of the extent to which melancholic states are part of the human condition, rather than rare forms of mental disorder. It is clear that melancholia is a condition of loss, but mystery attaches to the question of what is lost and whether adult states relive or merely mimic earlier infantile experiences. In addition, we remain uncertain of the relation between melancholia and hysteria, as of that between melancholia and mania. The notions of the ego-ideal, the super-ego, and the part played by ambivalence also remain vague and unresolved. I would be the first to grant the resonance and charm of the essay. Who can resist the image of the shadow of the object falling across the ego, or fail to be intrigued that "a man must become ill before he can discover truth" (Freud 1917:156)?[1] Here, however, I want to examine not only the brilliance and appeal of "Mourning and Melancholia" but its strange opacity.

In the following pages is a discussion of the ambiguities in this text which allow us to wonder whether Freud's melancholia is a universal propensity or even a universal experience. I note two later and influential psychoanalytic theories, those of Melanie Klein and Julia Kristeva, which develop on, and exploit, this ambiguity. I also identify what is innovative in Freud's essay. Some importantly new ways of portraying melancholia are to be found in "Mourning and Melancholia," which diverge quite markedly both from the psychiatric thinking of Freud's own era and from the much earlier, more literary tradition of writing about melancholy. But alongside these new ideas are older associations and assumptions apparently derived from that earlier tradition. The curious compound that results, I suggest, accounts for some of the puzzling and elusive aspects of the piece. (It probably also accounts for some of its special appeal.)

Previously published in *The Analytic Freud*, edited by Michael Levin. New York: Routledge, 2000, pp. 211-230. Reprinted with permission of the publisher, Taylor & Francis Ltd.

Innovations such as Freud's bold theory of narcisissism and introjection have been widely adopted by later neo-Freudian thinkers, and widely credited. But less commonly recognized to be Freud's original contribution are two constituents of melancholic states, loss and self-loathing. In addition to offering a diagnosis of the essay's opacity, I draw attention to these insufficiently acknowledged innovations in "Mourning and Melancholia."

The following discussion falls into three sections. In section 1, I discuss the seeming ambiguity that has allowed neo-Freudian interpretations to portray melancholia as very widespread or even a universal propensity, and I note some of the implications of that reading. In section 2, I identify aspects of Freud's essay that seem to harken back to earlier traditions about melancholy and melancholic states. While not new to Freud, these elements reflected a tradition absent in the writing of Freud's contemporaries, I show. The purpose of this discussion is twofold. By identifying the residue from past traditions on melancholy, I will be able to isolate those of Freud's own innovations which I believe have been neglected. These, the notions of melancholia as a condition of loss and as comprising self-critical attitudes, are explored in section 3. Despite its echoes of past writing on melancholy, Freud's was also a throughgoing reconstruction of melancholia, and I want to elucidate the extent and depth of that reconstructive effort. Also in section 3, I note the influence of Freud's loss model on twentieth-century analyses of melancholia and clinical depression, analyses in which it has been appropriated, but misunderstood and even trivialized.

One last preliminary: until rather recent attention by contemporary theorists outside analytic philosophy and psychoanalysis, commentaries on Freud's writing have more often quoted from than thoroughly analysed "Mourning and Melancholia." Philosophers have not provided much by way of systematic analysis of this particular text, either, in comparison with their close examination of other writing of Freud's, and the philosophical analyses that do exist differ widely in their view, and use, of this work. For those who cast melancholia as a form of neurotic or unresolved grief, and a failure of proper mourning, Freud's is an essay about melancholia understood as a rare, pathological condition (Mitchell 1974; Cavell 1993). For those who read the introjection, identification, and narcissism Freud introduces here as a feature of all mourning, it is an essay about narcissism and (normal) mourning (Rorty, 2000). For those directing their attention to the splitting of the ego proposed by Freud as the source of later melancholic states, it is merely the first intimation of the super-ego concept (Wollheim 1971).

Those within the fields of literary, feminist, and cultural studies have shown a welcome interest in Freud's essay, and their recent work provides a sustained and illuminating commentary (Schiesari 1992; Enterline 1995). Nonetheless, this work also, I show, fails to recognize and acknowledge the extent of Freud's innovative reconstructive effort.

1. Melancholia as Loosely Bounded and Ambiguous

In drawing attention to the blurring of the boundaries around melancholia, let me comment briefly on Freud's term "melancholiac". The essay begins with a warning. Even in descriptive psychiatry, Freud remarks, "the definition of melancholia is uncertain; it takes on various clinical forms...that *do not seem definitely to warrant reduction to a unity*" (Freud 1917:152: my emphasis). In light of this admission, Freud may be judged to speak of "melancholiacs" incautiously. Uncertain over the extent to which melancholia constituted a recognizable unity or "syndrome" in the medical or psychiatric sense, and understood as a permanent or semipermanent ascription, we might today suppose he would better have referred to "those suffering melancholic states". Such niceties may not have troubled Freud or his translators as much as they do us, however. In the psychiatry of his time, the term "melancholiac" had begun to acquire a narrower meaning. But in the long tradition of writing about melancholy that preceded Freud, "melancholiac" refers indifferently to those suffering occasional melancholic states and to those permanently afflicted with a more serious disorder.

Several aspects of Freud's account seem to contribute to a blurring of the difference between melancholic states as rare disorders and as more common propensities. To understand these, it is important to distinguish the object of melancholic states from their occasion: Freud appears to adhere to a structure whereby an affective state is over or about some object (which may itself be unconscious), while often precipitated by another state of affairs that is merely its immediate occasion. First, then, the "object" of melancholic states is vaguely specified, suggesting that our primal narcissistic object choices dispose us all to subsequent melancholic states; second, the occasions of melancholia are not only (adult) loss of a loved one but every possible kind of human suffering; finally, melancholia is somehow linked with two other universal propensities—mourning and conscience.

Who or What Is the Object?

To understand the notion of the object in Freud's analysis, it is necessary to examine the machinations by which, according to Freud, love of another may be transformed into melancholic self-accusation. The narrative of loss and transformation in "Mourning and Melancholia" goes this way:

> First there existed an object-choice, the libido had attached itself to a certain person; then, owing to a real injury or disappointment concerned with the loved person, this object relationship was undermined. Then...the free libido was withdrawn into the ego and not directed to another object...[where]...it served simply to establish an *identification* of the ego with the abandoned object. Thus the shadow of the object fell upon the ego, so that the latter could henceforth be criticized by a special mental faculty like an object, like the forsaken object. In this way the loss of the object became transformed into a loss in the ego, and the conflict between the ego and the loved person transformed into a cleavage between the criticizing faculty of the ego and the ego as altered by the identification. (Freud 1917:159)

Who or what is the object? Freud's specification is loose, even careless. In the case of the "deserted bride," he points out, it may be the missing groom (155); in other cases, it may be an ideal or an idea rather than a person (155). What is more, we cannot always know what the object is, because it may be unconscious.

This is an important qualification. As in mourning, melancholia starts with the loss of an object of love, but *the patient may not consciously recognize what that object is.* Then, "This, indeed, might be so even when the patient was aware of the loss giving rise to the melancholia, that is when he knows whom he has lost but not *what* it is he has lost in them" (155). In contradistinction to mourning, in which "there is nothing unconscious about the loss," Freud concludes, melancholia is "in some way" related to loss of an unconscious love-object (155). Moreover, he later emphasizes that this unconscious aspect of melancholic states is of the greatest importance: what is conscious, a conflict as he says between one part of the ego "and its self-criticizing faculty," is insignificant. What is "essential" is the unconscious part (168).

Is the object ever—or always—the mother or the image of the mother? Remarks in the succeeding pages of Freud's essay suggest that if the object is not the mother, then nonetheless the process of narcissistic identification which allows the ego to incorporate the other in melancholia is a process in every way analogous to "the way in which the ego first adopts its object"—that is, first adopts its mother-image. The ego "wishes to incorporate this object into itself, and the method by which it would do so, in this oral or cannibalistic state, is by devouring it" (169). This process described as the "regression from narcissistic object choice to narcissism" (161), which marks melancholia, is also found in the progression by which the ego "first adopts an object"—that is, in normal object-relational, or interpersonal, development.

Melancholia is "in some way" related to loss of an unconscious love-object, but how? What remains opaque is the extent to which adult suffering is not only like the early loss of the mother but also over, or about, that loss. Adult melancholia at the least mimics, but perhaps even reenacts, the psychic incorporation of the mother by the infant.[2] If all melancholiacs resort to regression from narcissistic object-choice to narcissism, then our primal narcissistic object-choices apparently dispose us all to subsequent melancholic states. The distinction blurs between melancholy as part of the human condition and melancholia as an infrequently occurring mental disorder.

What Are the Occasions for Melancholic States?

Freud's essay introduces a sustained analogy between normal mourning over the loss of a loved one and melancholia, and interpreters of Freud have sometimes cast melancholia as a form of unresolved and inappropriate grief. But melancholic states arise on occasions both related *and unrelated* to adult grief. Indeed, Freud asserts that, for the most part, the occasions giving rise to melancholia extend beyond the clear case of a loss by death. They include "all those situations of being wounded, hurt, neglected, out of favour, or disappointed, which can import opposite feelings of love and hate into the relationship or reinforce an already existing ambivalence" (Freud 1917:161). Almost any kind of disappointment may rekindle the infantile experience of loss that marks melancholia.

This is merely to extensively rewrite the range of possible occasions for melancholia; it is not, of course, to say we all experience melancholic states when such occasions arise. Nonetheless, even for Freud, melancholic states are now potentially associated with almost every kind of human suffering, and this passage encourages us to regard melancholia as an aspect of the human condition. As adults we all experience some form of suffering and distress, and we all have experienced early loss, the enactment of which may be occasioned by such suffering and distress.

Melancholia is portrayed as a pathological condition. But mourning is also a quasi-pathological condition, Freud makes clear. That mourning does not *seem* to us pathological, he insists, "is really only because we know so well how to explain [it]" (Freud 1917:153). If a tendency to melancholic states parallels normal mourning in being an aspect of the human condition, then partial recognition of this deeper parallel between mourning and melancholia—not only are they each conditions of loss with earily similar psychic and behavioural manifestations, they are also each universal, though pathological, propensities—may have motivated Freud's development of other comparisons between the two states of melancholia and mourning which I explore in section 3 of this essay.

Freud wrote little on melancholia after the 1917 essay. At the outset of "Mourning and Melancholia," he notes that the various clinical forms of melancholia in descriptive psychiatry "do not seem definitely to warrant reduction to a unity" (152). We can surmise that this doubt over its unitary status dampened his interest in the alleged syndrome of melancholia. If melancholia were without clear boundaries, then it would not readily submit to close theoretical analysis of the kind to which Freud would wish to subject it. When melancholia recurs in his writing (it is in *The Ego and the Id*, published in 1923), the processes that were earlier used to explain it are recognized to have much broader application. The universal feature allied to the early splitting and introjection revived in melancholia has become moral development, conscience, and character. *Character formation results from the splitting of the ego and the emergence of the super-ego.*

Looking back at the time of his earlier work, Freud now remarks:

> we did not [then] appreciate the full significance of this process [splitting and introjection] and did not know *how common and how typical it is*. Since then we have come to understand that this kind of substitution has a great share in determining the form taken by the ego and that it makes an essential contribution towards building up what is called its "character." (Freud 1923:18; my emphasis).

By this later analysis, a distinction not remarked in the 1917 essay provides Freud a means of separating the melancholiac from the normal person. Early loss and early object relationships are the source of all adult character, but the nature and resolution of that loss determines what kind of character ensures. In the normal person the super-ego is present, but not unduly strong. In the melancholiac, by contrast, are the self-critical attitudes which received such stress in the 1917 essay. Now "the excessively strong super-ego...rages against the ego with the merciless violence" (Freud 1923:43). This criterion for separating the melancholiac is absent from the earlier work; moreover, because Freud attributes conscience to the same processes explaining melancholic states, even in this later work melancholic states seem at risk of being seen as a common and central part of our human condition—as common and central, perhaps, as is the conscience that springs from the same source.

Klein and Kristeva

Thus far I have employed an interpretive contrast between presenting melancholic states or propensities as rare and pathological and as common and normal. But this alignment is explicitly collapsed by Freud when he regards mourning as both common and pathological or quasi-pathological. And in the influential neo-Freudian interpretations and developments of Melanie Klein (dating from the 1930s and 1940s) and Julia Kristeva (1970s), we find melancholia, also, portrayed as common while still pathological.

The roots of the developmental stage that Klein termed the "depressive position," a stage she judges of paramount importance to psychological development, can be found in Freud's discussion of mourning and melancholia and in Freudian ideas of introjection and identification. The depressive position is the distressed state with which the infant responds to the loss associated with the early, and inevitable, separation from the mother such as that occurring during weaning. The experience of all infants, the depressive position is nonetheless a neurotic or disordered condition of which Klein remarks that "it is a melancholia in *statu nascendi*" (Klein 1935:345).[3]

The depressive position, then, which is sometimes reactivated in adult life, is universally experienced. We are all mothered and weaned, we are all frustrated and disappointed by, and ambivalent over, our first "object." Moreover, not only other adult neuroses and excessive grief but all and any adult mourning reactivate the depressive states of infancy. Echoing Freud, Klein remarks that the mourner is in fact ill, "but because this state of mind is common and seems so natural to us, we do not call mourning an illness" (Klein 1935:354).[4] This means that not one but two different aspects of the Kleinian analysis suggest melancholia or depression as universal states or propensities: the infantile experience of the "depressive position" and the "illness" undergone in all adult mourning.

Carrying forward Freud's best-known innovation in "Mourning and Melancholia", his theory of projective identification, or introjection, Klein employed the same concepts as Freud in describing the infant's psychic incorporation of the mother. But Klein also elaborated. Hatred and rage, as well as love, are directed toward the other; bad as well as good aspects of the other are incorporated. In later writing, Klein still represented feelings as clustered around the depressive position, but the depressive position became an affective structure, reflecting differences in ego integration. (Psychoanalytic theories have continued to cast the depressive position as a mode of relating to objects based on ego integration. Rather than an infantile stage to be overcome, the depressive position is a relatively mature psychic achievement. Fluctuation between the depressive and more primitive paranoid-schizoid modes, on this elaboration, is a central factor in psychic life [Bion 1963].)

In a controversial development, Julia Kristeva also inherits Freud's model of infantile "mourning" for the maternal object. But Kristeva's analysis construes this experience of early loss in such a way as to render melancholia or depression a universal state or propensity, at least for women. We are all alike subject to the loss of the object, she explains, and thus inclined, as Freud believed, to incorporate or "introject" the other. But due to the identification with the same-sex mother peculiar to the female infant, combined with a universal matricidal drive, there is a proneness to depression peculiar to women. The "inversion of matricidal drive," which in the male child is transformed into misogyny, takes a different course in women. For the female infant, "the hatred I bear her [the mother] is not oriented toward the outside but is locked up within myself. There is no hatred, only an implosive mood that walls itself in and kills me secretly, very slowly, through permanent bitterness, bouts of sadness" (Kristeva 1989:29).

For the woman, on Kristeva's account, avoidance of this painful depression may be impossible in heterosexual development. The extent to which homosexual adjustment is women's only way to avoid melancholia and depression is left ambiguous. Nonetheless, the broad meaning of Kristeva's analysis is apparent: for women, at least, melancholic states may be next to inevitable.

Freud's essay invites speculation over the commonness or even universality of melancholic states, and these Kleinian and Kristevian developments on Freud's work offer a certain resolution on the matter. Melancholic states are human nature for Klein; for Kristeva, they are women's nature. Although I cannot deal with them in any detail here, the implications of adopting either analysis are clearly profound. If melancholic states are part of human nature, then two features attaching to this century's conception of clinical depression seem to be thrown into question—the "medicalization," by which it is construed on the model of symptom clusters or syndromes in clinical medicine, and its gender association. Even if melancholic and depressive states are part of women's nature, as Kristeva suggests, then at least their construction as medical diseases and as abnormal must become problematic.

2.   The Older Tradition

In allowing the distinction between common and uncommon states to remain unresolved, Freud's work echoes a long, earlier tradition of writing on melancholy, melancholia, and melancholic states. (These three variations are not distinguished in any systematic way in that tradition.) There, rather than a limited disorder in some adults, melancholy is often portrayed as a condition common to all, an "inbred malady in every one of us," in Robert Burton's words.

And, while a remarkably innovative work, "Mourning and Melancholia" is strongly evocative of earlier writing on melancholia. Freud's exemplar of the melancholiac was Hamlet, and, as this suggests, he was familiar with the rich vein of European traditions around melancholy. (Freud was an attentive student of European literary traditions, reading several languages, including Shakespeare's and Burton's English.)[5] These traditions originated in the humoral theories of the Greek physicians and flowered in works of the Renaissance such as Ficino's *Three Books on Life*, Burton's *Anatomy of Melancholy*, and literary and artistic representations like Hamlet and Dürer's engravings on melancholia.[6]

At least three features of this older tradition appear to have found their way into Freud's essay. The first: the categories of melancholy and melancholia elude definition. The second: melancholy is characterized by groundless fear and sadness (fear and sadness "without cause"). The third: melancholic states have a glamorous aspect. The melancholy man (and it is a man, as contemporary writing has emphasized [Radden 1987; Schiesari 1992]) shows artistic genius and intellectual greatness; moreover, the melancholy man knows states of passion and exaltation not allowed to other mortals. I shall take these three characteristics in turn and show how they match, and may be reflected in, Freud's thinking in "Mourning and Melancholia."

Melancholic States as Undefinable

Consider the passage quoted earlier in which Freud remarks that the definition of melancholia is "uncertain" and that melancholia takes on various clinical forms, which "do not seem definitely to warrant reduction to a unity" (Freud 1917:152). This phrasing affirms so much in past writing on melancholy that it reads like a self-conscious allusion to such writing. Again and again, we find this theme of melancholy eluding capture because of the multitude and variety of its forms. (The tower of Babel, Burton remarks, "never yielded such confusion of tongues as this Chaos of Melancholy doth variety of symptoms" [Burton 1621:395]).

Related to this issue of melancholy's elusiveness is ambiguity in the term "melancholy." We in the twenty-first century are inclined to separate melancholia as a mental disorder from melancholy as a temporary or more long-lasting state or trait in an otherwise normal person. Yet until the end of the nineteenth century saw the advent of psychiatry in something like the form we know today, this distinction was rarely stressed in writing about melancholy and melancholic states. It is not merely that the borders between mental disorder and normalcy were recognized to be vague and uncertain. Nor is it that floridly disordered states were not encountered, or not included, in the category of melancholia, for they were. It is, rather, that, due to certain unifying factors, on the one hand, and in the absence of a set of disciplinary interests and purposes associated with psychiatry, on the other, the divisions and categories that today seem so obvious often went without remark. The humoral theories served to unite all forms of melancholy as disorders and manifestations of the black bile (Foucault 1973; Jackson 1986). In a late-nineteenth-century shift the hitherto encompassing category of melancholy divided, leaving a sharper distinction between the despondent moods and temperamental differences of essentially normal experience, on the one hand, and the clinical disorder known as melancholia or clinical depression, on the other. But this shift resulted only when a complex set of distinctions such as those arising from seventeenth- and eighteenth-century faculty psychology combined with developments in medical thinking and practice to lay the base for a distinct science of psychiatry (Radden 1987, 1996).

Just as the distinction between melancholy as part of the human condition and melancholy as an infrequently occurring mental disorder is blurred in the earlier, pre-psychiatric, and pre-Freudian tradition, so "Mourning and Melancholia" reaffirms the elusive and encompassing nature of melancholy expressed in the older tradition.

Fear and Sadness without Cause and the
Unconscious Object of Loss

The second them from pre-Freudian writing on melancholy that seems to make its way into "Mourning and Melancholia" concerns the traditional characterization of melancholy as groundless fear and sadness. (To speak of fear and sadness "without cause" is not to deny that the fear and sadness were occasioned by something, but to deny that their "object"—that is, what these feelings are about or over—is known to their subject.) Freud's analysis of melancholia as a state of loss parallels these older accounts in two ways: it emphasizes the subjective and affective, and it introduces a phenomenologically objectless mental state, a mood.

First, in contrast to the prevailing psychiatric ideas of his time, Freud's analysis of melancholia as a condition of loss is a subjective and affective one. The somatic and behavioral elements of melancholia rather than the subjectivity of melancholic states were more commonly emphasized in the psychiatric thinking of Freud's contemporaries. Freud's recognition of the growing emphasis on the behavioral and somatic in his time is conveyed by his opening remark that melancholia takes on a variety of clinical forms, some of them suggesting somatic rather than "psychogenic" affections (1917:152). But his qualification aside, Freud's analysis nonetheless offers melancholia as a "psychogenic affection," characterized, just as Burton's had been, by references to its sufferer's affective subjectivity.

The second parallel is between Freud's particular, and I will insist, new, emphasis on the subjectivity of melancholia in terms of *loss* and earlier accounts in terms of fear and sadness without cause. The characterization of melancholy subjectivity as fear and sadness without cause is found as early as Hippocratic and Aristotelian writing and is a recurring theme for as long as a century after Burton.[7]

Familiar and long lived as they are, however, fear and sadness without cause introduce ambiguity as symptoms of melancholy. In particular, the phrase "without cause" is a confusing one. Does it mean without any cause, or is it elliptical for without sufficient cause, it is necessary to ask? Some commentators have read Burton and those who followed him to mean the latter (without sufficient cause), rather than the former (without cause) (Jackson 1986). Others have emphasized the former, and in so doing highlighted that the subjective state is a nebulous and pervasive mood rather than an affective state with any more sharply delineated cognitive content.

The philosophical distinction sometimes maintained between moods and emotions is the one identified here. If fear and sadness are *without sufficient cause*, then they are still accompanied by "intentional objects"—that is, they are over or about something which the sufferer understands to be so or to exist (Gordon 1986). But their objects do not appear to warrant the degree of feeling attributed to them. (An example would be excessive fear over a clearly minimal danger, or excessive distress over a trifling event.) In contrast, if melancholic fear and sadness are *entirely without cause*, then they are not over or about anything in particular (in one sense, they are so pervasive as to seem rightly judged about everything). If so, then they are moods. This distinction is sharpened by focus on the cognitive content of emotions that came with Brentano's theory of intentionality at the end of the nineteenth century (Brentano 1874 [1955]). (Brentano's theory, it is worth remembering, was one with which Freud was familiar.)[8] Nonetheless, its retrospective application suggests that Renaissance and later writing about melancholia is concerned as much with nebulous, pervasive, and nonintentional *moods* of fear and sadness (no cause) as with the *emotions* of fear and sadness in excess of their occasions (without sufficient cause).

In "Mourning and Melancholia," we saw, Freud makes an important qualification about the object of the loss suffered in melancholia: the object may be unconscious in melancholia, as may some aspect of the object's *meaning*. By allowing this, Freud has linked his analysis with traditional accounts of melancholic states. There is something, the sufferer knows not what, toward which his nebulous mood of loss is directed. An affective mood state, *a sense of loss without a (consciously recognized) cause*, now makes up part of melancholic subjectivity. (I emphasize this to point out that Freud is not suggesting that every aspect of the loss is unconscious. Some aspect, the sense or *mood* of loss, and even sometimes some recognition of its object, may be an item of conscious awareness.)

Freud characterizes the symptoms of melancholia as "painful dejection, abrogation of interest in the outside world, loss of the capacity to love, inhibition of all activity, a lowering of the self-regarding feelings to a degree that finds utterance in self-reproaches and self-revilings, and culminates in a delusional expectation of punishment" (1917:153). Of the characterizations of the earlier eras, only the affective state of sadness ("painful dejection") remains part of that subjectivity. With his strong—and innovative—emphasis on melancholic subjectivity characterized by *moods of (often) objectless loss*, rather than groundless fear, and in addition to groundless sadness or dejection, Freud has at the same time revived the earlier Renaissance tradition and rung significant changes upon it.

Brilliance and Inspiration and the Compensations of Mania

Melancholy's link with genius, creative energy, and exalted moods and states is the third feature of earlier accounts that can be found in Freud's essay. This is an alignment that traces back to Aristotelian writing.[9] Reawakened and transformed during the Renaissance, the "glorification of melancholy" gathered strength from the new category of the man of genius. It waned during the early eighteenth century, only to be revived with the Romantic movement. Now the suffering of melancholy was again associated with greatness; again, it was idealized, and the melancholy man was one who felt more deeply, saw more clearly, and came closer to the sublime than ordinary men (Klibansky et al. 1964).

By the time Freud wrote "Mourning and Melancholia," much of the luster had left melancholia. Nonetheless, as Juliana Schiesari has pointed out, there are signs that it was only with difficulty that Freud relinquished the associations with inspiration, genius, and exaltation (Schiesari 1992). For Freud, as for the earlier tradition, Schiesari argues, the figure of the melancholic is a male one. (Schiesari's own theory is that in the gender economy of our patriarchal structures men suffer melancholia while women merely mourn. Other contemporary theorists such as Jacques Lacan and Luce Irigaray have also precluded women from the satisfactions of melancholic expression, although for slightly different reasons than Schiesari's).[10] For Freud also, the glamorous Hamlet is the developed case example. The interests of patriarchal ideology and of psychoanalysis, remarks Schiesari, are both served by the mad prince:

> When Freud refers to Hamlet, he signals the fact that a well-known *male* character such as Hamlet is indeed [in contrast to the unnamed female patients referred to in the essay], a *nameable* subject and a subject of literary and psychoanalytic interest precisely because the canon legitimizes his "neurosis" as something *grand*. (Schiesari 1992:59; my emphasis)

For Freud, finally, melancholia provides inspiration and a privileged knowledge. The melancholic "has a keener eye for the truth than others who are not melancholic" (1917:156). This and similar remarks of Freud's seem on their face most notable examples of an uncritical embrace of the earlier Romantic traditions. On the other hand, the observation rings curiously true, today, in light of empirical studies showing the unsurpassed realism of the mildly depressed and the consistent link between accurate appraisal, mild depression, and low self-esteem (Taylor and Brown 1988).

The boundary separating melancholia, the mental disorder, from other dejected states and melancholy dispositions was sharpened with the advent of modern psychiatry in the late nineteenth century. And as this occurred, something of the tradition of associating melancholy with creative energy and brilliance reemerged as a focus on the connection between melancholy and the more enlivened states of mania. "Cyclical insanity," otherwise known as *folie à double forme* or manic depression, became a central category.

Freud also is alert to the suggestion that manic moods are melancholia's twin and compensation. We see this in remarks on mania at the end of "Mourning and Melancholia." These remarks constitute no more than a "first sounding" (Freud 1917:164), and Freud calls off the investigation in the very last paragraph of the essay. Moreover, he earlier resists the assumption that all melancholia has the capacity to transform into the joy, triumph, and exultation which, as he says, "form the normal counterparts of mania" (Freud 1917:164). Nonetheless, the essay ends with an allusion to mania. Narcissism remains, but melancholia will end. After the work of melancholia is completed, mania is possible (Freud 1917:169–70). So, supported this time by the more orthodox German psychiatry of his day, Freud also seems to glimpse in mania the balance and compensation for the bereft states of melancholia.

3. The New

Several aspects of "Mourning and Melancholia" deserve the title of innovations, both relative to Freud's own earlier writing and when judged from the perspective of psychiatric writing about melancholia in his own time. Best known is the elaborate theory of narcissism, identification, decathexis, and ego "splitting." But his notion of melancholia as loss is another innovation, as is his association between melancholia and expressions of self-loathing and self-criticism, and the following discussion focuses primarily on the identification of melancholia with loss and self-loathing, as it is the status of these, *as innovations*, which has been ignored.

Loss and Self-Loathing

Most contemporary writing about melancholia and depression, not only within psychoanalysis but in much contemporary psychology and psychiatry as well, presupposes the link between melancholia and loss. Recent theoretical attention to melancholy and depression within feminist psychoanalysis, literary criticism, and cultural studies, for example, treats loss as an inevitable component of those conditions (Kristeva 1982; Irigaray 1991; Schiesari 1992; Enterline 1995). A passage from Julia Kristeva will serve to illustrate: depression, she remarks in *Black Sun*, "is the hidden face of Narcissus.... I discover the antecedents to my current breakdown in a loss, death, or grief over someone or something that I once loved" (Kristeva 1989:5).

But to a great extent this modern framing is attributable to Freud. Melancholia takes on stronger connotations of loss, as it does themes of self-loathing, only in — and after — Freud's essay. Indeed, through its emphasis on the theme of loss and self-critical attitudes, Freud's writing on melancholia may be seen to have *reconstructed* melancholic states. From a condition of humoral imbalance and a mood of despondency, melancholia has become a frame of mind characterized by a loss of something — and also by self-critical attitudes. As the result of Freud's work, the latter aspects of melancholic subjectivity, hitherto granted little importance, become attenuated, elaborated, and central. Far from the nebulous and pervasive mood states of Elizabethan melancholy, Freud's melancholiac experiences self-directed emotional attitudes of criticism and reproach which Freud regards as definitive of melancholia. Dissatisfaction with the self on moral grounds, as he says, is "in the clinical picture...the most outstanding feature" (Freud 1917:157).

My thesis here concerning Freud's reconstruction of melancholia as loss and self-loathing represents a significant departure from some interpretations. Recent writing on melancholy and melancholia from cultural and literary studies, in particular, explicitly notes and emphasizes an alignment between melancholy, melancholia, and loss (or lack) in the earlier traditions going back to the Renaissance. There is some force to this interpretation. Undoubtedly for Ficino and Burton, as also for Shakespeare, melancholy was a narcissistic condition; moreover, it was recognized to parallel normal grieving. Nonetheless, while conceding certain similar themes in earlier writing, I think it a mistake to overemphasize these similarities. It is implausible because Freud's ideas on loss in "Mourning and Melancholia" can be shown to derive seamlessly from earlier work on melancholia and loss in the letters to his friend, Wilhelm Fliess, written in 1902, and these earlier ideas bear less resemblance to Renaissance accounts of melancholy. It is also wrong because it depends on an inexact translation whereby "loss" (literally, in German, *Verlust*) becomes "lack," which is not an equivalent of "loss" or of *Verlust*. (And this is a difference, we shall see, which is significant.) The influence of Renaissance accounts of melancholy and melancholic states is not absent from "Mourning and Melancholia". In various ways, his essay reveals Freud's familiarity with the category of melancholy known through the writing of earlier eras. But in the case of his notion of melancholia as a condition of loss, Freud's idea is his own.

The theme of loss in "Mourning and Melancholia" is foreshadowed in comments on melancholia to be found in letters to Fliess. This series of letters to Fliess during their intense ten-year correspondence and friendship in which they shared observations and hypotheses are a valuable source for Freud's earliest theoretical developments. In light of these letters, we can identify two stages in Freud's thinking about melancholia, loss, and mourning. In the first stage, found in letters written in 1902, Freud identifies the loss he sees in melancholia as a lack of sexual excitement. Normal mourning is the longing for something lost; in melancholia, this something lost is "loss in instinctual life." Thus he says, "melancholia consists in mourning over a loss of libido."[11]

At this early stage, Freud identifies the loss of libido or (sexual) "anaesthesia," which at the first stage he sees as inviting melancholia, as predominantly a characteristic of women—although for reasons of cultural and not biological difference. (Women, he observes to Fliess, become "anaesthetic" because they are brought up to repress sexual feeling and because they are often required to engage in loveless sex.) Despite this, and the fact that the medical psychiatry of his time had already established a gender link between women and melancholia or depression, Freud does not in "Mourning and Melancholia" present melancholia as a women's disorder. (He does not do so, arguably, precisely because of the influence on his thinking of the Renaissance tradition in which melancholia is associated with the man of genius.)

By the 1917 paper, Freud has developed both his notions of projection and identification and his understanding of narcissism. Now, two new themes predominate. First, melancholia represents loss of the "object"—that is, another person: the mother or mother-image. Second, self-accusation and self-hatred have become a *central characteristic* of the melancholic state, and the sole characteristic allowing us to distinguish melancholia from normal mourning (Freud 1917:153). The attitudes of self-accusation and self-abasement represent a form of rage toward the once-loved object, now redirected toward one part of the ego by another. Having incorporated the object, the self attacks that object within it. The conflict between the ego and the loved person or object, as he puts it, results in a schism "between the criticizing faculty of the ego and the ego as altered by the identification" (159). (This last conclusion Freud derives from his observation that there is a quality of disingenuousness about the protestations of the patient: "we get the key to the clinical picture—by perceiving that the self-reproaches are reproaches against a loved object which have been shifted on to the patient's own ego" [158].)

The parallel between the despondent frame of mind of melancholia and the frame of mind found in the normal mourning occasioned by the loss of loved ones was not Freud's invention, as I have said. We know that writing about melancholy had repeatedly drawn such parallels, at least since Elizabethan times. In addition, Freud attributes to his follower Karl Abraham recognition of the importance of this parallel between melancholia and normal mourning. Yet the standard comparsion likening the despondent mood and characteristic dispositions of sorrow, lethargy, and low interest in normal mourning to melancholic states was merely Freud's starting point. He constructed a more elaborate parallel. The mourner has *lost* something (someone, that is) and grieves his loss; thus, the melancholic also must have suffered a loss.

The operative term is "loss," notice, not merely "lack." The two words (loss and lack) are sometimes interchanged in contemporary discussions of these ideas, such as Schiesari's. But this represents a distortion of Freud's intent and leads, I believe, to a failure to recognize the originality and importance of Freud's loss theory of melancholia. Let us see why, and consider James and Alix Strachey's decision to render the German *Verlust* not into the English "lack" but into "loss" in the English edition of Freud's work which—importantly, since Freud was a fluent speaker and reader of English—Freud himself authorized and oversaw.

The German *Verlust* was Freud's consistent choice in passages discussing this aspect of his analysis. This word translates literally as "loss," and "loss" was the Stracheys' consistent choice, as a glance at these passages in the German will reveal. The German *fehlen* corresponds most closely to our "lack" in the English sense of "lacking" something ("I lack courage", "Something was lacking"). *Fehlen* is not found in these German passages, nor does "lack" occur in the translation.

By contrasting the two English words "lack" and "loss," we can perhaps see some of what was at stake in the Stracheys' choice. We may *lack* many things, including qualities (tact) and particulars (money) and including things we have never had (stamina). But we *lose* particulars (persons, sets of keys); and we only lose particulars we have once possessed, in some sense of that term. The loss we associate with grief is loss, not lack. A particular love, once known to us ("possessed"), is gone. The loss Freud attributes to the melancholic parallels the loss of mourning. Although not always recognized as such by its sufferer, the object lost(the mother or mother-image) is a particular, once possessed. Recognizing this, the Stracheys and Freud relied on the English word best able to convey not only the literal meaning of *Verlust* but also the broader theoretical context within which the term was embedded: Freud's sustained analogy with mourning. (For illumination on the sensitivity with which James and Alix Strachey approached the task of translating Freud, see Meisel and Kendrick 1985.)

We can now summarize the two stages of Freud's lack/loss theory. At first, in the 1895 unpublished letter and writing to Fliess, Freud proposes that the lack, or want, is of libido. There is no hint here that the object of lack is personified (i.e., that it is a loss). Only later in the essay does he complete the parallel with mourning; now the lost object is not libido but another person, or, more exactly, the distorted idea of another person (the *imago*).

The formation of Freud's loss theory of melancholia may now be traced. The parallel with mourning, itself triggered by a long literary tradition on the subjective mood states of melancholy and also, apparently, by Abraham's work, directs Freud through a series of recognitions: first that melancholia must be identified in terms of lack, eventually that it must be the loss of someone. Only then come the ideas of self-accusation and self-loathing which form a central and much-repeated theme in "Mourning and Melancholia."

These attitudes, also, are something rather new. They are to be found neither in the clinical psychiatry of Freud's own time, I shall now demonstrate, nor in the writing on melancholic states from earlier eras.

Self-accusation and self-loathing are absent from the portrait of melancholia found in the elaborate case summaries of Kraepelin and in more-casual clinical references from his era. Kraepelin notes self-accusation as a feature of *one* kind of melancholia, but it is not treated as a central feature. (In the more severe melancholia gravis, Kraepelin notes, ideas of sin and self-reproach are often present, but so also are ideas of persecution. The less severe melancholia simplex, which is arguably closer to the kind of disorder suffered by the patients Freud describes in his essay, is for Kraepelin characterized as much by world-loathing as by self-loathing: "*everything* has become disagreeable to him [the melancholic patient]" [1921:76; my emphasis].) Kraepelin's findings are mirrored in William James's more casual observations on melancholic states from the same era. James identifies what he calls the sense of sin as only one of three themes found in milder forms of melancholia (those, that is, that "fall short of real insanity") in *The Varieties of Religious Experience*: he lists as well the vanity of mortal things and the fear of the universe (James 1902:158). So rather than a central theme, self-accusation is merely one of three possible themes characterizing the melancholic frame of mind.

Although it has widely been accepted as central to depressive subjectivity as the result of Freud's influence, self-accusation is not a theme associated with melancholic subjectivity in writing from the Renaissance. Garrulous, complaining, self-obsessed these melancholiacs were, but not self-hating. In a tradition deriving from as far back as the Greek physicians and Aristotle, the subjective moods of melancholy and melancholia were identified as groundless mood states of sadness and fear; less-central characteristics included disinterest, despair, inertia, and dullness, moreover, but not self-loathing.

Interestingly, recent cross-cultural studies of depression from our own era also fail to reveal any emphasis on guilt and self-accusation in the symptom idiom of other cultures (Ihsan Al-Issa 1955; Kleinman and Good 1986).

We must conclude that Freud's listing of the "distinguishing mental features" of melancholia in "Mourning and Melancholia" includes some that are widely accepted, consonant both with more recent and empirical, and older and more literary, accounts, and others that are new. "Painful dejection, abrogation of interest in the outside world, loss of the capacity to love, inhibition of all activity" (Freud 1917:153)—these correspond to the traditional and modern psychiatric notions of melancholic subjectivity. But "a lowering of the self-regarding feelings to a degree that finds utterance in self-reproaches and self-revilings, and culminates in a delusional expectation of punishment," do not. These attitudes of self-loathing and self-reproach became and remain today central parts of the symptom description and symptom idiom of melancholia and depression, transforming melancholic and depressive subjectivity. And it is to Freud that a great measure of this transformation is due.

The influence of Freud's loss analysis of melancholia is also evident in later twentieth-century analyses, where it is a commonplace in medical, behavioral, and psychoanalytic theories of depression that "loss" is a constituent of depression. But Freud's account of that loss is today identified with clinical depression, an oversimplified loss model wherein loss conveys any lack, any disappointment, any sorrow, and any source of suffering. There is no place for Freud's separation of loss from lack: any lack is a "loss." The influential "learned helplessness" model of depression is identified as a loss theory (Seligman 1975), for example. But although it is trivially true that helplessness corresponds to a deprivation of opportunity to act, the state of helplessness identified by Seligman implies no loss of a personified object of the kind intended by Freud. In other theories, moreover, depression is defined as a loss of self-esteem, of self, of relationships, of agency, and even, rendering such accounts entirely circular, a loss of hedonic mood states.

Conclusion

In this essay I have explored some of the unresolved and confusing elements in Freud's essay on mourning and melancholia, offering an explanation of those elements, and of the essay's resonant appeal, by analyzing it as the effort of a brilliant innovator enmeshed in his history and culture. Much in the essay is breathtakingly new, I have argued; the rest is breathtakingly old.

The rich complexity of "Mourning and Melancholia" stimulated theoretical writing important even today within object-relations psychology and psychoanalysis. Melanie Klein's "depressive position" remains a central category within these fields, and Julia Kristeva's recent loss analysis of women's depression is today influential among feminist theorists and those working in cultural studies. Nonetheless, the fate of melancholia as a mental disorder has not been what Freud's innovative and striking reframing at the start of this century deserved. Increasingly, even in his own era, melancholia the category came to be subsumed under and eclipsed by the broader diagnostic grouping of clinical depression. With this change, the connotations from earlier eras' writing on melancholy dwindled in medical and psychiatric analyses. Left, was a disorder of abject despair. Clinical depression had become a condition identified with feminine subjectivity and with a set of metaphors conveying oppression, wretchedness, apathy, and, others have suggested, mute suffering. It also came to be a condition identified by its bodily and behavioral symptoms.

The fortunes of the two particular features of melancholia discussed here, loss and attitudes of self-criticism and self-loathing, have differed widely. Evidence from cross-cultural psychiatry suggests that it is a culture-bound and thus an apparently fragile association by which Freud found melancholia to express itself in attitudes of self-loathing and self-criticism. Yet self-loathing and self-criticism continue to be elevated to the status of central symptoms in accounts of clinical depression. Loss, on the other hand, has been transformed. In twentieth-century writing about Freud's essay, as we have seen, a failure to distinguish the narrower "loss" from the broader "lack" has led to a misinterpretation of Freud's analysis and obscured its originality. More significantly, an oversimplified loss model wherein depression is understood in terms of loss and loss now conveys a lack or want of any kind, has come to dominate a range of theories of clinical depression. A failure to honor Freud's careful separation of loss from lack renders many of these claims little better than trivially true.

Acknowledgments

I am grateful to Michael Levine, an anonymous contributor to *The Analytic Freud*, Joan Fordyce, Neal Bruss, David Flesche, and members of PHAEDRA—Jane Martin, Janet Farrell-Smith, Ann Diller, Beebe Kipp Nelson, and Barbara Thayer-Bacon—for helpful criticism and commentary on this essay.

Notes

1. All page references are to the *Standard Edition* (Freud. 1917 [1967]). That there is no authoritative interpretation of Freud's essay is part of my thesis. For the sake of those readers who may not be familiar with this work, however, let me provide one brief interpretation of

it. When some adults (melancholiacs) experience despondency and inertia notably like that experienced during mourning, a disappointment or loss undergone in adult life has reignited an unresolved early loss. That unresolved early loss was marked by the psychic incorporation of the simultaneously loved and hated other, or mother. There was a splitting of the ego or self into two parts, one judging and the other judged, and as a result the melancholiac, unlike the mourner, reveals attitudes of self-loathing and self-criticism.

2. For useful explication of the notions of narcissism, "splitting," and projective identification introduced in this passage, see Bruss (1986), Bollas (1987), Wollheim (1984, 1971), Cavell (1993), Mitchell (1974).

3. Klein's (often-criticized) development of these ideas goes like this: "In the very first months of the baby's existence it has sadistic impulses.... The development of the infant is governed by the mechanisms of introjection and projection. From the beginning the ego introjects objects "good" and "bad," for both of which the mother's breast is the prototype — for good objects when the child obtains it, for bad ones when it fails him. But it is because the baby projects its own aggression on to these objects that it feels them to be "bad" and not only in that they frustrate its desires: the child conceives of them as actually dangerous — persecutors who it fears will devour it...compassing its destruction by all the means which sadism can devise. These imagoes, which are a phantastically distorted picture of the real objects upon which they are based, become installed not only in the outside world, but, by a process of incorporation, also within the ego" (Klein 1935:262).

4. Klein's account of mourning is as follows: "Mourning the subject goes through a modified and transitory manic-depressive state and overcomes it, thus repeating, though in different circumstances and with different manifestations, the processes which the child normally goes through in his early development" (Klein 1935:354).

5. Did Freud read Burton? I surmise that he probably did, based on his love of English literature (he apparently restricted his leisure reading to English for a decade of his life) and his affinity for Shakespeare. See Jones (1953–57 [1961]); see also Gilman, Birmele, Geller, and Greenberg (1994) and Gay (1990, especially ch 4, "Reading Freud through Freud's Reading"). But he would not need to have read Burton to have absorbed the features of the tradition discussed in this essay; they are recurrent and inescapable themes in a great part of the best in English literature from Chaucer to the novelists and poets of the nineteenth century.

6. For a thorough discussion of the ideas in this tradition, see Klibansky et al. (1964) and Jackson (1986).

7. Well into the seventeenth century, we find Thomas Willis offering an explanation of the fear and sadness of melancholia without challenging their centrality as symptoms. (This is in *Two Discourses Concerning the Souls of Brutes*, published in 1672.)

8. Freud is known to have attended more than one philosophy course taught by Brentano at the University of Vienna between 1874 and 1875 (Jones 1953–57 [1961]:59–60).

9. It is believed to have probably been one of Aristotle's followers, most likely Theophrastus, who penned the famous section on melancholy in the *Problematica*, which begins by asking why all brilliant men suffer melancholia.

10. For example, Lacan (1982), Irigaray (1991).

11. Even earlier than these letters to Fliess, Freud analogized melancholia to mourning and introduced the notion of a loss of libido. In an unpublished letter dated January 1895, Ernest Jones informs us, Freud defined melancholia as grief at some "loss," probably of libido, and emphasized the link between melancholia and sexual anaesthesia. Reference to this letter is found in Jones (1953 [1961]). In it Freud offers a quasi-physiological explanation of the link between melancholia and sexual anaesthesia, which Jones conveys as follows: "When the libido loses strength, energy is correspondingly withdrawn from associated "neurones," and the pain of melancholia is due to the dissolving of the associations" (245).

References

Bion, W. (1963) *Elements in Psycho-Analysis*. London: Maresfield Reprints.
Bollas, C. (1987) *The Shadow of the Object: Psychoanalysis of the Unthought Known*. New York: Columbia University Press.
Brentano, F. (1968) *Psychologie von empirischen Standpunkt*, ed. Kraus. Hamburg: F. Meiner.
Bruss, N. (1986) "Validation in Psychoanalysis, and 'Projective Identification.'" *Semiotica* 60(1/2):129–92.
Burton, R. (1621[1927]) *An Anatomy of Melancholy*, ed. Floyd Dell and Paul Jordan-Smith. New York: Farrar and Rinehart.
Cavell, M. (1993) *The Psychoanalytic Mind: From Freud to Philosophy*. Cambridge: Harvard University Press.
Enterline, L. (1995) *The Tears of Narcissus: Melancholia and Masculinity in Early Modern Writing*. Stanford: Stanford University Press.
Ficino, M. (1489 [1989]) *Three Books on Life: A Critical Edition and Translation* by Carol Kaske and John Clark. Binghampton, NY: Medieval and Renaissance Texts and Studies.
Foucault, M. (1973) *Madness and Civilization: A History of Madness in the Age of Reason*. New York: Vintage.
Freud, S. (1917 [1957]) "Mourning and Melancholia". In *Collected Papers*, vol. 4, pp. 152–70. Authorized translation under the supervision of Joan Rivière. London: Hogarth Press.
——. (1923 [1966]) *The Ego and the Id*. trans. Joan Rivière; rev. and newly ed. James Strachey. London: Hogarth.
Gay, P. (1990) *Reading Freud: Explorations and Entertainments*. New Haven: Yale University Press.
Gilman, S., Birmele, J., Geller, J., and Greenberg, V.D. (eds) (1994) *Reading Freud's Reading*. New York: New York University Press.
Gordon, R. (1986) "The Passivity of Emotions." *Philosophical Review* 95:371–92.
Ihsan Al-Issa (1995) *Handbook of Culture and Mental Illness*. Madison, CT: International Universities Press.
Irigaray, L. (1991) *The Irigaray Reader*. Ed. and intro. Margaret Whitford. Oxford: Blackwell.
Jackson, S. (1986) *Melancholia and Depression*. New Haven: Yale University Press.
James, W. (1902) *The Varieties of Religious Experience*. New York: Modern Library.
Jones, E. (1957 [1961]) *The Life and Work of Sigmund Freud*. ed. and abr. Lionel Trilling and Steven Marcus. New York: Basic Books.
Klein, M. (1935 [1975]) *Love, Guilt and Reparation and Other Works*. London: Hogarth.
Kleinman, A., and Good, B. (1986) (eds) *Culture and Depression: Studies in the Anthropology and Cross-Cultural Psychiatry of Affect and Disorder*. Berkeley: University of California Press.
Klibansky, R., Panofsky, E., and Saxl, F. (1964) *Saturn and Melancholy: Studies in the History of Natural Philosophy, History and Art*. New York: Basic Books.
Kraepelin, E. (1899) *Lehrbuch der Psychiatrie*. Leipzig: Abel.
——. (1904) *Lectures on Clinical Psychiatry*. Authorized translation. New York: Hafner.
——. (1921) *Manic Depressive Insanity and Paranoia*. Trans. R. Mary Barclay from the 8th ed. of the *Textbook of Psychiatry*. vols 3 and 4. Edinburgh: E. and S. Livingstone.
Kristeva, J. (1982) *Powers of Horror: An Essay in Abjection*. Trans. Leon Roudiez. New York: Columbia University Press.
——. (1989) *Black Sun: Depression and Melancholy*. Trans. Leon Roudiez. New York: Columbia University Press.
Lacan, J. (1982) *Feminine Sexuality: Jacques Lacan and the École Freudienne*. Trans. Jacqueline Rose. Ed. Juliet Mitchell and Jacqueline Rose. New York: Norton.

Lloyd, G. (1979) "The Man of Reason." *Metaphilosophy* 10(1) (Jan.):18–37.

———. (1984) *The Man of Reason: "Male" and "Female" in Western Philosophy*. Minnesota: University of Minnesota Press.

Lutz, C. (1986) "Emotion, Thought, and Estrangement: Emotion as Cultural Category." *Cultural Anthropology* 1:287–309.

Meisel, P., and Kendrick. W. (eds) (1985) *Bloomsbury/Freud: The Letters of James and Alix Strachey 1924–1925*. New York: Basic Books.

Mitchell, J. (1974) *Psychoanalysis and Feminism: Freud, Reich, Laing and Women*. New York: Basic Books.

Radden, J. (1987) "Melancholy and Melancholia." In David Michael Levin (ed.), *Pathologies of the Modern Self: Postmodern Studies in Narcissism, Schizophrenia and Depression*. New York: New York University Press.

———. (1996) "Lumps and Bumps: Kantian Faculty Psychology, Phrenology, and Twentieth Century Psychiatric Classification," *Philosophy, Psychiatry, and Psychology* 3(1):1–14.

———. (1998) "Melancholy, Melancholia and Depression: Contemporary Reflections". Unpublished ms.

Rarty, A. O. 2000. "Freud on Unconscious Affects, Mourning and the Erotic Mind." In *The Analytic Freud: Philosophy and Psychoanalysis*, ed. M. P. Levine. London: Routledge.

Schiesari, J. (1992) *The Gendering of Melancholia: Feminism, Psychoanalysis, and the Symbolics of Loss in Renaissance Literature*. Ithaca, NY: Cornell University Press.

Seligman, M. (1975) *Helplessness: On Depression, Development, and Death*. New York: W. H. Freeman.

Taylor, Shelley, and Jonathan Brown (1988) "Illusion and Well-Being: A Social Psychological Perspective on Mental Health." *Psychological Bulletin* 103:193–210.

Willis, T. (1683) *Two Discourses Concerning the Souls of Brutes*. Trans. S. Pordage. London: T. Dring, C. Harper and J. Leigh.

Wollheim, R. (1971) *Sigmund Freud*. New York: Viking.

———. (1984) *The Thread of Life*. Cambridge: Harvard University Press.

PART III

SUBJECTIVITY

*Melancholy as Subjective, Sad,
and Apprehensive Moods*

10

My Symptoms, Myself

Reading Mental Illness Memoirs
for Identity Assumptions

Portrayals of the relationship between self and psychological symptoms in first-person narratives about psychiatric illness and recovery are conspicuously varied.[1] Much of this variation will obviously be attributable to the symptoms themselves—not only their degree of disabling severity but also their nature more generally. Some of these states and traits are more abhorrent and painful than others, for example, and some affect moods, capabilities, and responses more central to self and self identity than others—as, I shall argue, does depression.

An additional source of these variations is the beliefs and assumptions such narratives reveal about the symptoms of disorder and their relation to personal or self-identity. In some narratives, for example, the narrators' symptoms are depicted as emanating from alien, sometimes diabolical, sources of agency outside the self, while in others, narrators, "identify with" their symptoms as closely as they do their other experiential states.

Taking more and less explicit form, and acknowledged in varying degrees, such variations can be discerned in many mental illness memoirs, including those from today's mental health care consumers' movements. These movements have changed the landscape of mental health care in recent years. They reflect burgeoning participation by the users of mental health services in their care, treatment, and self definition. They acknowledge the importance of the voices of "survivors" and those who are in "recovery," the efforts of "mad pride" movements modeled on other liberation movements, and an alignment with other disabilities. They offer and emphasize new, positive models of recovery for those with psychiatric illness.

Drawing on some of these recent narratives along with earlier memoirs, I here illustrate some assumptions people have held about the relation between self and symptoms, while showing the epistemological complexity of such an inquiry. I then

First published in *Depression and Narrative*, edited by Hillary Clark. New York: SUNY Press (2008). Reprinted with permission from SUNY Press.

note implicit models and analogies found in the recent narratives and explore some of their theoretical implications. And I point to particular aspects of depression, and hence depression narratives, as they intersect with these ideas.

The term "symptoms" here refers to the manifestations in psychological states and behavioral dispositions of what to observers appear to be psychopathology.[2] Although the term is primarily a medical one, and forms part of a disease model in which symptoms (like signs) are the causal byproducts of an underlying disease process, "symptom" is also used in more theoretically innocent ways and occurs in some mental illness memoirs that explicitly reject further medical presuppositions. This simpler use will be employed here until otherwise stated.

Illness Narratives, Some Variations

The approach I am employing here sets apart the symptoms and episodes described in these accounts from their framing presuppositions and assumptions, explicit and implicit. This is not always an easy contrast to maintain, we shall see, but two pre-modern narratives will provide an initial illustration. The fifteenth-century *Book of Margery Kempe* is an account (dictated, for she was illiterate) by a troubled, pious woman whose life was interrupted by episodes when she believed herself touched by divine intervention and others when, in her words, she entirely lost her reason. Written in the eighteenth century, George Trosse's memoir is the spiritual autobiography of a nonconformist minister looking back from middle age on his youthful experience with visions, voices, and suicidal thoughts.

Beliefs about spiritual intervention and causation frame the experiences described in these two narratives, and the person subject to those experiences is in each case conveyed as a relatively—or entirely—passive victim of nonearthly interference. Control, and at least to that extent "ownership," of symptoms is attributed to an agency external to the self.

Prolonged, uncontrolled wailing, tears, and shouting were Margery Kempe's characteristic traits throughout her life—although whether many of these were a divine blessing or symptoms of disorder was contested. At least during one twelve-day episode of what she seems to accept as an "affliction," however, she represents herself as the recipient of unbidden thoughts sent by the devil. During this time, she reports:

> The devil deluded her, dallying with her with accursed thoughts....And...*she could not say no*; and *she had to do his bidding*, and yet she would not have done it for all the world....Wherever she went, or whatever she did these accursed thoughts...remained with her. When she should see the sacrament, make her prayers, or do any other good deed, such abomination was always *put into her mind*. (Kempe 1985:183–84; my emphases)

In a description apparently sharing some of the same assumptions, Trosse describes how during great inner turmoil he heard a voice bid him to cut off his hair, to which, he says, he replied: "I have no Scissors." " *It was then hinted*," he goes on, "that a Knife would do it; but I answer'd I have none. Had I had one, I verily believe, this Voice would have gone from my Hair to my Throat, and have commanded me to cut it" (Trosse 1982:30; my emphasis). He was "thus *disturbed*," as he later sums it up, with "silly ridiculous Fancies, and Thousands of unreasonable and nonsensical Delusions"(Trosse 1982:68; my emphasis).

It was "put in her mind"; it was "hinted"; Trosse was "disturbed." Phenomenologically, we usually feel ourselves to direct our thoughts. Yet the language in each of these accounts indicates thought processes in the receipt of which their subjects are as passive as in their receipt of perceptual experiences.

Experiences of unbidden thoughts and alien commands are typical of psychosis, now as much as then. Phenomenologically, psychiatric symptoms often involve ruptures and divisions within consciousness, and inner voices, thoughts, and feelings are not merely framed but *experienced* as alien. Caution is required here, then: an epistemic indeterminacy prevents us from unreservedly attributing the depiction of the self/symptoms relation to framing rather than treating it as a phenomenologically accurate report. This indeterminacy makes for ambiguity and confusion as we try to interpret narratives such as these.

That said, the particular framing in these narratives whereby such thoughts are directed *as if from an unearthly external agency* in a form of possession, a framing common to early modern memoirs, is less frequently found in memoirs nearer to our own time. By the modern era, different conceptual possibilities suggest themselves and other ideas and assumptions—including some sense of the proprietary self as owner of and constituted by the totality of its experiences and corporeal states—seem to have gained salience.

This more recent conception emerges in John Perceval's 1838 memoir, written after a year in a private madhouse which followed an episode of severe disturbance. Perceval looks back on earlier states of hallucination and delusion and judges them to have resulted from a "natural but often erroneous...confused judgement," a source within himself which is *not* himself.[3] The mind, Perceval explains, is "a piece of excellent machinery" and "there is a power in man, which independent of his natural thought and will, can form ideas upon his imagination—control his voice—and even wield his limbs." His recovery from this condition comes, as Perceval understands it, when he recognizes that he can resist the directives from this unconscious source: "On one occasion...I yielded my voice to the power upon me, and forthwith I uttered the most gross and revolting obscenities, by the influence of a similar power." But now, he chose to be silent "rather than obey." Finally, he says, he was cured of the "folly that I was to yield my voice up to the control of any spirit...without discrimination, and thus my mind was set at rest in great measure from another delusion; or rather, the superstitious belief that I was blindly to yield myself up to an extraordinary guidance was done away" (Perceval 1964:253).

Although not attributing them to any agency external to his body, Perceval denies his symptoms are *his*, and in that sense "disowns" or "alienates" them. This kind of framing is regularly found in later writing, such as the following, reported in the middle of the twentieth century. The author apparently speaks of experiences similar to Kemp's, Trosse's, and Perceval's here, yet reasons not to the presence of an alien agency but to a state of compromised personhood and a sense of objectification: "Things just happen to me now and I have no control over them. I don't seem to have the same say in things any more. At times, *I can't even control what I want to think about.* I am starting to feel pretty numb about everything because I am becoming an object and objects don't have feelings." (quoted by McGhie and Chapman 1961:109; my emphasis).

From the same era comes Lisa Wiley's *Voices Calling* (1955), in which she describes "darkness...closing in " and frames the relation between herself and her symptoms in terms of depletion and deadness:

> I could see everything and saw it as it was, but it was all a dead, lifeless mass. I was dead mentally, having no conscience of anything and having no emotion. I could still think and apparently reason but it was all silent thoughts....There was no future and no past. Everything was just an endless black nothingness. (Wiley 1982: 281)

The alienation of her mental states here, it seems, renders them unreal or even nonexistent for their subject.

John Custance's long memoir about his manic-depressive condition *Wisdom, Madness and Folly* (1952) provides a final illustration of a symptom alienating framing from these mid-twentieth-century memoirs. Speaking of the preceding manic period, he describes experiencing "unearthly joys." But of his depression, he remarks:

> A crumpled pillow is quite an ordinary everyday object, is it not ? One looks at it and thinks no more about it. So is a washing rag or a towel tumbled on the floor, or the creases on the side of a bed. Yet they can suggest shapes of the utmost horror to the mind obsessed by fear. Gradually my eyes began to distinguish such shapes, until eventually, whichever way I turned, devils which seemed infinitely more real than the material objects in which I saw them. (Custance 1964:58–59)

Recounting what he experienced, imagined, and saw, Custance employs a more active voice than is found in early modern narratives and leaves no doubt that his own mind is the source of his hallucinated "devils." Custance positions all his experiences within a psychiatric understanding. This was illness. Though painful, exhilarating, and *seemingly* unearthly, his experiences were merely the symptoms of a disordered brain.

These ways of representing symptoms as alienated from the self, sometimes no more, perhaps, than reports of the actual phenomenology of unbidden and alienated states, must also be distinguished from another kind of framing, this one as apparent in pre-modern as in contemporary memoirs: *reframing*. Most mental illnesses are episodic. Few such memoirs are completed, although they have sometimes been begun, during the severest throes of disorder.[4] (Such episodes might prevent, and eclipse, the writing, or at least the time it takes.) In reading these works, we must be alert to the inevitable reconfigurations imposed on all self narratives in their retelling, but very often heightened, here, by efforts to explain or excuse states so extreme, unsought, unwelcome, and stigmatized.

Moralistic and religious reframing typifies early modern memoirs such as Trosse's. A previous, disordered, and sinful self is viewed from the perspective of one morally restored or saved. While not denying the presence of illness, when he looked back on the "Sin and Folly" of his youth ("going from Place to Place...prating and drinking"), Trosse had come to see the presence of disorder as invited, and made possible, by his own iniquities, for all that its seat was a disordered brain. "A crack'd Brain," in his words, was "impos'd upon by a deceitful and lying Devil" (Trosse 1982:28).

Attitudes in our times are less immediately moralistic, if still stigmatizing. And although a repositioning of self with respect to symptoms can be found in contemporary narratives, that repositioning is construed in a different way. What were seen in the throes of the episode as reasons, and as "my" reasons" for "my" conclusion, "my" resolve, or "my" action, are represented—with the shift in standpoint provided by recovery—as more like invasive and alien states bearing no comprehensible connection to the self. My experiences become things that befell me—or things I mistakenly thought were "my" experiences, reasons, and actions.[5] (Thus the commonly heard assertion: "It was my depression talking, not me. ")

Adding to the complexities of interpretation introduced thus far, memoirs from our present era introduce new elements, such as the reductionistic assumptions of modern biological psychiatry where symptoms are dismissed as the meaningless causal products of a disordered brain. These assumptions are almost inescapable, given the ubiquity, authority, and influence of medical psychiatry today. Moreover, the medical psychiatric perspective *enforces its own adoption*. Understood as a failure to acknowledge the medical nature of one's condition, "lack of insight" is uniformly treated as a sign of illness. Very often it is only by acknowledging that their experiences are medical symptoms of underlying pathology, and thus acceding to the presuppositions of the medical perspective, that patients can demonstrate restored health or evidence of healing.

This influence of the medical model is self-consciously acknowledged in Lauren Slater's 1998 *Prozac Diary*. "Having lived with chronic depression," she writes, "a high-pitched panic, and a host of other psychiatric symptoms since my earliest years, I had made for myself an illness identity, a story of the self that had illness as its main motive. I did not sleep well because I was ill. I cut myself because I was ill." "Illness, for me," she says, "had been the explanatory model on which my being was based" (Slater 1998:50).

Slater looks back here, transformed by Prozac to the unexpected experience of wellness. This description easefully employs the psychiatric language of "chronic depression" and "symptoms" and nods toward the explanatory power and reductionistic tone of psychiatric framing. Yet—as is true of many such sophisticated, contemporary memoirs—there is a tone of irony, and we sense the author's reservations over this limiting identity she had woven for herself.

The reductionistic aspect of a medical framing and the coercive way it is imposed are often more openly challenged by today's memoirists. Writing of his breakdown, Peter Campbell charges the medical psychiatric system with disempowering patients and thwarting their capabilities:

> By approaching my situation in terms of illness, the system has consistently underestimated my capacity to change and has ignored the potential it may contain to assist that change. My desire to win my own control of the breakdown process and thereby to gain independence and integrity has not only been ignored—it has been thwarted. The major impression I have received is that I am a victim of something nasty, not quite understandable, that will never really go away and which should not be talked about too openly in the company of strangers. (Campbell 1996:56–57)

And of her experiences with a diagnosis of schizophrenia, Patricia Deegan observes:

> My *identity had been reduced to an illness* in the eyes of those who worked with me.... Treating people as if they were illnesses is dehumanizing. Everyone loses when this happens.... People learn to say what professionals say: "I am a schizophrenic, a bi-polar, a borderline, etc.".... Most professionals applaud these rote utterances of "insight."... the great danger of reducing a person to an illness is that there is no one left to do the work of recovery. (Deegan 2001: 5-6; my emphasis)[6]

Campbell's and Deegan's narratives exemplify a growing, new emphasis. In the era of identity politics, group identification and self-identity have come to receive unparalleled attention—the question "Who am I?" is inescapable. Similarly inescapable, as we saw above, is the influence of medical framing, bringing an increased interest in the disease status of mental disorder and hence in "symptoms" in the medical sense. Today, the relation between self and symptoms is frequently addressed in memoirs such as these with explicit and sustained attention (for example, Read and Reynolds 1996; Barker, Campbell, and Davidson 1999).

Contemporary Models

One or the other of two apparently incompatible frameworks or "models" representing the relationship between self or identity and symptoms are to be found in many of today's first-person descriptions.[7] On a "symptom-alienating" model, we find distancing and controlling metaphors. The person describes living and strives to live, "outside" rather than being pulled "inside" the illness; the illness and its symptoms are at most a peripheral aspect of the whole person; essential to recovery is hope, and the hope of everyone with mental illness is the absence ("remission") of all symptoms. Thus symptoms are alienable from, rather than integral to, the self. Through an active process of "recovering" or taking back an identity hitherto reduced to these symptoms, the symptoms are controlled ("managed"), their effects and importance minimized and diminished. Often, showing the influence of medical psychiatry, symptoms appear as the meaningless by-products of inherent, biological disorder with no intrinsic interest, meaning, or relevance to the person from whose dysfunctional brain they emanate.

Rhetoric from the "recovery" movement echoes, likely grows out of, and also nourishes this set of assumptions in first person narratives. And these ideas also underlie new definitions of "recovery": defining a self apart from the symptoms of disorder is said to constitute part of, and has been established to foster, healing.[8] In prescriptions for getting "outside" mental illness, emphasis is placed on resuming "control" and "responsibility" by "managing" symptoms.

In contrast to the symptom-alienating model, some narratives reveal "symptom integrating" assumptions and a picture of symptoms as less easily alienated and, in some cases, as central to, and constitutive of, the identity of the person. Instead of alienated and controlled, symptoms are embraced, even valorized. Rather than inconsequential effects of a diseased brain, they are depicted as meaningful aspects of experience and identity. When they are alienated, the goal of recovery is also sometimes understood to be integrating them *into* the self. Simon Champ, in "A Most Precious Thread" (1999) illustrates the integrative aspect of this kind of narrative, describing how he has come to think about his symptoms. He speaks of a "communication with himself" that allows him to overcome the initial sense of disintegration accompanying the onset of his symptoms. This communication with himself "has given me the most precious thread, a thread that has linked my evolving sense of self, a thread of self reclamation, a thread of movement toward a whole and integrated sense of self, away from the early fragmentation and confusion" (Champ 1999:12).

Symptoms are not only integrated and valued but valorized in Simon Morris's narrative, "Heaven Is a Mad Place on Earth"(2000), in which he employs the metaphor of deep sea fishing to capture the extreme states wrought by his disorder:

> All who have experienced "deep sea fishing" will know the sensation of heightened awareness, of consciousness enhanced far better than LSD could ever do it, of feelings of wonder and terror that can't be verbalized…and then have these visions which effortlessly outstrip the alienation of daily life dismissed as "delusion" by some fucking shrink.…I was always mad—I hope I always will be. My crazy life is wonderful. The "sane" really don't know what they're missing. (Morris 2000:207–8)[9]

Although it is found in narratives describing other disorders as well, this symptom-integrating framing is particularly apparent in narratives about depressive states (and in such writing it long predates the current consumer movements). Memoirs such as Kay Jamison's *Unquiet Mind,* William Styron's *Darkness Visible,* and Meri Nana Ama Danquah's *Willow Weep for Me* emphasize the depth of appreciation and feeling that come with depression, not simply accepting that these moods are integral to who they are but insisting that there is great personal meaning and value in them. Acknowledging that she is identified with and at least in part constituted by her depression, Danquah writes, "For most of my life I have nurtured a consistent, low-grade melancholy; I have been addicted to despair." Honoring her mood states, she comments:

> Depression offers layers, textures, noises. At times it is flimsy as a feather.…Other times…it offers new signals and symptoms until finally I am drowning in it. Most times, in its most superficial sense, it is rich and enticing. A field of velvet waiting to embrace me. It is loud and dizzying, inviting the tenors and screeching sopranos of thought, unrelenting sadness, and the sense of impending doom. (Danquah 2000:151–52)

Why should depression, particularly, lend itself to the "integrative" conception of self and symptoms? Speculation here takes at least three distinct directions. First, affective states appear to be more integral to self-identity than cognitive ones: our emotions and moods are not easily separated from our core selves. Mood states, such as depression, are pervasive and unbounded in their psychological effects. In this they differ from beliefs. We may distance ourselves from any given belief in several ways— by doubting or disbelieving, rather than embracing it, for example. But no comparable separation allows us to distinguish our moods from ourselves. Moods by their nature color and frame all experience. In this respect, at least while they last, they are inescapably part of us. (Consistent with this, of course, is a subsequent reframing that affects that distance, although arguably such reframing still takes the form of "That [person] was not me" rather than "That mood was not mine." In contrast, reframing a state when a now-relinquished delusional belief was entertained simply involves saying, as Trosse does in the passage quoted earlier, "I was [then] subject to nonsensical and unreasable delusions"—*not* "That [person] was not me.")

Second, the effect of depression on reasoning, and on perceptual, cognitive, and communicative capabilities, is often less disabling than is the effect of other severe conditions: moods of despair and sadness may be easier to integrate than the jarring and disruptive intrusion of symptoms such as inner voices. Severe, psychotic depression can occur, and the subtler effects of depressive moods on judgment are not inconsiderable. Nonetheless, reasoning, judgment, and interpersonal communication are not as immediately compromised by most depressive moods as by the delusions and hallucinations associated with other severe disorders such as schizophrenia.

And last, glamorous associations still cling to the notion of melancholia and even extend to today's depression. In the afterglow of the long tradition in which melancholy bespeaks brilliance, creativity, and inspiration, the drawbacks of depressive moods are not entirely unalloyed. (In Styron's memoir, for instance, although emphasizing the excruciating and terrifying aspects of his depression, Dante's *Inferno* is used as a frame, and the great depression sufferers of the past are listed, as if to remind the reader of the ennobling value of such suffering.)

Some Theoretical Implications

Some additional theoretical implications appear to attach to the models outlined above and may in turn account for their adoption in some cases. For example, theories of self-identity and agency vary. Some analyses portray the "author" of the self-narrative as actively engaged in selecting the experiences that comport with a story she constructs rather than as passively receiving whatever life experiences she is dealt. On this analysis, arguably, a person's psychiatric symptoms may not even enter her story. The narrative self-analysis is widely adopted today and seems to play an important part in much of the rhetoric and prescriptions associated with the recovery movements. Other theories of self-identity deriving from Kantian traditions, in which the self is the recipient and proprietor of the totality of its life experiences, will perhaps better accommodate a symptom-integrating approach, such as illustrated in Champ's memoir, than a symptom-alienating one.

A second theoretical implication of these contrasting models concerns the analogy between psychiatric and other kinds of symptoms. Much symptom-alienating recovery movement rhetoric is styled on that of the broader disabilities movement wherein differences between the symptoms of bodily and psychiatric disorders are diminished and deemphasized. Such a perspective denies psychiatric disorders exceptional status. Symptom-integrating assumptions, in contrast, seem more hospitable to such exceptionalism. The extent and persuasiveness of the analogy between ordinary, bodily symptoms and "psychiatric" symptoms, then, is also implicated in this contrast between symptom-alienating and symptom-integrating framings of the self/symptom relationship.

The extent and persuasiveness of that analogy is a complex and problematic matter. Holistic thinking concerned to avoid unacceptable forms of dualism would insist on the strong analogy between all symptoms, whether they resulted from bodily or psychological dysfunction or disorder. On a strict, medical understanding, symptoms, in contrast to signs, are by definition psychological and subjective; they are the patient's "complaint" or avowal—communicative acts. (Signs are observable aspects of the situation, not requiring cooperation or even consciousness from the patient.) Arguably, then, "I cannot walk on my leg" and "My thought processes are being interrupted by distracting inner voices" belong to the same ontological order of things.

Yet even limiting our focus to symptoms strictly so called, the deficits and problems included among psychiatric symptoms come in many forms that are less-hospitable to the analogy with the complaint that "I cannot walk on my leg." The silence of catatonia; incomprehensible "word salads"; neologisms; apparently self-contradictory claims ("I am dead"; "Someone has stolen my thoughts"); words addressed to unseen or unheard others—all these bear little resemblance to what we mean when we think of communication about ordinary, bodily symptoms.

The thoroughgoing analysis required to resolve these questions of analogy cannot be undertaken here. But at least two seeming differences between psychiatric and nonpsychiatric symptoms compel our attention. First, the attitudes and expectations customarily accompanying more ordinary bodily symptoms are not as reliably present with psychiatric symptoms.[10] These include the presumption that those experiencing them (at least in the face of medical knowledge) will accept the disorder status of their symptoms: want to be rid of them and want to cooperate in their removal.

Second, psychiatric symptoms regularly compromise the capabilities required for the expression of any symptoms, so understood—speech, and the shared, intersubjective responses that allow words to successfully convey meanings, actions to make apparent sense, and understanding and communication to take place. While mental disorder may not often be so devastating in its effects as the above examples portray, and the statement "My thought processes are being interrupted by distracting inner voices" may be more common than "I am dead" or "Someone has stolen my thoughts," nonetheless, these examples of fundamental dysfunction in the means of expressing and communicating symptoms seem to raise a challenge for the general analogy between the symptoms of psychiatric and bodily disorders.

Conclusion

Some factors influencing how illness narratives portray the relation between self and symptoms were introduced here. Most generally, rather than mere phenomenological reports, individual narratives reflect the "framing" ideas and explanations accepted and imagined at their given time and place in history. But several further features of these narratives were shown to complicate our efforts to identify this framing. Because the relation between self and symptoms may itself become disordered as the result of mental illness, any separation between accurate report and cultural framing is problematic and leaves epistemic indeterminacy at the heart of our interpretive efforts. Further interpretive complexity comes from the element of "reframing": these narratives will likely reflect the temporal standpoint from which they were written rather than the framing within which the symptoms were first experienced. These each intersect with the last factor that was our particular focus: the assumptions, ideas, and explanations—including the theory of self and the perceived analogies with bodily symptoms—guiding how the self is seen in relation to its psychological symptoms.

Variation among these narratives vis à vis depictions of the self/symptom relation is most obviously attributable to variation in the kind of symptoms experienced, it was pointed out at the outset of this discussion. And here, too, there appear to be patterns of interaction with the above ideas about the relation between self and symptoms. The distinctive nature, and cultural place, of mood states, it was proposed, likely explain why memoirs of depression more often adopt symptom-integrating assumptions.

Notes

1. I use the word "symptoms" here for simplicity, and because that will be the main focus of my discussion. In some narratives, the relationship between self and the broader "disorder," "disease" or "illness" also appears, but these terms introduce additional considerations and will not receive systematic analysis here.

2. Symptoms include behavioral dispositions, as well as psychological states, but this discussion is limited to examples of the latter.

3. Interestingly, although Freud's work on the unconscious was still half a century away, this account seems to anticipate the belief in unconscious mental states that frames some twentieth-century narratives.

4. Nijinsky's *Diaries* constitute one valuable exception to this generalization.

5. This raises some epistemic puzzles: particularly when it involves a recurring disorder, such as depression, or manic depression, we must ask why the perspective of the later, "recovered" author of the illness narrative, which alienates the self from its symptoms, should be privileged over the account of the earlier, ill subject, which did not (Radden 1996:12–14; 170–71).

6. Deegan's discussion illustrates Hilda Lindemann Nelson's work on the healing achieved through replacing others' subordinating "master narratives" (You are a schizophrenic) with one's own "counter stories" (I have schizophrenia) (Nelson 2001).

7. In using the term "model" here, I mean to suggest a cluster of ideas that are very often found together and appear to form a harmonious set although they are not joined by entailment.

8. For example, Jacobson and Greenley 2001; Barham and Hayward 1991, 1995, 1998; Corrigan and Penn 1998; Ridgeway 2001; Davidson 2003.

9. Some of the political rationale for the "mad pride" model is clarified in the following passage from a U.K. Mad Pride website: "The word 'mad' is basically a term of abuse. Remember so once was the word 'black.' But people reclaimed the word and used it as a proud badge to be worn along the long march to freedom. There was Black Power. There is Black Pride" (www.madpride.org.uk/about.htm, accessed June 2004).

10. Some psychiatric symptoms are of course bodily sensations, such as pain and discomfort in the head. So we can at best speak of typical psychological or psychiatric symptoms in these ways.

References

Barham, P., and Hayward, R. 1991. *From the Mental Patient to the Person.* London: Routledge.

———. 1995. *Relocating Madness.* London: Free Association Books.

———. 1998. In sickness and in health: Dilemmas of the person with severe mental illness. *Psychiatry* 61:163–70.

Barker, P., Campbell, P., and Davidson, B. (eds.) 1999. *From the Ashes of Experience: Reflections on Madness, Survival, Growth.* London: Macmillan.

Champ, S. 1999. In *From the Ashes of Experience: Reflections on Madness, Survival, Growth.*, ed. P. Barker, P. Campbell, and B. Davidson. London: Macmillan.

Corrigan, P., and Penn, D. 1998. "Disease and discrimination: Two paradigms that describe severe mental illness. *Journal of Mental Health* 6:355–66.

Custance, J. 1952. *Wisdom, Madness and Folly.* New York: Farrar, Straus & Cudahy.

Davidson, L. 2003. *Living outside Mental Illness: Qualitative Studies of Recovery in Schizophrenia.* New York: New York University Press.

Deegan, P. E. 1996. Recovery and the conspiracy of hope. At http://www.intentionalcare.org/articles/articles_hope.pdf. (accessed July 8, 2005), 4.

Jacobson, N., and Greenley, J. 2001. What is recovery? A conceptual model and explication. *Psychiatric Services* 52(4):482–85.

Jamison, K. R. 1995. *An Unquiet Mind.* New York: Knopf.

Kempe, M. 1985. *The Book of Margery Kempe.* Trans. B. A. Windeatt. London: Penguin.

Luhrmann, T. 2000. *Of Two Minds: The Growing Disorder in American Psychiatry.* New York: Knopf.

McGhie, A., and Chapman, J. 1961. Disorders of attention and perception in early schizophrenia. *British Journal of Medical Psychology* 34:103–16.

Morris, S. 2000. Heaven Is a Mad Place on Earth. In *Mad Pride: A Celebration of Mad Culture,* ed. T. Curtis, R. Dellar, E. Leslie, and B. Watson, 207–8. London: Spare Change Books.

Nelson, H. L. 2001 *Damaged Identities: Narrative Repair.* Ithaca, NY: Cornell University Press.

———. 2003. *Rationing Sanity: Ethical Issues in Managed Mental Health Care.* Washington, DC: Georgetown University Press.

Ohio Department of Mental Health. 2004. *Recovering from Mental Illness.* <city>: Mental Health Association of Summit County.

Perceval, J. 1964. A narrative of the treatment experienced by a gentleman, during a state of mental derangement. In *The Inner World of Mental Illness,* ed. Bert Kaplan., 235–53. New York: Harper & Row.

Radden, J. 1996. *Divided Minds and, Successive Selves: Ethical Issues in Disorders of Identity and Personality.* Cambridge, MA: MIT Press.

Read, J., and Reynolds, J. (eds.) 1996. *Speaking Our Minds: An Anthology.* London: Macmillan.

Ridgeway, P. 2001. Re-storying psychiatric disability: Learning from first-person narrative accounts of recovery. *Psychiatric Rehabilitation Journal* 24 (4):335–43.

Slater, L. 1998. *Prozac Diary.* New York: Penguin.

Styron, W. 1990. *Darkness Visible.* New York: Vintage.

Trosse, G. 1982 Life of the Reverend Mr. George Trosse: Written by himself, and published posthumously according to his order, Reprinted in *A Mad People's History of Madness,* ed. Dale Peterson, 27–38. Pittsburgh, PA: Pittsburgh University Press.

Wiley, L. 1982. Voices calling. Reprinted in *A Mad People's History of Madness,* ed. Dale Peterson. Pittsburgh, PA: Pittsburgh University Press.

11

Melancholy, Mood, and Landscape

A wintry, northern landscape stretches before us in monochromatic tones, with few or no signs of habitation, and overcast skies. Such a scene is gloomy, and mournful, we say, or melancholy. My question is why we say "melancholy"; my challenge is to identify and explain the way in which the bleak landscape is related to the state or condition of melancholy.

This inquiry takes place in the shadow of art historical and aesthetic theorizing about how works of art can be said to variously express, stimulate, represent, convey, and symbolize affective states. Yet that theorizing is in significant ways different from the task that will be undertaken in this essay. Although melancholy is associated with characteristic affective states, it is equally, and perhaps even primarily, tied to states of disorder and to temperament. In addition, the relation between observers and works of art contains elements not present between observers and natural phenomena. So asking why we call a landscape melancholy is both more and less complicated than asking why we attribute other, so-called expressive properties (such as sadness or cheerfulness) to works of art. It is more complicated because most expressive properties refer solely to the inner states and moods by which they have been identified, whereas the notion of melancholy conveys much else besides; it is less complicated because the additional features distinguishing works of art are absent.

This exploration concerns natural phenomena—a category that includes not only sights, such as landscapes, but also sounds. Whatever conclusions can be drawn about why we describe landscapes as melancholy, then, may also extend to why we refer to certain sounds as melancholy (for instance, the hoot of an owl or the cry of departing geese). However, even though pictures of landscape are also sometimes described as melancholy (think of the scenes of Casper David Friedrich or Corot),

Reprinted from *Grey Hope: The Persistence of Melancholy*, edited by Sigrid Sandström. Aberdeen & Northamptom: Atopia Projects, 2006. Reprinted with permission from Sigrid Sandström and Atopia Projects, Aberdeen & Northamptom.

"landscape" here refers only to natural landscape. Without qualification, my findings will be unlikely to apply to, and are not intended for, such representations. Finally, when we speak of landscape as natural, "natural" is used loosely: few of the landscapes that we have an opportunity to see are entirely unaffected by human design.

My approach here is to explore the ways in which ascriptions of melancholy to natural phenomena might have their source in associations and ideas about melancholy which, reinforced by and entwined with iconographic traditions in the visual arts, are our Western European cultural legacy. Notable among these associations are the characteristic mood states, forming an important part, though only a part, of that tradition. In a brief rider to this discussion, theories about the "expressive" or affective properties of works of art will be introduced. These suggest an additional explanation—the landscape causes us to *feel* melancholy—that, though unproven, is complementary to the one developed here. While it may also sometimes leave us melancholy, my contention will be that the melancholy landscape makes us think of, rather than feel, melancholy, and particularly to think of mood states of unexplained disquiet and sadness.

As part of a broader, and broadly Foucaultian inquiry into the cultural origins of images of otherness, Sander Gilman has offered a theory of psychiatric illustration which seems a good place to begin. Gilman's method is to identify the visual motifs that make up the image of the insane in representations varying from artworks to medical illustrations. Such motifs, "visual stereotypes," or "structures," are ubiquitous even today, he reasons, due to the inherent, frightening inexplicability of madness. We learn to see the world through the prism of art, Gilman believes: "it is not art which imitates insanity, but the perception of insanity which imitates art" is his particular version of Oscar Wilde's famous remark that "External Nature imitates Art."[1]

Gilman's concern has been to identify cultural conceptions of insanity or madness (he uses the two interchangeably) framed and formed by visual *representations* of it. Because most kinds of mental disorder were identified with melancholy during this time, Gilman's approach is readily demonstrated using the extensive iconography of melancholy found in medieval images of the four humors and elaborated throughout the early modern period. This iconographic tradition culminates in sixteenth- and seventeenth-century works such as Dürer's *Melancholia* series and Ripa's images of *Melancholicus*. In Dürer's engravings, for example, the shadowed or darkened face alludes to the blackness of mood and countenance associated with melancholy from traditions that trace to Greek humoral medicine. The lowered head and cheek resting on the hand are motifs from the earliest medieval images of the melancholy temperament. And the purse reminds us of later medieval associations connecting the melancholic character with miserliness. Other elements such as the geometer's tools bespeak links, forged in the Renaissance, between melancholy, intellectual and artistic pursuits, and genius. The bright star in the sky denotes the planet Saturn, the sign of the melancholy temperament. And there are many other examples.[2] These artists knew the many tropes and motifs making up the language of melancholy and offered them in personifications of "Melancholy" and "Homo melancholicus" to be read as if from a book.

Adopting Gilman's broad approach toward our melancholy landscape, we might expect such iconographic conventions to transfer to natural phenomena. Why do we call our bleak landscape melancholy? Because, with its dark and drear features, the scene before us exhibits some of the elements associated with the familiar pictorial language of melancholy. The landscape is often wintry, suggesting cold; or it is autumnal, hinting at cold to come. It is dark, or monochromatic, with overcast skies. Its spaces are featureless, or barren and isolated. These examples each reflect motifs familiar from the extensive canon of writing about melancholy and the associative thinking that it embodies. In the ancient tables of opposites, containing humors, contrary qualities, and other contrasting elements, melancholy was always placed with coldness (and dryness). As the seasons came to be added to such schemas, melancholy was associated with things autumnal. The link with darkness is similarly ancient: as a disease of the black bile, melancholy was described as common in those of dark hair and complexion. (Faithful to this notion, the earliest images of the melancholy man, whether as one afflicted with the disease or merely possessing the melancholy temperament, showed a shaded or darkened face.) The emphasis upon out-of-the-way, unpeopled landscapes seems to hearken to the isolation and (self-imposed) loneliness of misanthropy, which from the earliest descriptions has been noted as an aspect of melancholy.

These features are to be found in *representations* of melancholy as far back as such representations can be found, and, although we are not here focusing on artworks, the impact and influence of such visual motifs must be considered in any account of why we describe a natural landscape as melancholy. Indeed, we must suppose that written and visual motifs fed upon and reinforced one another, as Gilman suggests.[3] I should add here that while all the motifs described thus far are from classical and early modern sources, cultural constructions are dynamic edifices. More current associations with melancholy, such as the link with the visual property of blueness, would need to be included in a complete, contemporary account.[4] Moreover, the above examples were restricted to visual properties or traits that could be conveyed in visual terms (for example, the spatial composition suggesting social isolation). An analysis of natural phenomena known through nonvisual sense modalities (the owl's hoot, for example) would include auditory and tactile properties of melancholy, such as low tonality and heaviness, respectively.[5]

It is significant that two of the properties noted thus far—darkness and isolation— are not affections of any kind. And as a disease of the black bile, melancholy was long understood in terms of its bodily and behavioral traits as well as its subjective symptoms. But whether construed as a humoral disorder or a lifelong temperament, melancholy has also been associated with certain affective states; when Burton finds our universal lot, and the very "Character of Mortalitie" in "that transitory Melancholy," which "goes & comes upon every small occasion of sorrow, need, sickness, trouble, feare, griefe, passion or perturbation of the Minde," it is to those affective states he refers. As symptoms of a disorder, as traits and tendencies of the melancholy temperament, or as fleeting moods, these states are likely to be involved when we speak of the natural landscape as melancholy, just as when we say it is sad or mournful.

The affective states that form part of the associations with melancholy in the long cultural tradition noted above require special attention. But in stressing the link between these feeling states and the melancholy landscape, I will distinguish such states as objects of thought (about melancholy) rather than as states directly caused in any more immediate way by the sight of the landscape.

Klibansky, Panofsky, and Saxl identify, in lyric writing, narrative poetry, and prose romances of the early modern era, what they call a poetic sense of melancholy as a "passing subjective mood state." They distinguish this from two previous meanings of melancholy (melancholy as a disease of the black bile and melancholy as a temperament). These authors argue that the poetic notion of melancholy as a temporary mood of sadness and distress came partially to eclipse these earlier meanings. In all modern European literature, they assert, the word melancholy lost the sense of a quality and acquired instead that of a "mood" that could be transferred to inanimate objects.

It is perhaps true that a new sense of melancholy, as a temporary mood state, gained prominence in this period. Much evidence indicates that all three sets of associations by which melancholy was identified—as a disorder or disease state, as a naturally occurring temperament, and as a passing mood—coexisted throughout the early modern era, receiving greater and less emphasis according to context. But, more important, reference is made to something like the melancholy mood well before the early modern era, as a subjective and affective accompaniment to, or expression of, the melancholy temperament, as well as a symptom of the humoral disorder of melancholy. And there is remarkable consistency in these descriptions. Since the very earliest writing from the Greek physicians and philosophers, melancholy has been linked to two kinds or clusters of states identified as "groundless": those of fear, disquiet, anxiety, and apprehension on the one hand and, on the other, sadness, despondency, and dispiritedness.[6]

Thus, appealing to the Hippocratic corpus, Galen notes that all melancholic patients' symptoms can be classified into two groups: fear and despondency. The patient is rendered melancholic when such states last "for a long time." The reasoning here appears to be that since in most people such states are short-lived, prolonged fears and despondencies must be ungrounded, unfounded, or without sufficient cause. Emphasizing the same set of presuppositions, the Aristotelian text notes that when temperament is exceptionally cold ("beyond due measure") it produces "groundless" despondency. Renaissance writers continue, and embellish, this theme: Ficino writes that in suffering melancholy "we *fear everything*." Our fears, in their indiscriminate and encompassing nature, he suggests, exceed what it can be reasonable or normal to fear. With Ficino comes another theme, elaborated by Timothiy Bright and others in the sixteenth century: some of the fear and apprehension the melancholic suffers when "adustion" results in more severe forms of the disorder are engendered by the alarming specters wrought by their disordered imaginations.[7] In what became the standard medical definition of melancholia for the early modern era, Andre Du Laurens describes a "dotage without any fever, having for his ordinaryie companions, feare and sadness, *without any apparent occasion*" (my emphasis). By the seventeenth century, Robert Burton writes that while not always sad and fearful, melancholics are "usually so: and that *without a cause*."[8]

Fear and sadness are customarily thought of as universal human emotions. Due to our shared makeup, we respond to our experiences in similar ways, and there is some agreement over the norms of what are reasons for sadness and grounds for fear.

In light of that, this persistent emphasis on these states as without "cause," and their centrality to conceptions of melancholy, leaves them in need of further analysis. First, the phrase "without cause" is ambiguous in several ways. All psychic states have some cause, which is often their external occasion, an event or state of affairs in the world that brought them about. Thus, most immediately, "without cause" is to be understood as without any known cause or without an identifiable occasion. (For no accountable reason, you wake on the "wrong side of the bed," as the saying goes. The *cause* of your ill temper is unknown.) When the subjective state referred to is a nebulous and pervasive mood, it will also sometimes lack what, in philosophical writing, is known as an "object" (that which it was directed toward, over, or about). Its cause may be recognized, yet it may be over or about nothing identifiable to its subject. (A sudden shock or surprise might leave you inexplicably unsettled and anxious. The cause is evident, but the anxiety is undirected and diffuse—it has no *object*.) When Ficino says that the melancholic fears everything, he identifies a state he believes is *caused* by humoral imbalance, the scholarly life and temperament, and so on. But this state pervades all of its subject's experience, and thus is about *nothing*, because it is about everything. The notion of a state "without cause" is further complicated by the analysis noted above, where fears and apprehensions were sometimes portrayed as irrational or unreasonable. In this final sense of "without cause," the delusional apprehensions resulting from their subjects' disordered imaginations were unsoundly based.

Summing up, the several ways in which states of sadness and fear might be without cause include instances when (i) the cause or occasion is not identified; (ii) there is cause but the affection lacks any object; (iii) the "object" is global rather than specific; and, finally, (iv) the object, while recognized, results from unsoundly based reasoning or beliefs. Attributions of each of these deficits to the effects of melancholy can be found in past writing; the first three of these feeling states, I want to emphasize, are kinds of moods rather than more precise emotions.

Martin Heidegger's discussion of moods and their importance sets the stage for this contrast between moods and emotions. For "die Stimmung," translators of Heidegger use "mood" or "state of mind." But the term "Stimmung," Heidegger points out, derives originally from the tuning of a musical instrument, so that "mood" could be said to be (a person's) "attunement," or "temper." We are always in some mood or another, Heidegger insists, and although they are not as transparent to us as our cognitive states, our moods have an ontological primacy over those states.[9]

By their nature, then, moods are important and ubiquitous, yet elusive and unbounded, blurring into other states. (Melancholy merges with nostalgia, ennui, unease, sadness, gloom, and despondency—to name a few—and perhaps also with nebulous bodily or quasi-bodily sensations, such as heavy-heartedness and inertia.) They pervade the world we experience. Some of these aspects of moods allow us to place them in contrast to other affective states such as emotions. Emotions, like other belief-based subjective states, are accompanied or constituted by ("intentional") objects. Melancholic fear and sadness are "objectless" affective states or moods when they are not over or about anything in particular.

Contemporary philosopher Gabriele Taylor has considered this distinction between moods and emotions. She notes that with moods there is no specific thing, situation, or event that can be picked out and described independently of the mood itself, and moods therefore spread to color everything: "It is a constitutive feature of moods that they involve a way of seeing the world. They are distinguished from each other by the particular way in which the world is seen: in moods of elation everything is perceived as attractive and attainable, in moods of depression, everything appears gloomy or irritating, the worthwhile out of one's reach."[10]

This way of distinguishing moods from emotions, it should be added, is not always honored in the naming and classification of affective states. Some emotions are always intentional—for example, curiosity, hopefulness, and shame; but others such as anxiety, sadness, and excitement seem to arise both as emotions and as moods. (On occasion, we feel anxious over a particular thing; at other times, we experience anxiety as a generalized, "free-floating" state, unattached to the specificity of an object.)

The distinction between the cause and object of an emotion has been consistently acknowledged only since the eighteenth century, and that between moods and emotions since the early twentieth century. But we can read much in earlier writing about melancholy to concern nebulous, pervasive, and nonintentional moods of fear and sadness *without* any (consciously recognized or apparent) cause or object. Melancholy is many things: cognitive defects, errors of judgment, bodily states of humoral imbalance and their sequelae, behavioral tendencies, a character type, and a bundle of affective states—of emotions, attitudes, and feelings. Within the rich lode of associations and ideas about melancholy subjectivity that are our Western cultural heritage, melancholy appears as an objectless mood state as much as or more than it does as a specific emotion.

Interestingly, it has been remarked that, in general, works of art "seem to affect our feelings *more by putting us into a mood than by exciting a directed emotion*."[11] In a parallel observation, I would draw attention to the relative ease with which we attribute objectless mood states—compared with emotions—to *natural phenomena*. The landscape may be unsettling, sad, or gloomy: states that often occur as moods. The landscape cannot as readily be seen as hateful or curious: states that are, or are more often, intentional. The bird song can be cheerful, gay, or grave, but although we may say it *sounds* impatient, we would not so readily say it *is* impatient. The landscape, in contrast, does not merely *look* melancholy, it *is* melancholy. To be worried, angry, curious, impatient, or troubled is usually to be in these states over or about something, to entertain beliefs. Because many affective states—like sadness—may occur as a mood or an emotion, it is easy to lose sight of this difference.[12] Today, we speak of melancholy, as we do of sadness and depression, as both mood and emotion. Thus, I may be melancholy over a particular, known loss; or, equally, I may be sunk into a pervasive melancholy, which colors all that I contemplate.

Ascriptions of melancholy to natural landscape involve—although they do not reduce to—moods, rather than emotions. They invite us to briefly acknowledge parallels with the attribution of what are known as expressive properties to art objects. (The music, we say, is cheerful, the scene in the painting dismal.) It has been proposed, on the one hand, that there might be naturally occurring resonances that make some musical tones and keys sound sadder, some colors and compositions look brighter and happier.[13] In a related line of speculation, the presence of actual subjective states—invoked in the audience or perhaps experienced, or intended, by the artist—has been hypothesized.[14]

With our natural landscape, there is no artist. But the variant of these theories where expressive properties are said to be ascribed *because the work of art invokes such feeling states in its audience or observer* remains applicable. It may be supposed that we attribute expressive properties such as melancholy to natural phenomena because those phenomena directly induce particular feeling states in us. Moreover, if there are naturally occurring resonances that make some colors and compositions sadder, it might be expected that such resonances would affect our apprehension of natural phenomena *in the same way* as they do our apprehension of works of art. We may be constituted or "hard wired" so that dark tones—whether in a picture or in a natural landscape—make us feel, as well as think of, melancholy. And, conceivably, this springs not solely from our particular cultural inheritance but from something deep within our human nature.

Applied to natural phenomena, these theories require qualification.[15] When we ascribe melancholy to a landscape, we sometimes remain unmoved. Or we may be affected, though not with melancholy. We may be calmed or soothed, transported into a pensive mood, or a faintly pleasurable one, revived and restored, or moved to gentle merriment. So the natural resonance theory is at best true in some instances. Nonetheless, as a complement to the explanation from our cultural legacy of associations attached to melancholy, it cannot be ruled out that sometimes this more direct kind of affection occurs as well.

Summing up, then, we say the landscape is "melancholy" because it apparently posesses some of the visual properties and other elements associated with the familiar iconography and cultural lore of melancholy. This multi-stranded conception or structure of melancholy includes subjective states, particularly moods of sadness without cause.[16] Melancholy landscapes may also affect us with such mood states in a more direct way. Primarily, though, we attribute melancholy to landscapes by some alchemy derived from the associative attachment between visual and affective aspects of our conception of melancholy. Aspects of the landscape make us *think* of, not (or not merely) feel, melancholy.

Notes

1. Sander L. Gilman, *Seeing the Insane* (New York: John Wiley and Sons, 1982), preface iii.

2. R. Klibansky, E. Panofsky, and F. Saxl, *Saturn and Melancholy: Studies in the History of Natural Philosophy, Religion, and Art* (New York: Basic Books, 1964).

3. The canon on melancholy goes back much further than extant images, which suggests, *pace* Gilman, that the originating source of this concentrated alloy was likely texts rather than illustrations.

4. As an expression denoting melancholy, "the blue devils" traces to the sixteenth century.

5. Notable among more recent and nonvisual properties are the musical associations that have braided a particular style and chord progression with moods of sadness, depression, and dispiritedness to give us blues music.

6. The Greek word *dusthumia* may be variously translated as despondency, sadness, ill-temper, or despair.

7. For an interesting exploration of these ideas, see Claire Bartram, "Melancholic Imaginations: Witchcraft and the Politics of Melancholia in Elizabethan Kent," *Journal of European Studies*, Dec., Vol. 33, No. 3–4 (2003):203–11.

8. Translations of Aristotle, Galen, Ficino, Bright, and Burton are taken from *The Nature of Melancholy: From Aristotle to Kristeva*, ed. Jennifer Radden (Oxford: Oxford University Press, 2000).

9. Martin Heidegger, *Being and Time*, trans. John Macquarrie and Edward Robinson (New York: Harper and Row, 1962), 173–75.

10. Gabriele Taylor, "Deadly Vices?" in *How Should One Live? Essays on the Virtues*, ed. Roger Crisp (Oxford: Clarendon, 1996), 165.

11. William Charlton, *Aesthetics* (London: Hutchinson, 1970), 97 (my emphasis).

12. Charlton's confidence may gain false support from the chameleon feeling (of sadness) he has chosen for his example in the following passage where he disposes of the problem of how natural phenomena like landscape can have expressive properties. What is primarily sad, no doubt, is a certain feeling on the part of a person, he notes, "but other things may be called sad because they are related to that feeling. A man is sad if he has it; someone's death may be sad if it causes it in survivors; a sigh may be sad because it indicates or results from it." When we are told that a piece of moorland is sad, "we need not wonder how a feeling can be attributed to…tract of earth and rock; our task is…to say in which of the many possible ways the moorland is related to the feeling." Ibid., 94, 95.

13. For a discussion of this view, see, for example, Richard Wollheim, *Art and Its Objects* (New York: Harper and Row, 1968).

14. Benedetto Croce. *Aesthetic*, 2nd ed., trans. Douglas Ainslie (London: Macmillan, 1922). See also R. G. Collingwood, *The Principles of Art* (Oxford: Oxford University Press, 1938).

15. And, indeed, they have been criticized in application to works of art as well (Wollheim 1968).

16. An investigation into when and why moods of sadness and despondency eclipsed those of fear and apprehension in accounts of melancholy, and in the cultural legacies which persist today, though intriguing, must be pursued elsewhere.

12

Review of *Against Depression* by Peter Kramer

The broad framework of Peter Kramer's book, *Against Depression*, is familiar. In response to repeated questions appearing to romanticize the pathology of great artists ("what works of genius might have been lost if Van Gogh had been dosed with Prozac?"), Kramer sets out to show depression for what, he is sure, it is—nothing more than a disease, a scourge, and a medical and public health problem of unmatched proportions.

To this end, in a long, rather discursive book, he develops his case. Depression is a disease; he summarizes the range of intriguing biological findings from the 1990s that support such a claim, outlining a model of brain function wherein resilience, the ability to bounce back from life's inevitable slings and arrows, is apparently compromised in some people. He takes on the long-held cultural tropes that link depressive states, and the related states earlier known as melancholia, with artistic and intellectual achievement, creativity, and a more profound understanding and wisdom than is vouchsafed to more sanguine folk. He sketches a future time at which depression will be recognized to be no more attractive, "charming," or profound than are tuberculosis or heart disease today. And finally, he hints at a utopian era when, due to genetic and perhaps also social engineering, depression has gone the way of the Black Death or, in the West, leprosy.

In many respects, this is an admirable and welcome book. Kramer's clearly written, even-handed discussion of the causes of depression, for example, provides a nuanced and layered counter to the oversimplified explanatory stories still sometimes issuing from the respective nature and nurture camps. As Kramer explains recent brain science, it will be biological fragility (the result both of genetic tendencies and of damage and deficit), together with some trigger from experience

Review of *Against Depression* by Peter Kramer (Viking 2005), published June 15, 2005, on Metapsychology (www.mentalhelp.net/books/). Reproduced with permission from Metapsychology.

(a loss, a defeat, a trauma), which generates an episode of the disease, and each such episode, in turn, will contribute its own, additional damage. This eclectic and multi-causal "stress and impaired resilience" analysis allows Kramer to propose a range of remedies for depression: a future in which the fragility gene can be identified and removed before it causes harm; the prescription of those combinations of psychotherapy and antidepressant medications that have been found to help some weather their depressive episodes; public policy and reform aimed at reducing the social causes and triggers of depression such as want, war, and abuse. Much here is sensible, mainstream, and unexceptional.

For Kramer, depression is a disease understood according to the neo-Kraepelinian model, a categorical entity whose underlying, stable core process is the cause of its clinical features, the characteristic signs and symptoms we observe through its apparently episodic course (or "career"). One of the more controversial themes in the book is provided by this analysis, for depressive states, particularly, seem to invite a dimensional rather than a categorical analysis. They shade from more to less severe, and from less severe to mild, for example, and show themselves in acute episodes, but also in long-term traits and temperaments. They are the quintessential conditions of gradation and even boundlessness, seemingly rendering arbitrary and artificial the lines we attempt to draw around them.

Kramer takes this particular conceptual bull by the horns. Studies of depression have shown, he points out, that the number, severity, and duration of depressive episodes "sit on a continuum of risk"—that is, depression is solidly continuous, in the manner of high blood pressure. And the milder depressive symptoms form a "halo" around depression, so that even low-level depression precedes major depression or follows it, and all these instances of depression are, as he says, "part of a single picture." Spectrum diseases are common in medicine, he insists, and "we understand their manifestations as *pathology all* along the spectrum" (my emphasis).

We may concede with Kramer that the vast range of mild to severe symptoms of depression all form a unity and a categorical whole. Yet further along this apparent continuum lie qualitatively similar states and traits we want to classify not as disease, mild or severe, but as normal and, perhaps, adaptive responses to stress and loss. Kramer sometimes acknowledges this fact, making space for states of sadness, grief, and loss and for bleaker temperaments, but he does not do so entirely consistently, and his account is somewhat muddy on these points. Thus, the milder temperamental condition known as dysthymia is part of the disease category, by his reckoning and "can be a devastating condition." He speaks of himself, in contrast, as a person who, without qualifying for a diagnosis of even low-level depression, is reasonably depressive or melancholic in terms of "personality style or humor" ("I brood over failures; I require solitude"). Clear enough thus far. But then he goes on: "in the face of bad fortune, I suspect that I might well succumb to mood disorder."

The latter remark may be read to suggest that the "mood disorder" or disease of depression is something we are all heir to. If so, then on the diathesis-stress model Kramer has adopted, where preexisting vulnerability combines with some adverse experience to yield the depressive response, the implication is that we *all* bear *within us* the potential for disease.

The view that melancholy tendencies are universal, the lot of humankind, can be found in as great an authority as Robert Burton, writing in the seventeenth century. From "Melancholy Dispositions," Burton asserts, "no man living is free," and melancholy in this sense is "the Character of Mortalitie." But Burton wanted to set aside those states which are part of our human legacy and distinguish them from melancholy the "Habit," even though, in some people, "these Dispositions become Habits" and, eventually, disease. The difference between that melancholy which is the human condition and the melancholy of disease was for Burton a difference in kind, not degree. Kramer, too, had proposed a strict categorical analysis of depression, but his later remarks seem to jeopardize any attempt to hold separate the category of suffering that is the normal response to stress and loss.

If we are all heir to depression, then depression cannot easily be regarded as a disease. If it is so regarded, then insufficient conceptual space seems left for normal responses to life's troubles.

Accounting for our squeamishness in acknowledging that minor states of distress be labeled as part of the monolithic disease of depression, Kramer remarks that for most of the twentieth century,

> under the rubric of "neurosis," yet more minor depressive states might be labeled illness. I suspect that...we may have tolerated a loose understanding of mood disorder because we did not imagine psychotherapy to be radically effective....Contemplating treatment via more hard-edged means—think of genetic engineering, think of a campaign of eradication—demands that we own our beliefs regarding minor depression and its status as disease.

Kramer seems to suppose the prospect of genetic engineering to eliminate milder states of distress will reconcile us to according those states disease status. But surely it is precisely the prospect of such radical "cures" that alarms us most about this blurring of the line between depression the disease (including its disease penumbra) and milder states of distress that seem normal and, indeed, part of what make us most, and perhaps most appealingly, human.

The argument in *Against Depression* breaks into two broad facets, establishing first what depression is (a disease) and then what it is not (heroic). The broad strokes are exciting, imaginative, and often compelling in this second aspect of Kramer's argument and reveal a sensitive and informed awareness of cultural and literary traditions. Before turning to these discussions aimed at showing that we must divest depression of its charm, let me express a general historical concern.

The heroic view of melancholy, which dates to ancient times and texts, found one of its strongest expressions in the Romanticism of the early nineteenth century. Arguably, we are seeing a modest resurgence of that view in the present era, expressed in works such as Kay Jamison's *Touched with Fire* and heard in the newly articulate voices of depression sufferers recounting their own experiences. Yet to some considerable extent through the last part of the nineteenth century and most of the twentieth, the deromanticizing of depression that Kramer supports *was taking place*. Though still remembered, the glamorous associations of melancholy were considerably muted and even eclipsed when—and arguably because—depression became "gendered," a women's condition in epidemiological terms, and, in cultural ones, linked with disvalued feminine traits. Kramer's account makes no mention of these historical shifts or of the nineteenth-century gendering of depression. (He does put forward a Darwinian explanation for the gender link between women and depression, citing it as a possible cost of women's caring roles. But then, again, such theorizing fails to take into account the broad "gendering" of depression not evident until the end of the nineteenth century.) These omissions, to my mind, detract from the effectiveness of his overall argument against depression as heroic.

Our long Western fascination with melancholy and the cultural traditions linking melancholic states with brilliance, creativity, and other valued and heroic states and achievements contain, Kramer recognizes, distinguishable hypotheses. Some of these are causal, others not; some point to achievements, others to traits of mind and character; others still to ideas and ideals. A real asset of this book is the way these different strands of the "charm" argument are subject to separate discussion and analysis. Nonetheless, the many-headed hydra that constitutes the "charm" argument(s) proves a daunting adversary, which Kramer's efforts are less than equally successful in defeating.

Though not the most persuasive of these various ways of explaining the charm of melancholy, the causal claims pointing to creative achievements may be the best known and come to us weighted with the authority of long-held lore. The geniuses of the Renaissance would not have achieved greatness, it has been insisted, without their black moods and bile; the dour states of "spleen" were the noxious side effects of creativity and brilliance—unwanted, but unavoidable. Other causal claims, these often asserted in the literary memoir of depressives (their autopathographies, in Kramer's term), allow that through depressive suffering people discover truths about themselves and the universe. Kramer deals with each of these causal claims. For example, the evidence linking depression to creativity is, he shows, "shaky," especially since, on the face of things, depression "looks like a straightforward handicap." No formal studies confirm the link between depression and creative achievement, in his view, and whatever link there may seem to be invites a more nuanced interpretation of the causal story. For instance, *difference* helps in the creative process, and depression is "a form of difference"; if self-consciousness is the subject of art, "depressives are ideal chroniclers"; literary achievements might arise by default: "mustering the stamina for a regular job may be difficult," and so on. As he sees it, there is likely "a complex process of mutual adaptation, between the disease and the medium."

A first step is to separate out analogous claims about the glamour and achievements of those suffering manic-depression (apparently stronger because of the energy and inflated self-esteem of the manic phase); if we accept this restriction—there are some who challenge the concept of unipolar depression as a separate disorder, and would not—then Kramer's assessment seems reasonable and appropriate to the kinds of achievement identified in these claims.

Claims about the profundity and depth of character alleged to result from depressive episodes leave Kramer equally dubious. In his estimation, and their own avowals notwithstanding, a close study of depressives' autopathographies does not indicate that depression brings depth and profundity to the character of the sufferer. But questions of method arise here and complicate Kramer's assessment. An outside observer, however skillfully trained, does not readily assess depth and profundity of

character any more than the value of a life. And we usually accord to the person herself the role of judge on these matters, on Mill's grounds: the individual knows best
the personal values and interests integral to any such assessment. These judgments
are not open to the easy objective tests by which we measure artistic achievements.
Arguably, Kramer too quickly dismisses the claims made in these memoirs, for all
that they smack of banality and unseemly "hints of pride."

His dismissal of the Aristotelian association between melancholy and greatness
in the public world may be similarly premature, moreover. Recent historical work
on Abraham Lincoln's severe, debilitating, and recurrent melancholic states indicates a twentieth-century historical revisionism tantamount to a "cover-up" (Joshua
Wolf Shenk, *Lincoln's Melancholia: How Depression Challenged a President and
Fueled His Greatness*, 2005). While only one, the example of Lincoln encourages
general suspicion over biographies of great men written in an era when depression
had been much, though not entirely, deromanticized and come to be relegated to a
woman's condition and a weakness unworthy of great men.

The tie between depressive states and greatness, meaning, and human truths
goes beyond these sorts of causal claim. For example, depressive or melancholic
states are believed emblematic of the attitude it is *appropriate* to adopt in the face
of the meaninglessness of life in modernity—emblematic of, not, or not merely,
responsible for. Kramer rightly leads us to Kierkegaard here, noting that the isolation one feels in depression is what it is believed one "ought to feel in a mechanical,
chaotic, and uncomprehending universe." He calls the tragic view of life the "grand
hypothesis of melancholy—not just that it creates art but that it *describes our place
in the universe*" (my emphasis).

That said, Kramer's conclusion—that by eliminating depression, we could
expect to see an end to this tragic view and see, as he says, the linkage with heroism
as "a . . . delusion"—may also be overly hasty. The philosophical attitude toward life
known as the tragic attitude, while neither arising from the depressed mind nor giving rise to it, may still represent, or find unique resonance in, depressive subjectivity.
Thus, other, stronger versions of the associative link between depressive states and
cultural "structures" such as the tragic attitude point to something different from
causal claims: something closer, perhaps, to a mimetic relation. Though not causally necessary for profound understanding of the world, subjective states of melancholy and depression may echo and seem to correspond to such states.

The tragic view is in this sense epistemically independent of depressive states.
For that reason, we need not suppose that changes in our view of depression will
alter its currency or popularity. There are passages in *Against Depression* expressing
both this recognition that the relationship is not causal and the recalcitrance of the
associative link between depressive states and the tragic view. "The despair that is a
symptom of depression *mimics* the despair that might accompany full awareness of
the absurdity of our lives," Kramer observes. Yet he seems to resist the implication of
this view, asking: "Why is depression, in particular, the fit metaphor?" His answer:
"If we recognize depression as a particular disease, we will no longer treat it as the all
purpose affliction, the stand-in for suffering in general." Depressive states resemble
the states appropriate to the tragic view, this seems to suggest, because as a reversible
and arbitrary accident of cultural history, we have forged a link between the two.

My disagreement with Kramer here is that feelings of depression, at least, *are* a stand-in, or metaphor, for suffering in general. Depression may be a disease, but it is a disease whose central symptoms involve moods, feelings, attitudes, and beliefs, and not, for instance, bodily sensations. So it is no ordinary disease. Thus some of the trouble here lies with the disease framework by which each sign and symptom of the condition is understood as an inseparable part of a whole: the disturbances of sleep, appetite, and energy, as much as the depressive subjectivity. Only these latter, "mental" states making up depressive subjectivity correspond to the states we think it appropriate to adopt in the face of our troubled world, and a more careful statement of the thesis that depression is somehow deeply reflective of those attitudes would protect it from some of the force of Kramer's critique.

The affinity between depressive states and the tragic view of life is one form of noncausal relation. That between depressive states and a certain aesthetic is another. When depression, "like dysentery and epilepsy and the rest, declares itself a disease" Kramer predicts, "our valuation of depressive art might seem an anachronism, the remnant of a tradition required to mitigate and justify otherwise inexplicable sorrow." Later, affirming his own literary preference for the more sanguine writing of John Updike, Kramer contrasts the "mutedly optimistic and American style" to that which is "thoroughly bleak and European." These differing aesthetics, he implies, are matters of taste, and can be expected to change, through time. Yet just as philosophers might want to assert the *truth* of the tragic view of life, which at once ensures its causal independence from and its mimetic relation to depressive states, so it seems legitimate to accord more enduring value to the bleak, European aesthetic and to rank it over its sunny "American" alternative. Tracing as the "European", aesthetic does to works as profoundly grave as Aristotle's *Poetics*, it seems unlikely that our traditional aesthetics will be soon undone by changes in our attitude toward depression.

In addition to his attempts to rebut each of the several "charm" arguments identified here, Kramer eventually offers his personal and autobiographical credentials as a man of feeling, sensitivity, and profundity—as *Homo melancholicus*, one might even say. And, indeed, some passages in *Against Depression* convey a strangely melancholy tone. Kramer speaks as if the tragic (bleak and European) aesthetic, linked as it has been all these years through a mistaken valorizing of depressive states and traits, will wither and be replaced by something more upbeat when depression comes to be understood for what it is. Yet he finishes his chapter on the end of melancholy with the elegiac comment that "in our lives, depth seems to endangered and happiness so overblown, so commercial, so stupefying, that we may be inclined to cling to some version of melancholy, never mind what doctors say about depression."

Ironically, in his nuanced approach, Kramer exemplifies the ambivalence and self-doubt whose devaluation in the melancholy self of Western literary and philosophical traditions, and eventual decline, he has tried to persuade us to anticipate without regret. But that is perhaps what sets his book apart and makes it, as was *Listening to Prozac* before it, a wonderfully stimulating and enjoyable one to read.

INDEX